The Great Angel

Margaret Barker

The Great Angel   A Study of Israel's Second God

concepts of 'the other'
in the ancient
Near East
in ancient
Near Eastern
texts?

Westminster/John Knox Press
Louisville, Kentucky

First published in Great Britain 1992,
SPCK, Holy Trinity Church, Marylebone Road,
London NW1 4DU

First American edition
Published by Westminster/John Knox Press
Louisville, Kentucky

PRINTED IN GREAT BRITAIN
9 8 7 6 5 4 3 2 1

Library of Congress Cataloging-in-Publication Data

Barker, Margaret, 1944–
    The great angel: a study of Israel's second god/by
Margaret Barker. — 1st American ed.
        p.   cm.
    Includes bibliographical references.
    ISBN 0-664-25395-4

    1. Jesus Christ—Messiahship.   2. Jesus
Christ—History of doctrines—Early church, ca. 30-
600.   3. Jesus Christ—Name.   4.
Messiah—Judaism.   5. Angels (Judaism)   I. Title.
BT230.B27   1992
232'.1—dc20   91-43042

For Hugh Montefiore

Yahweh —
a maker God - irony
only dead matter!

toward
death by projecting
/delivering death (anality)
in sublimated form
1) de sanctify matter
2) purity obsession
3) greed /(boundary)
4) sexual anorexia-bulimia
5) war /power

All through my boyhood I had the profound conviction that I was no good, that I was wasting my time, wrecking my talents, behaving with monstrous folly and wickedness and ingratitude and all this, it seemed, was inescapable, because I lived among laws which were absolute, like the law of gravity, but which it was not possible for me to keep.

George Orwell, *A Collection of Essays*

"I AM"

And he said, 'Who are you, Lord?'
And he said, 'I am Jesus ...'

(Acts 9.5)

Yeshya

Ye Ne
Shem
hyya

Contents

oldest
religion,
in Samaria

doxy
praise   { temple
             ritual
            + ceremony

same

incarnate
bar Enosh

vs

Preface

Some of the reviewers of my first book, *The Older Testament*, recognized that I had left several things unsaid. The theory which I set out in this present volume was already very much in my mind when *The Older Testament* was being written, and it was inevitable that these ideas should break the surface from time to time. My first three books have been, in effect, an extended introduction to *The Great Angel*. It was necessary to show how I thought the religion of Israel had developed (*The Older Testament*), and then to show how its oldest form had survived into the New Testament period. Thus *The Lost Prophet* showed the extent to which the so-called apocalyptic world view (in reality the world view of the first temple) permeated the whole of the New Testament and *The Gate of Heaven* showed, among other things, the extent to which the first characteristically Christian theology was expressed in the imagery and symbolism of the temple.

At first I hesitated to write *The Great Angel*. It ranges over an enormous amount of material from ancient Canaan to mediaeval Kabbalah and nobody can hope to be competent let alone expert over so great a field. Nothing but a broad sweep, however, could have done justice to the evidence. In addition, I feared the consequences of presenting these ideas. There are many who will be disturbed by them and even angered.

What finally prompted me to write was an article (I will not specify!) which I came across one day whilst browsing in the library. Like so many recent contributions to New Testament study, this one assumed that the idea of Jesus's divinity was brought relatively late to Christianity, invented by Greek converts who had not really left their paganism behind. It was a painstaking study of one minute area with no attention to the broader context and showed clearly the dangers inherent in that over specialization which characterizes the contemporary scene. Kasemann once described it as the situation of a man in a private pit looking out at the world around and the sky above (NTS 19 1973).

Ideas grow over a long period of time and it is not possible to say when the Great Angel first began to appear. Several publications

xiii

stand out in my memory as significant points: Emerton's 'The Origin of the Son of Man Imagery' (JTS 1958); Segal's *Two Powers in Heaven* (1978); Fitzmyer's 'The New Testament Background of the Kurios Title' (1979); Fossum's *The Name of God and the Angel of the Lord* (1985); and Whybray's *The Making of the Pentateuch* (1987). Their influence is apparent throughout.

Writing can be a very frustrating business. I should like to thank my friend Robert Murray SJ for his constant support and encouragement and the staff of the Hallward Library at Nottingham University for their help. Finally, I should like to dedicate this book to one of my university teachers who went on to become a much loved bishop of Birmingham.

Margaret Barker, Michaelmas 1991

Abbreviations

VT Vetus Testamentum

ZAW Zeitschrift fur alttestamentliche Wissenschaft

ZNW Zeitschrift fur neutestamentliche Wissenschaft

Introduction

Jesus was worshipped by his followers and hailed as Son of God, Messiah and Lord. For centuries the churches have used these titles, and they now mean something very important to millions of people. Scholars of the ancient texts, however, are less certain about them, and how it could have been possible for monotheistic Jews to have *worshipped* Jesus. Here lies the great problem. Did the first Christians worship Jesus and what did they mean when they used these words to describe their beliefs about him? What would a man from first-century Galilee have understood when he heard 'Son of God', 'Messiah' and 'Lord'?

The titles have been explained in various ways, but often so as to show that their original meaning was other than that which the Christians eventually adopted. They were brought into Christian thought from a pagan background, it is said, and thus represented a later understanding of Jesus which became incorporated into the New Testament, or they were a paganized understanding of what had originally been Palestinian titles. The worship of Jesus cannot possibly have begun among the first Jewish Christians since their monotheism would have made such a practice unthinkable. The problem is solved by explaining that 'Son of God' was adopted from Greek mythology or the claims of contemporary royal families; that 'Messiah' was no more than the usual designation of nationalist leaders who wanted to rebel against Rome; and 'Lord' was a courtesy title which unfortunately was confused by the Greek Christians with the Old Testament's version of the divine Name and thus Jesus became divine and was worshipped like one of the local Greek gods.

Versions of these ideas have been popular with New Testament scholars for most of the twentieth century, their hidden agenda being to emphasize the humanness of Jesus and to show that his 'divinity' was a later development and an unfortunate one at that. Hengel has shown how there was an alliance between Jewish and Protestant scholars in this task; the former wished to reclaim Jesus for Judaism, but obviously only on their terms, and the latter felt unhappy with the

1

more mysterious and supernatural aspects of the Gospel stories.[1]

A straightforward reading of the New Testament, however, does suggest that Jesus was seen from the beginning as more than simply human. Long before the first Gospel was written down, Paul could quote a Christian hymn, presumably one which his readers would recognize, and therefore one which was widely known.

... though he was in the form of God, did not count equality with God a thing to be grasped, but emptied himself, taking the form of a servant, being born in the likeness of men. And being found in human form he humbled himself and became obedient unto death, even death on a cross. Therefore God has highly exalted him and bestowed on him the name, which is above every name, that at the name of Jesus every knee should bow, in heaven and on earth and under the earth, and every tongue confess that Jesus Christ is Lord, to the glory of God the Father. (Phil. 2.6–11)

Similarly, at the beginning of Romans, Paul quotes what seems to be an early statement of Christian belief:

the gospel of God ... concerning his Son, who was descended from David according to the flesh and designated Son of God in power according to the Spirit of holiness by his resurrection from the dead. (Rom. 1.3–4)

All the titles are there: Son of God, Lord and Messiah.

It has been the practice to treat the titles separately, as if each designated a different aspect of belief, and the separate strands were only brought together by the creative theologizing of the first Christians. I should like to explore a different possibility, namely that these three titles, and several others, belonged together in the expectations and traditions of first-century Palestine, and that the first Christians fitted Jesus into an existing pattern of belief. The rapid development of early Christian teaching was due to the fact that so much of the scheme already existed; the life and death of Jesus was the means of reinterpreting the older hopes. This is not a new idea; from the beginning Christians have claimed that Jesus was the fulfilment of the hopes expressed in the Old Testament. Our problem is to know exactly what those hopes were, and how they were expressed in first-century Palestine. What did the key words mean?

The discovery of the Dead Sea Scrolls has forced us to redraw the picture of Judaism in the time of Jesus; many of the old certainties have been destroyed by this new knowledge. Many of the 'sources' for New Testament background studies (writings of the rabbis, the gnostic texts) have now been shown to belong to a period two or three centuries later than the time of Jesus. They cannot be used to illuminate the world in which the Christian message was first formulated.[2] Perhaps it would be more accurate to say that they cannot be used as evidence for Christian belief as we usually understand it. We have to use these materials differently, and to listen carefully to what they are saying. In the course of reading in this area I have become increasingly aware of another set of possibilities for understanding them, and it is this I want to explore.

canaanite

The investigations range over a wide area, and cannot be in any sense comprehensive. What has become clear to me time and time again is that even over so wide an area, the evidence points consistently in one direction and indicates that pre-Christian Judaism was not monotheistic in the sense that we use that word. The roots of Christian trinitarian theology lie in pre-Christian Palestinian beliefs about the angels. There were many in first-century Palestine who still retained a world-view derived from the more ancient religion of Israel in which there was a High God and several Sons of God, one of whom was Yahweh, the Holy One of Israel. Yahweh, the Lord, could be manifested on earth in human form, as an angel or in the Davidic king. *It was as a manifestation of Yahweh, the Son of God, that Jesus was acknowledged as Son of God, Messiah and Lord.*

Please note that I have kept the Hebrew divine name as Yahweh wherever the Old Testament is quoted. In the New Testament and in the early Christian writers I have used 'the Lord' as the conventional translation of *kyrios*.

Notes to Introduction

1 M. Hengel, *The Son of God.* ET London 1974, ch.2.

2 P.S. Alexander, 'Rabbinic Judaism and the New Testament', ZNW 74 (1983), pp. 237–46.

Chapter one The Son of God

So much has been written on this subject that it seems presumptuous even to attempt to say more. I do not want to survey the evidence for the use of the term in other religions, or in the contemporary Hellenistic world. Rather, I should like to concentrate on one aspect which I have not found explored elsewhere, namely the distinction between the different words for God in the Old Testament and the effect that this must have upon our estimate of what it meant to be a son of God.

It is customary to list the occurences of 'son of God' in the Old Testament, and to conclude from that list that the term could be used to mean either a heavenly being of some sort, or the King of Israel, or the people of Israel in their special relationship to God. Thus Dunn in his *Christology in the Making* deals with what 'son of God' might have meant in Hellenistic circles and then discusses Judaism thus:

Even those whose cultural horizons were more limited to the literature and traditions of Judaism would be aware that 'son of God' could be used in several ways: *angels or heavenly beings* – 'the sons of God' being members of the heavenly council under Yahweh the supreme God (Gen. 6.2, 4; Deut. 32.8; Job 1.6–12; 2.1–6; 38.7; Pss. 29.1; 89.6; Dan. 3.25); regularly of *Israel or Israelites* – 'Israel is my firstborn son' (Ex. 4.22; Jer. 31.9; Hos. 11.1; see also e.g. Deut. 14.1; Isa. 43.6; Hos. 1.10); *the king* so called only a handful of times in the OT – II Sam. 7.14 (taken up in I Chron. 17.13; 22.10; 28.6) Ps. 2.7 and 89.26f.[1]

This comprehensive treatment does not, however, distinguish between the two different words for God and therefore *ignores a crucial distinctions* There are those called sons of El Elyon, sons of El or Elohim, all clearly heavenly beings, and there are those called sons of Yahweh or the Holy One who are human. This distinction is important for at least two reasons; Yahweh *was* one of the sons of El Elyon; and Jesus in the Gospels was described as a Son of El Elyon, God Most High. In other words he was described as a heavenly being. Thus the annunciation narrative has the term 'Son of the Most High' (Luke 1.32) and the demoniac recognized his exorcist as 'Son of the Most High God' (Mark 5.7). Jesus is not called the son of Yahweh nor the

4

son of the Lord, but he is called Lord. We also know that whoever wrote the New Testament translated the name Yahweh by *Kyrios*, Lord. (See, for example, the quotation from Deuteronomy 6.5: 'You shall love Yahweh your God ...' which is rendered in Luke 10.27 'You shall love the Lord [*Kyrios*] your God.') This suggests that the Gospel writers, in using the terms 'Lord' and 'Son of God Most High', saw Jesus as an angel figure, and gave him their version of the sacred names Yahweh (see chapter 10).

The heavenly sons of God appear in the Old Testament in several places, often by name but sometimes also by implication. Their first appearance is in Genesis 6.2, 4, where they are the sons of the *'elohim*. This is the account of the sons of God who fell from heaven and became the fathers of the giants. It is generally agreed that the account in Genesis is a fragment survival from an early myth.[2] A longer version of the tale appears in 1 Enoch, and this may be an expansion of the biblical fragment, or it may be the fuller form of the story from which the Genesis account was taken. Whichever explanation is adopted, 1 Enoch shows how the story was understood in the period of the second temple when the Enoch literature was being preserved and developed. The sons of God brought wisdom, i.e. divine knowledge of the secrets of creation, but because this wisdom was brought to earth in rebellion against God Most High, it corrupted the creation. 1 Enoch lists the names of these angel figures in two places (1 Enoch 6.7; 59.2). Most of the names end in *-el*, meaning god: *Kokabiel*, star of God, *Tamiel*, perfection of God, *Barakiel*, the lightning of God and so on. Were these angels, then, envisaged as aspects of God, manifestations of God, rather than as separate divinities? Notice that they do not have names compounded with Yahweh except in the Apocalypse of Abraham where there is a great angel called Yahwehel.

The second sons of God text is Deuteronomy 32.8, one on which a great deal has been written:

When the Most High gave to the nations their inheritance,
   when he separated the sons of men,
he fixed the bounds of the peoples
   according to the number of the sons of God.

The problem lies in the difference between the Hebrew and the Greek versions. The MT does not mention sons of God, but has sons of Israel instead. The Qumran Hebrew has sons of God (sons of *'el*) and the

5

Greek has angels of God.[3] This text shows two things: that there was some reason for altering sons of God to sons of Israel, or vice versa (the Qumran reading suggests that the earlier Hebrew had read 'sons of God'); and that the sons of God were the patron deities of the various nations. Elyon the High God had allocated the nations to the various sons of God; one of these sons was Yahweh to whom Israel had been allocated (Deut. 32.9). This fossil incorporated into Deuteronomy is thought to be one of its oldest components; how such a 'polytheistic' piece came to be included in Deuteronomy, with its emphasis on monotheism, is a question we cannot answer, although it is possible to guess why 'polytheism' was removed from the later Hebrew text, as we shall see. The angels of the nations are probably the same as the 'messengers' (it is the same word in Hebrew) of the nations who appear in Isa. 14.32 and who are warned that Yahweh's people are protected by Zion which he has founded. The angels of the nations appear in a later form in Daniel, where they are the princes of Persia and Greece, attacking the unnamed angel who fights for Israel with the help of the archangel Michael (Dan. 10.13–14).

The third set of son of God texts is in Job. The prologue describes how the sons of God (sons of the *'elohim*), one of whom was Satan, came to Yahweh and challenged him to test the loyalty of Job. The usual English renderings of Job 1.6 imply that Yahweh was superior to the sons of God: 'the sons of God came *to present themselves before* Yahweh.' This is not necessarily what the Hebrew implies since the same verb is used in Ps. 2.2, and there it means '*set themselves against* Yahweh'. Thus the prologue to Job depicts a heaven where Yahweh is one among many and is challenged to test the loyalty of his servant. This is a world of heavenly rivalries, where suffering is seen as a test of loyalty to one's own God, not as a punishment for wrongdoing. It is almost a pre-moral polytheism, and Yahweh, one of the sons of God, is a part of this world.[4] The sons of God (sons of *'elohim*) also appear in Job 38.7. Yahweh asks Job: 'Where were you when I laid the foundation of the earth? (...) when the morning stars sang together, and all the sons of God shouted for joy?'

Yahweh is the creator and the sons of God are there too, closely linked to the morning stars. It is interesting that there is no mention of the sons of God in the Genesis account of creation but Jubilees has a longer account which does describe the creation of the angels: 'For on the first day he created the heavens which are above and the earth and the waters and all the spirits which serve before him ... the angels of the presence, and the angels of sanctification ... And on the second day he created the firmament' (Jub. 2.1, 4). The question we cannot answer is: How is it that Jubilees and Job have an account of the creation which includes the angels, which Genesis does not mention, even though it does have an evil serpent figure of whose origin we are told nothing? Later traditions knew that an elaborate heavenly world had been created before the material world and this heaven was totally integrated with the earth.

The psalter gives several glimpses of the sons of God. The sons of gods (sons of 'elim) appear in Ps. 29.1, where they are told to acknowledge the glory and strength of Yahweh the creator who is enthroned as king. The setting of this psalm is probably the same as that of Pss. 58, 82 and 89 which depict the divine council. Ps. 58 describes the 'elim who have acted unjustly and are to be judged for it. It does not mention the sons of God, but its theme is identical with that of Ps. 82 which describes the judgement upon the sons of God, (sons of Elyon). The opening verse illustrates well the problem of names which is apparent throughout this investigation: 'Elohim has taken his place on the council of El, in the midst of Elohim he gives judgement' (Ps. 82.1) and then: 'You are Elohim, sons of Elyon all of you ...' (Ps. 82.6) The sons of 'elim also appear in Ps. 89.6; none among the sons of 'elim is like Yahweh who is a god feared in the council of the Holy Ones.

Then we should note Dan. 3.25, where one like a son of the gods (a son of elahin) appears as the fourth figure in the fiery furnace; he has human form. In 2 Esd. 13.22–6 the deliverer of Israel is the one whom the Most High has kept hidden, his Son to be revealed as the Man coming from the sea; here the son of Elyon has human form, but a comparison with 2 Esd. 2.42–8 shows that this man is an angel figure, the Son of God who crowns the martyrs in heaven. Finally there is the Qumran fragment known as 4Q Son of God: 'He shall be hailed as the son of El and they shall call him the son of Elyon.' It is not known of whom this was said but he was to rule on earth and be a conqueror. The setting is apocalyptic, with comets in the sky and the triumph of the people of God. The figure is not named, but he is recognizable.[5]

These were the sons of God Most High, angel figures who were manifested in human form. In the coded language of the apocalypses they were described as 'men' or like men or even as son of man; thus

Daniel saw 'the man Gabriel' (Dan. 9.21) and John saw the angel measuring the heavenly city 'by a man's measure, that is, an angel's' (Rev. 21.17). Mortals were described as animals.

The sons of Yahweh on the other hand are never called this by name; it is always by implication: 'You are my son,' says Yahweh. The king was the first to be called a son of Yahweh. How this was understood we do not know, but it is quite beyond the evidence to say that Israel did not understand the term in the same way as did other ancient nations who believed their kings to be divine. We have only the texts of the Old Testament as evidence, and these suggest overwhelmingly that Yahweh was 'present' in the one called his son. Ps. 2 shows that the king could deliver the words of Yahweh:

> I will tell of the decree of Yahweh:
> He said to me, 'You are my son, today I have begotten you.' (Ps. 2.7)

There are also the last words of David:

> The spirit of Yahweh speaks by me,
> His word is on my tongue. (2 Sam. 23.2)

We do not know when the king was thought to become divine; it is generally assumed that this is a coronation psalm, but there is no proof. The king has been set on the holy hill of Zion (Ps. 2.6) and he has received an oracle (Ps. 2.7); this is all we are told. Ps. 110 is similar; the Greek of Ps. 110.3 reads 'I have begotten you', implying divine sonship, instead of the customary form 'your youth'. The Hebrew consonants can be read either way; it is interesting that the Greek read them as of divine kingship, and the Hebrew as we have it today has pointed them to mean something else. We shall never know what the original was, but in view of the similar change away from 'sons of God' in the Massoretic text of Deut. 32.8, the Greek seems more likely to have kept the original meaning. Isa. 9.6–7 belongs in this setting, although exactly what the oracle means is still debated. The child was born 'to us' and named 'Wonderful Counsellor, Mighty God, Everlasting Father, Prince of Peace'. Perhaps these were birth names given at the physical birth, or perhaps they were throne names, given at the kingmaking ceremony. Perhaps, as has been suggested,[6] these names were given by the heavenly host who were rejoicing at the birth of their son. The Greek of this text has not four titles but one, The Angel of Great Counsel, and this angel was to be the ruler of Israel. Isaiah's other oracle of a royal birth (Isa. 7.14–17) suggests

chief

protector

that the child was a sign of God's presence from his birth. How else are we to understand '... bear a son and call his name Immanuel, God with us'? Ps. 89 is another royal psalm which compares the power of Yahweh in the heavenly assembly to the power of his king on earth. Just as Yahweh is acknowledged by the heavenly beings as supreme, so his son will be acknowledged as supreme on earth. The king will cry to Yahweh 'You are my Father' (Ps. 89.26) and he will be *made* the firstborn, the highest of the kings of the earth. This royal sonship is a statement of power; the king is the agent of Yahweh, his representative and therefore the channel of his power.

The other texts describing royal sonship are all related to the tradition of the Davidic covenant. The Deuteronomic formulation of it in 2 Sam. 14 has eclipsed all other ideas of the royal covenant, and may well have distorted our picture of it. The king is described as a son of Yahweh: 'I will be his father and he shall be my son.' Such an expression completely excludes any literal meaning for the words. The king's heirs will be sons of Yahweh. The Chronicler is equally clear: 'It is Solomon your son who shall build my house and my courts, for I have chosen him to be my son, and I will be his father' (1 Chron. 28.6). What we cannot know is how accurately the Deuteronomic and post-exilic representations of the idea of kingship reflect actual belief during the time of the monarchy. They show what was believed in retrospect by those who produced these writings, but this was not necessarily the only point of view in the period of the second temple and therefore in the period of Christianity's origins.

Israel as *a people* was also described as the son of God. They were to be restored as 'Sons of the living God' (Hos. 1.10), and had been called from Egypt as a son of the Holy One (Hos. 11.1, 9). All the other references come from writings compiled during the exile, and reflect the democratization of the royal covenant. What had formerly been believed of the kings was then interpreted to apply to the whole people. Thus Israel, instead of the king, was the firstborn son (Exod. 4.22). Yahweh was the father of Israel, and Ephraim was his firstborn (Jer. 31.9). The family of Yahweh the Holy One, sons and daughters, would be gathered in (Isa. 43.6), and the sons of Yahweh would be distinguished from all other people by their observance of ritual laws: they could not disfigure themselves nor eat unclean foods (Deut. 14.1 and 3ff). Some called on Yahweh as their Father and Redeemer even when the rest of Israel did not acknowledge them (Isa. 63.16). The family imagery continued in the later literature. 'Solomon' ruled over the sons and daughters of his God (Wisd. 9.7), and warned his Egyptian contemporaries that Israel had been acknowledged as God's son in the earlier encounters with Pharaoh (Wisd. 18.13). The pattern was further developed to describe the ultimate triumph of the upright man in the face of his enemies. The child/servant of the Lord had knowledge of God and lived an upright life. He was persecuted by those who mocked his claim to be God's son (Wisd. 2.12–20). Later the persecutors were amazed to find that he had been 'numbered among the sons of God' (Wisd. 5.5).

These passages are based on the Servant poems of Isaiah, especially Isa. 52–3)[7] and the suffering of Yahweh's servant has been used to explain the sufferings of the righteous man. This later text associates the triumph of the persecuted one with his recognition as a son of God, thus increasing the possibility that the poems originally described the Davidic kings in their relationship to Yahweh. The *Psalms of Solomon* compare the suffering of the righteous to the disciplining of a firstborn son (Ps. Solomon 13.8; 18.4), and the expected Davidic king would reign over the sons of God (Ps. Solomon 17.30). Sirach offers three very different examples of the usage: in Sir. 4.10 the righteous man is exhorted to be like a son of Elyon, the Most High; in Sir. 23.1 he prays to the Lord, Father and Ruler of his life; and in Sir. 51.10 he prays to the Lord, the father of his Lord, using *kyrios* each time. The 'two Lords' will prove to be a very important piece of evidence.

All the texts in the Hebrew Bible distinguish clearly between the divine sons of Elohim/Elyon and those human beings who are called sons of Yahweh. This must be significant. It must mean that the terms originated at a time when Yahweh was distinguished from whatever was meant by El/Elohim/Elyon. A large number of texts continued to distinguish between El Elyon and Yahweh, Father and Son, and to express this distinction in similar ways with the symbolism of the temple and the royal cult. By tracing these patterns through a great variety of material and over several centuries, Israel's second God can be recovered.

Notes to chapter one

1 J.D.G. Dunn, *Christology in the Making*, London 1980, p.15.

2 e.g. G. von Rad, *Genesis*, ET London 1961, pp.109-10.

3 P.S. Skehan, 'A Fragment of the "Song of Moses" (Deut. 32) from Qumran', BASOR 136(1954), pp.12-15.

4 See my *The Older Testament*, London 1987, ch.4.

5 J.A. Fitzmyer, 'The Contribution of Qumran Aramaic to the Study of the New Testament' in *A Wandering Aramaean: Collected Aramaic Essays* SBL Monograph 25, Missoula 1979.

6 H. Graf Reventlow, 'A Syncretistic Enthronement Hymn in Isa. 9.1-6', Ugarit-Forschungen 3 (1971), pp.321-5.

7 G.W.E. Nickelsburg, *Resurrection, Immortality and Eternal Life in Intertestamental Judaism*, Cambridge, Mass. 1972, pp.62-3.

Chapter two **The Evidence of the Exile**

The exile in Babylon is a formidable barrier to anyone wanting to reconstruct the religious beliefs and practices of ancient Jerusalem. If we are to discover any possible reason for the distinction between the sons of El/Elyon and the sons of Yahweh it is a barrier which has to be acknowledged. Enormous developments took place in the wake of enormous destruction, and these two factors make certainty quite impossible. They make *all* certainty impossible, and this too must be acknowledged, for the customary descriptions of ancient Israel's religion are themselves no more than supposition. What I shall propose in this chapter is not an impossibility, but only one possibility to set alongside other possibilities, none of which has any claim to being an absolutely accurate account of what happened. Hypotheses do not become fact simply by frequent repetition, or even by detailed elaboration. What I am suggesting does, however, make considerable sense of the evidence from later periods, as I shall show in subsequent chapters.

The great destruction wrought by the Babylonians at the beginning of the sixth century followed hard upon the so-called Deuteronomic reform. What was destroyed was therefore in a state of flux, since we are by no means certain that the Deuteronomic reform was the wholesale success claimed for it. The two accounts of what happened in the reign of Josiah differ in detail and emphasis: the Chronicler (2 Chron. 34–5) described finding the lawbook, renewing the covenant and keeping a great Passover; the Deuteronomist (2 Kings 22–3) described in detail all the abominations that were swept away and wrote but briefly of the great Passover. We do not know, therefore, what happened at the time. All we know is that the Deuteronomists wrote themselves into history at this point, since, in 2 Kings, they clearly identified the programme of reform with their own ideals. If this is accurate, then we have evidence for a sweeping away of everything that did not accord with one particular point of view; if it is not accurate, i.e. if it is only a retrospective improvement on fact, then we have evidence for a rewriting of history on a massive scale, to the point where it becomes extremely difficult for us to call it history in any modern sense of that word. We should call it propaganda. It is a common enough phenomenon in this century to see a radical change of government or ruling philosophy accompanied by a rewriting of the past. If the keynote of the Deuteronomists was an emphasis on the sacred history, the Exodus and the saving acts of Yahweh to the exclusion of all other gods, then it is easy to see that any traces of earlier religious practices in Jerusalem, had they been concerned with things other than the sacred history, the Exodus and the cult of Yahweh alone, would have had little chance of surviving. It is a fact that the writings of the First Isaiah, our best source of information on the pre-Deuteronomic religion of Jerusalem, have no concern for just these things which the reformers made so central. Here then is the first question: What did they reform, either in fact, or by creative history writing? Was there more, far more, in the religion of pre-exilic Jerusalem, than the later writers wished to perpetuate?[1]

Other questions immediately present themselves. Why is Moses not a part of the religion of the pre-exilic prophets? It has even been suggested that Moses is not mentioned in any genuinely pre-exilic writing. How can we have any picture of Israel's older ways when so much of the Old Testament has been edited and transmitted by the reforming Deuteronomists or those whom they had influenced? The preface to Deuteronomy shows what they set out to remove; we always read this as though these were pagan practices, but a careful scrutiny shows that this was not necessarily so.

First, they were to have the Law instead of Wisdom (Deut. 4.6). Israel had had wise men of her own, so how did their wisdom teachings relate to the reformed religion, and what was the Wisdom which the Law replaced? Second, they were to think only of the formless voice of God sounding from the fire and giving the Law (Deut. 19.12). Israel had long had a belief in the vision of God, when the glory had been visible on the throne in human form, surrounded by the heavenly hosts. What happened to the visions of God? And third, they were to leave the veneration of the host of heaven to peoples not chosen by Yahweh (Deut. 4.19–20). Israel had long regarded Yahweh as the Lord of the hosts of heaven, but the title Yahweh of Hosts was not used by the Deuteronomists. What happened to the hosts, the angels?

These three examples will suffice to make the point: the religious practices which the Deuteronomists opposed are known to have had

13

a place in the earlier religion of Israel. If they removed these as a part of their reform, and removed most of the references to them, how can their writings be evidence for anything other than their own ideals? There are dangers of circularity in this process: one can either assume that what they wrote about the early history of Israel was an account of what actually happened and that their reform was a return to the ancient ways; or one can be more sceptical, and see in their ancient histories a call to return to a golden age which had never existed in reality, but which served the reformers' purposes. One can see the uniformity of so much of the Old Testament as a sign that Israel's history was a living sermon on the ways of God, or one can see the uniformity as a sign that the hand of improvers has been at work.

The sceptical viewpoint is corroborated by evidence in extra-biblical texts. 1 Enoch, for example, remembers the period of the exile and restoration as a time of disastrous apostasy, a time when wisdom was despised and impurity installed in the Temple. It would be very hard not to read this as comment on the Deuteronomic reform which so altered the form of Israel's religion. This text implies that the true religion of Israel, i.e. the pre-exilic religion of Jerusalem, was preserved only by those who wrote 1 Enoch and related works. They kept a role for Wisdom which the Deuteronomists had subsumed under the Law; they kept a tradition of the heavenly ascent and the vision of God, which the Deuteronomists denied; they were astronomers who had a complex theology of heavenly hosts and angels which the Deuteronomists had said were not for the chosen people. Whom do we believe? Do we work with the picture of a pagan religion which the Deuteronomists reformed and brought back to pristine purity, or do we work with a picture of an ancient religion virtually stamped out by the Deuteronomists, who put in its place their own version of what Israel should believe? This question is not just academic, a fine point to be debated about the religions of the ancient Near East. Our whole view of the evolution of monotheism in Israel depends on the answer to this question, for the Deuteronomists are recognized as the source of the 'monotheistic' texts in the Old Testament and as the first to suppress anthropomorphism. If the Deuteronomists do not represent the mainstream of Israel's religion (and increasingly they are being recognized as a vocal minority), was the mainstream of that religion not monotheistic and did it have anthropomorphic theophanies at its centre?

Traditions recorded centuries later by the rabbis remembered that there had been drastic changes in the cult at this time, not all of them for the better. Josiah had 'hidden away' the ark, the anointing oil, the jar of manna, Aaron's rod and the coffer which the Philistines had sent as a gift when they returned the ark, as a precaution against the exile prophesied in Deut. 28.36 (b. *Horayoth* 12a; also b. *Kerithoth* 5b). From this we may conclude that the reform of Josiah not only removed the objects associated with Ba'al, Asherah and the host of heaven but also objects associated closely with the cult of Yahweh. The ark had been the place of his presence (he spoke to Moses from above the cherubim: Exod. 25.22), and the sacred oil had consecrated the one who wore his name and was his anointed, i.e. his Messiah. The anointed high priest of the first temple cult was remembered as having been different from the high priest of the second temple cult since the latter was described simply as the priest who 'wears many garments', a reference to the eight garments worn by him on Yom Kippur: 'And who is the anointed [high priest]? He that is anointed with the oil of unction, but not he that is dedicated with many garments.' (m. *Horayoth* 3.4). It was also remembered that the roles of the anointed high priest and the high priest of many garments differed in some respects at Yom Kippur when the rituals of atonement were performed. The anointed high priest, they believed, would be restored to Israel at the end of time, in the last days.

The reform of Josiah/the Deuteronomists, then, reconstructed as best we can from both biblical and non-biblical sources, seems to have been a time when more than pagan accretions were removed from the Jerusalem cult. Wisdom was eliminated, even though her presence was never forgotten, the heavenly ascent and the vision of God were abandoned, the hosts of heaven, the angels, were declared to be unfit for the chosen people, the ark (and the presence of Yahweh which it represented) was removed, and the role of the high priest was altered in that he was no longer the anointed. All of these features of the older cult were to appear in Christianity.

One of the few certainties in this area is that the name Yahweh was linked to the Moses traditions, and in two places in Exodus the writer makes it clear that the El traditions of the pre-Mosaic period, i.e. the tradition that the patriarchs worshipped God by the name of El, are to be understood as the forerunners of the Yahweh traditions he is describing.

Yahweh, the God of your fathers, the God of Abraham, the God of Isaac and the God of Jacob has sent me to you; this is my name for ever, and thus I am to

15

be remembered throughout all generations. (Exod. 3.15)

I am Yahweh. I appeared to Abraham, to Isaac and to Jacob as El Shaddai, but by my name Yahweh I did not make myself known to them. (Exod. 6.2–3)

A traditional study of the Pentateuch would assign these two passages to the Elohist and Priestly sources respectively, and explain the fusion as a memory of Israel's remoter past. Recent scholarship has offered a different explanation. The passages represent a fusion, but a fusion of the several strands of Israel's religion practised in the period immediately before the exile. One of these was the veneration of El in addition to Yahweh. The pressures of the exile and the zeal of the Deuteronomic reformers combined to produce a fusion of all Israel's traditions. Everything that could possibly have been subsumed under the religion of strictest Yahweh worship, the religion of Moses and the Law, was absorbed and reformulated. The rest was dismissed as Canaanite and condemned.

The key to the issue of the divine names and the origin of monotheism must lie in the Pentateuch since it is here more than anywhere that a great variety of names for God is to be found. Unfortunately much scholarly argument in this field, for all its meticulous care, has been somewhat circular. Whybray recently surveyed the history of the study of the Pentateuch and concluded of one of the classic hypotheses of Old Testament scholarship, the documentary hypothesis: '[It] was unduly dependent on a particular view of the history of the religion of Israel.'[2]

Now the documentary hypothesis has dominated the field over since Wellhausen over a century ago, even though he was not the first to suggest it. The 'particular view' of the history of Israel was a framework into which the great literary compositions of J and E were fitted. These great epics reflected the moods and aspirations of the time of Solomon, or the eighth century, or whatever, and the monotheism of Israel's religion was never questioned. This presupposition as to the course of Israel's history and religion was never acknowledged; it was probably not even recognized, yet the conclusions based on it have been used to demonstrate the validity of the very assumptions on which it was based. If the great epics of J and E really *had* formed the basis of the Pentateuch, how is it that the authors of Israel's earlier literature had virtually no knowledge of them? The fact that the authors of the pre-exilic literature of the Old Testament outside the Pentateuch appear to know virtually nothing of the *hufshum galam + erva*

patriarchal and Mosaic traditions of the Pentateuch raises serious doubts about the existence of an early J or E.'[3]

If the great bodies of epic literature did not exist in the ninth and tenth centuries, what was Israel thinking about God at that time? And how was God addressed: as Yahweh only, or as El, or as two separate deities with these names? What period of Israel's thought does the Pentateuch represent with its many names and manifestations of God all gathered into one tradition?

One trend in Pentateuchal studies has been to move away from the study of supposed literary sources, to a study of the theologies of the various parts and especially of the theology which shaped the final form. There are several examples of this change of emphasis, but they do seem to have one significant factor in common, significant, that is, for an enquiry into the names of God. More and more the final form of the Pentateuch, and therefore its final theology, is being associated with the work of the Deuteronomists:

The redactional process in the patriarchal narratives ... cannot be attributed to any setting one cares to mention, but must be brought, as regards both time and content, into a connection ... with the Deuteronom(ist)ic process of tradition and interpretation which itself still needs differentiation. Literary hypotheses should always be tested by their theological implications and the probability of the latter. Thus the processes of redaction and growth within the Pentateuchal tradition could not be investigated without the accompaniment of the question of their place in the history of theology and their theological function.[4]

If the Deuteronomists had emphasized above all else that it was Yahweh who brought Israel out of Egypt and that this was the beginning of the nation, whatever this represents in terms of theology must be recognized as crucial for our reading of the Old Testament. Yahweh and history became fundamental; what happened to everything else? Even the least sophisticated study of the seaming of Pentateuchal traditions at Exod. 3.15 and Exod. 6.2–3 shows that it was Yahweh which became the dominant name for God. It was acknowledged that this had not always been the only name for God, but this was the name by which God was in future to be known. Presumably this means that any non-Yahweh traditions were either dropped, or rewritten of Yahweh. There are, as we shall see, examples of this in the Second Isaiah. The unanswerable question must be: How many traditions were rewritten in the wake of the great reform and did everyone go along with the new ways?

17

There are several ways in which it is possible to glimpse behind the reform of the Deuteronomists. One is to examine the remaining references to El. If there was a distinction between El and Yahweh, such as appears to be reflected in the distinction between the sons of El and the sons of Yahweh, then any evidence for a distinction between El and Yahweh must be crucial. There are several texts where El is simply a designation of Yahweh; this could be a sign of later reworking (as it undoubtedly is in the Second Isaiah), or it could be due to the fact that El is both the name of the High God of Canaan and also the noun meaning 'god'. In Ps. 104, for example, which is a paean of praise to Yahweh, the young lions seek their food from El who must here be Yahweh. In Deut 7.9 Yahweh is described as the faithful God (El). In instances like these there cannot be any suggestion that the Canaanite High God is to be understood; 'el' means simply God. The exclamation in Josh. 22.22 is similar: the Mighty One, God the Lord is El Elohim Yahweh. But if 'el' means no more than God, what are we to understand by the assertions of the Second Isaiah, when he emphasizes that Yahweh is El? Surely he cannot have been proclaiming that Yahweh was a god?

The prophecies of the Second Isaiah are from the period of the exile, the period in which we have reason to believe that there was a process of fusion. What he says makes most sense if we assume that he was taking the title El and using it of Yahweh.

'... you are my witnesses,' says Yahweh.
'I am El, and also henceforth I am He.' (Isa. 43.12–13)
'Turn to me and be saved, all the ends of the earth!
For I am El and there is no other.' (Isa. 45.22)

There was only one God; everything that had formerly been believed of El and Yahweh was to be believed of the one God, Yahweh.[5] In addition to making these declarations of monotheism, the prophet took the older titles of El and altered them; they became titles of Yahweh. Gen. 14.9 gives us the ancient title of El Elyon: 'Creator (goneh) of heaven and earth'. This is known elsewhere in the ancient Near East as a title of El, and we can be fairly certain that the account in Genesis is accurate, even if we cannot account for how it came to be in its present place. The Second Isaiah took the ancient title and expanded it:

'I am Yahweh maker of all things, who stretched out the heavens alone, who spread out the earth.' (Isa. 44.24)

18

'... Yahweh your *maker*, who stretched out *the heavens* and laid the foundations of *the earth*.' (Isa. 51.13)[6]

Here there is clear evidence of the reuse and expansion of the ancient El title and its application to Yahweh. Even more significant for an enquiry into the sons of God is the fact that the prophet altered the verb used to express the creative act. In the El epithet the verb is traditionally a form of *qnh*, 'procreate,' *in seminate* whereas in Isaiah it is '*śh*, 'make'. The prophet has removed the idea that the creator God was the procreator, the father of gods and men. In other words, *the idea of a procreator God with sons seems to have fallen out of favour among those who equated Yahweh and El.* (Those who retained a belief in the sons of God, e.g. the Christians, as we shall see, were those who continued to distinguish between El and Yahweh, Father and Son. This cannot be coincidence.)

There are five instances of this formula altered for Yahweh in the Psalter; in each case Yahweh is the Maker of heaven and earth, not the Procreator:

> May you be blessed by Yahweh, Maker of heaven and earth. (Ps. 115.15)
> My help is from Yahweh, Maker of heaven and earth. (Ps. 121.2)
> Our help is in the name of Yahweh, Maker of heaven and earth. (Ps. 124.8)
> May Yahweh bless you from Zion, the Maker of heaven and earth. (Ps. 134.3)
> Yahweh his God, Maker of heaven and earth. (Ps. 146.5–6)

If we could date these texts in their present form with certainty, and know with equal certainty that the divine names in them had not been altered, as seems to have happened in Isaiah and some parts of Genesis, it would be possible to establish when Yahweh came to be identified with El. We cannot.

Yahweh the maker of heaven and earth also became Yahweh the maker of history. The Second Isaiah frequently appeals to the power of the creator as proof that he can also create history:

> Thus says God, (*ha'el*) Yahweh,
> who created the heavens and stretched them out,
> who spread forth the earth and what comes from it
> (...)
> Behold the former things have come to pass,
> and new things I now declare;
> before they spring forth I tell you of them. (Isa. 42.5, 9)

Compare Isa. 43.1–2, 15–31, which has a similar theme. The signs and wonders of the natural order became the signs and wonders of the sacred history. Jeremiah (or rather, his Deuteronomic editor) also linked the two:

AH, Lord Yahweh it is you who ~~have~~ made the heavens and the earth by your great power and your outstretched arm ... you brought your people Israel out of the land of Egypt with signs and wonders, with a strong hand and with outstretched arm and with great terror. (Jer. 32.17, 21)

Ps. 136 is similar: the first part praises Yahweh the creator of the earth and the second praises Yahweh the creator of Israel's history.

The Pentateuch tells us that El was the more ancient name for God and that Yahweh, the name revealed to Moses and connected with the Exodus tradition, replaced it. Names such as El Shaddai appear in the 'early' stories of Genesis and Exodus, and in ancient poetry such as the Balaam oracles (Num. 24). If we assume that the Pentateuch is an account of the events in Israel's remotest past, then we should expect the name El to have disappeared from use long before the time of the exile. But it did not disappear; on the contrary, the writings from the exilic period and later use El more frequently than the earlier texts. This gives rise to some extraordinary explanations in order to keep the traditional view of Israel's history intact. The Second Isaiah and Job, both exilic texts, use El. This is explained as a 'revitalisation of old liturgical forms'. In the later Psalms, Daniel and the apocalyptic writings 'El returns to popularity'. In Hellenistic Jewish literature it finally takes over from Yahweh,[7] perhaps due to the influence of Zeus Hypsistos. Is this special pleading really necessary? Is it possible that El never fell out of use? The evidence for so much of the earlier period of Israel's history has come from the Deuteronomists, who are known to have reformed and unified Israel's traditions. Could the later texts' use of El be a sign of their freedom from the reformers' influences, rather than a sign of conscious archaizing?

Several pieces of evidence point in this direction. First, there is no polemic against El in the Old Testament. There is plenty of polemic against Ba'al and other deities, even though the references may sometimes be veiled, but there is none against the Canaanite High God El. Perhaps, as Eissfeldt suggested, this is because El was never viewed as a threat to Yahweh.[8] Ugaritic material shows how the Canaanite deities were envisaged; each had its own characteristics and modes of manifestation. Yahweh corresponds in many ways to Ba'al, and as such we can understand the rivalry between them. But Yahweh also has many of the characteristics of El; how were these assimilated if there was no conflict between the two deities? Second, there is the evidence of Genesis. The patriarchs set up rural altars and had sacred trees and pillars; all these practices were forbidden by the Deuteronomic reformers at the end of the seventh century, yet this prohibition is in itself proof that such pillars, trees and altars were still a part of popular piety at the time. It has been suggested that the stories in Genesis which associate the patriarchs with these altars and pillars were an alternative to the destructive methods of the Deuteronomic reformers. The writer of the Pentateuch advocated absorbing the local cults into the collective memory of the people, and treating the cult places as memorials to events in Israel's past. It is widely agreed that the Canaanite harvest festivals became associated with the celebration of events in Israel's history: barley harvest with the Exodus, wheat harvest with Sinai and the grape harvest with the enthronement of the king. Cult places were similarly absorbed and given a place in the history of the patriarchs.

Consequently, if one begins, as I have done, with the view that the stories of the patriarchs in Genesis, even in their Yahwistic form, date from the time of the exile, it is still possible to explain such features as the El epithets and the references to the sacred trees, pillars and altars as consistent with the theological concerns and religious practices of that period, they are not archaic remnants of a distant primitive stage of Israelite religion.[9]

The veneration of El, then, could have been a part of Israelite religion as late as the time of the exile, and references to the El cult could have been written over by the Yahwist who, working in the shadow of the Deuteronomists, was gathering everything into the tradition of Yahweh. There was no conflict with El; his cult was simply absorbed, because it had always had a place in Israel's religion. Such a hypothesis (and it is only a hypothesis *as are all other attempts to reconstruct the history of Israel's religion*), makes sense of much of the evidence from later texts. It would mean that those who had not experienced or accepted the reformulations of the exilic prophet and the Deuteronomists would have retained the older belief in El and Yahweh as separate deities, perhaps as a Father figure and a Son figure, which is what the Ugaritic texts lead us to suppose and what Deut. 32.8 (in the Qumran version) actually says. Yahweh received Israel for his portion when El Elyon divided the nations among the sons of God.

One recent and radical suggestion about the origin of the Pentateuch is that it was composed as a national history in the manner of the

21

early Greek histories of Hellanicus, Hecataeus and Herodotus. John van Seters has challenged many of the fundamentals of Pentateuchal scholarship, and, even if he is not correct in all details, he has performed a valuable service in reminding scholars that there are no 'facts' in this field. The most popular hypotheses have, by frequent repetition, been transformed into facts, and this they are not. There is no proof, he says, that J and E, the great bases of the documentary hypothesis, ever existed, let alone that they were a reflection of national pride in the golden age of Solomon. One or two influential scholars, through their own writings and those of their pupils, have constructed hypotheses which, though interesting, are only hypotheses and dependent works seem to have lost sight of this. Van Seters cites Albright, Cross and Freedman. There is no evidence for the ancient Hebrew epic cycle which they advocate. The Pentateuch resembles rather the work of Herodotus, and its compiler, the Yahwist, was collecting materials and constructing his histories in a similar way.[10] The Pentateuch was a sixth-century composition, he says. Herodotus wrote in the fifth century; the period between them is not so vast. Herodotus is also thought to have been influenced by the forms and ideas of the Near East. The earlier Greek historians had used a mixture of myths, legends and genealogies to demonstrate the origin of Athenian society, its customs and institutions. Herodotus compiled his histories from several sources; some were written, some were tales he had heard on his travels, and sometimes he used 'to fabricate stories and anecdotes using little or no traditional material, only popular motifs or themes from other literary works'.[11] The resulting anthology was written to give the Greeks a sense of self-identity and national pride. This emphasis on the needs of the audience is important; the story or history was told with a clearly defined purpose and recording fact was not the primary consideration. A Pentateuch written in the exile could have had an exactly similar purpose; the loss of their homeland would have necessitated some other means of bonding the people together, and this was done by appeal to a common heritage of tradition and history. (This is what the Deuteronomists did when they appealed to the common experience of the Exodus; the Second Isaiah appealed to Abraham as the common ancestor, and so on.) If this *is* how the Pentateuch was compiled, then we cannot expect to find in it evidence for anything but the concerns of the exiles, and one of these seems to have been to relate the El practices to those of Yahweh's cult.

An extension of this view of the Pentateuch, and one whose implications are even more important, takes account of modern work on oral literature and its transmission. These studies have called into question many of the cherished beliefs that Israel's traditions were handed down by word of mouth for centuries before they were written down. Tellers of tales were more likely to have adapted the tale at each new telling than to have kept rigidly for centuries to an exact form. It was a fluid, not a fixed, tradition. Thus the material in the Pentateuch, which had been used to reconstruct the early and outgrown religious practices of Israel is now seen to be 'a mass of material, most of which may have been of quite recent origin ... [which] had not necessarily formed part of any ancient Israelite tradition.'[12]

The complex patterns in the Pentateuch, both in small units and in the extended compositions, are now recognized as evidence of a literary artistry far beyond anything that can be called 'compilation'. The scissors and paste methods of the earlier hypotheses are now seen to be unrealistic. The Pentateuch as we now have it is probably the product of one mind, that of a genius. If we could be certain of the motive for his writing, we could begin to understand what he was doing, and perhaps to guess at how he used his sources. We might even discover whether he was reflecting an established point of view, or expounding something new which was later adopted by his fellow exiles. We think of the prophets as great innovators, bringing new insights into their troubled situations. Why should a historian not be similarly prophetic? The Pentateuch would then be evidence for one point of view subsequently adopted by some, but not all, of the heirs to Israel's traditions.

In the light of current uncertainty about the age of materials in the Pentateuch, it is interesting to look again at the Canaanite parallels to Old Testament motifs and themes. The classic study of these is *Canaanite Myth and Hebrew Epic* by F. M. Cross, which uses Ugaritic materials to set the Old Testament in its ancient context. We can see that El and Ba'al were separate and easily identifiable types of divinity; their mythologies and modes of manifestation were different. The Yahweh of the Old Testament seems to be an amalgam of the two types. This is not to say that Israel's religion was simply plagiarism from Canaan, but only that Israel expressed its experience of the divine in the imagery and poetry which were common to all the peoples of Canaan. Such similarities as do exist show that many

Canaanite elements, such as the ribald revelries of the heavenly court and the birth of the gods, have not been used. But, when the terrifying theophanies of Yahweh are described, they resemble the appearances of the Canaanite storm god Ba'al. When heaven is described it resembles the Canaanite court of El.

Yahweh was judge and warleader of the historical community. He revealed himself to the patriarch Moses, led Israel in the conquest; he was the god who brought Israel up from the land of Egypt, her saviour. There is also the second strain which entered Israel's primitive religion, that of the high and eternal one, El the creator of heaven and earth, the father of all.[13]

The question we have to answer is: when did the two fuse, and why?

Yahweh and Ba'al were seen as rivals in the traditions associated with the prophet Elijah. These, recorded in good Deuteronomic style, made it quite clear that Israel could have only one Lord, Yahweh. The presence of Ba'al characteristics in Yahweh show that he must at some stage have been perceived as a similar deity. There is no record of conflict with El; all we have is the cryptic declaration of the Second Isaiah.

The proposed date of the fusion of El and Yahweh characteristics is based on the assumed date of the materials in the Pentateuch, the tenth- and ninth-century epics which, in the older theories of Pentateuchal origins, were combined by editors in the early period of the monarchy. (Remember that this was only a theory; there was no actual evidence for the existence of these epics, nor for their having been combined at the suggested time.) Yahweh is recognized as having 'El' characteristics as 'early' as the epic texts, 'except in the Sinai pericope and in the archaic hymns cited in the epic sources'.[14] But if these epic texts were not early, and if much of the oral material was no older than the tale as it was told, *we have no certain basis for saying that the combination of the two divine types took place in the early period.*

There is a similar hiatus in tracing the tradition of Yahweh's theophany in the storm. The presupposition that Yahweh and El were one God in Israel has led to some extremely complicated explanations of how 'primitive' Yahweh material came to be in later texts. Appearances of Yahweh were associated with storm imagery in the 'early' period and 'returned to popularity in the sixth century in proto-apocalyptic and persisted into full blown apocalyptic'.[15] (Exactly the same arguments were used, it will be recalled, to explain how the name El was so popular in sixth-century texts, when it had fallen out of use several centuries previously once the great epic writers had fused El and Yahweh!) The storm theophany in Job 38 is explained as a sixth-century text using archaic language. (The Second Isaiah's use of El was also archaic language!) Ezekiel saw Yahweh in the storm cloud (Ezek. 1.4), but this was proto-apocalyptic (the implication being that apocalyptic is a curious aberration, and somehow does not count as real evidence). Isa. 24.19–23 and 34.8–10, neither of which need be later than the eighth century, the time of the First Isaiah, are said to be later insertions in an archaizing form. Isa. 42.13–15, from the exilic period, and Isa. 59.16–19, from the time of the return, are both evidence of the revival of old forms of expression. The old language forms were revived, transformed and reappeared as the eschatological warfare imagery of the apocalyptists. It is amazing that such contorted arguments should ever have been given a serious hearing. Not only have they been heard, they have been handed on as though fact. A more likely explanation is that the storm imagery of Yahweh's theophanies had never disappeared, and, in its latest appearances in the apocalypses, represents a link with the very oldest traditions. Similarly the name El did not enjoy a sudden revival which eventually eclipsed the name Yahweh. Both Yahweh and El survived as distinct deities, but not in the post-Deuteronomic tradition.

One would expect that, after the author of the Pentateuch had explicitly identified El and Yahweh, a certain amount of rewriting would have taken place. Cross suggested that this fusion of the El and Yahweh divinities led to just such a renaming process, although he put it in the tenth century because he used the older method of dating the Pentateuch. 'The substitution of Yahweh for El ... would be natural when Yahweh became the principal cult name.'[16] *The consequences of this for our reading and understanding of the Old Testament cannot be overestimated.* This is not just a question of divine names; it is also a question of how many divinities were acknowledged. To say that there are places in the Old Testament where Yahweh seems to have El characteristics may in fact mean that we have a rewriting of an El tradition, which had formerly been a part of Israel's tradition in its El form. That may seem to be stating the obvious, but if we do not know the date at which this renaming took place, we cannot know for certain how much of Israel's tradition was monotheistic.

One or two observations will illustrate this. Cross quotes a piece of Ugaritic poetry where El and Ba'al are in parallel, but still, we assume, separate deities:

> Lift up your hands to Heaven;
> Sacrifice to Bull, your father El.
> Minister to Ba'l with your sacrifice,
> The son of Dagan with your provision.[17]

Could this affect the way we read some of the psalms, where we have always assumed that two divine names in parallel were no more than a poetic repetition of the names of God? 'Yahweh thundered in the heavens, and Elyon uttered his voice (Ps. 18.13) *might* refer to two deities. The relationship between El and Ba'al in the Ugaritic texts is also significant; El sits on the throne in his council, with Ba'l Haddu at his right hand. Ba'l had the titles king and judge, but he was still subordinate to El.[18] This is exactly the picture assumed in the parable of the sheep and the goats (Matt 25.31–46) where the king sits in judgement but acknowledges a Father. The king in the Gospel is called Son of Man, and it has long been recognized that the son of man vision of Dan. 7 has similarities to the pictures of Ba'l and El in the Ugaritic texts.[19] How, it must be asked, could a second-century text such as Daniel have had a living knowledge of the Ba'l traditions of Ugarit? How could a text written at a time when the religion of Jerusalem was threatened by the paganism of a foreign ruler, how could such a text employ pagan ideas? And what are they doing in the Gospel? The answer must surely be that these ideas were not pagan, but deeply rooted in the most conservative of Israel's traditions. The picture of Ba'l ascending to El had not only been a picture of Ba'l and El; it had also been a picture of Israel's God and another, El and Yahweh.

The restructuring of Israel's traditions and writings during the exile and the years which followed must always be borne in mind when reading the Old Testament. So too must the fact that many traces of the older ways survived, as can be seen in Dan. 7, and *were still being removed at the beginning of the Christian era*, as can be seen from the significant differences between the Qumran versions of certain Hebrew texts and those we now use. Such traces of the older ways as escaped the ancient scribes are often removed by modern readers as they read, since we have all been steeped in one particular view of the Old Testament and its monotheism. The first Christians did not read it as we do; they still knew that Yahweh was the son of Elyon. To read the Old Testament without our customary presuppositions is an illuminating experience, and it is to this that we now turn.

Notes to chapter two

1 This is the theme of my *The Older Testament.*

2 R.N. Whybray, *The Making of the Pentateuch*, JSOT Supplements Series 53, Sheffield 1987, p.130.

3 Ibid., p.130.

4 H.H. Schmid, 'In Search of New Approaches in Pentateuchal Research', JSOT 3 1977, pp.36, 39.

5 *The Older Testament*, chapter 6.

6 N.C. Habel, ' "Yahweh, Maker of Heaven and Earth"; a Study in Tradition Criticism', JBL 91 (1972). See also B. Vawter, 'Prov. 8.22: Wisdom and Creation', JBL 99 (1980), who argues that none of the evidence compels us to translate *qnh* by 'create'. I do not find his case convincing in the broader context I am proposing.

7 F.M. Cross, *Canaanite Myth and Hebrew Epic*, Cambridge, Mass. and London 1973, p.60 n.60.

8 O. Eissfeldt, 'El and Yahweh', JSS 1 (1956), pp.25–37.

9 J. van Seters, 'The Religion of the Patriarchs in Genesis', Biblica 61 (1980), p.232.

10 J. van Seters, *In Search of History: Historiography in the Ancient World and the Origins of Biblical History*, New Haven and London 1983, pp.30ff.

11 Ibid., p.53.

12 Whybray, op.cit., p.242.

13 Cross, op.cit., p.75.

14 Ibid., p.183.

15 Ibid., p.169.

16 Ibid., p.71.

17 Ibid., p.181.

18 Ibid., p.185.

19 J.A. Emerton, 'The Origin of the Son of Man Imagery', JTS New Series ix (1958), pp.225–42.

Chapter three The Evidence of the Old Testament

The Old Testament must be allowed to speak for itself. We are accustomed to read it as the writings of a monotheistic faith which had one God with several names such as Elohim, Yahweh and Elyon. We assume that the angels which are so prominent in later texts were not an integral part of the older faith and that bizarre mythology such as developed in the other cultures of the ancient Near East had no real place in the religion of Israel. In such reconstructions as this, the faith of ancient Israel has been sanitized for the benefit of modern readers for whom mythology, ritual and mystery are too reminiscent of all that has been cast aside with the Reformation. History, archaeology and fact are all-important. The reforming Deuteronomists with their emphasis on history and law have evoked a sympathetic response in many modern scholars who have found there a religion after their own heart. Thus we have inherited a double distortion; the reformers edited much of what we now read in the Hebrew Bible, and modern interpreters with a similar cast of mind have told us what the whole of that Hebrew Bible was saying. The fact that most ancient readers of the texts read them very differently is seen as a puzzle. How could the first Christians have read the Old Testament in this way? How could those who translated the Hebrew Bible into Aramaic have chosen such strange ways to translate the various names for God? How could Philo have introduced alien ideas in order to fuse his Judaism with first-century Greek philosophy? and so on. The most crucial of all questions is: How was it that Christian theology grew so quickly into a complex system if the greater part of that system had not existed within the Judaism from which it grew? This system will have included the beliefs implicit in the earliest titles for Jesus and all the expectations associated with him. The first Christians related these beliefs closely to the Old Testament by means of proof texts. Were these simply pegs on which to hang new ideas or were they re-stating established ideas, derived from a way of reading the Old Testament which we have now lost? There are no simple answers, but an attempt to read the Old Testament *as it is* does point consistently in one direction.

Ps. 89 gives a glimpse of its world, the heaven and earth of the first temple. It extols Yahweh the god of Israel and the Davidic king. The supremacy of the king is a manifestation of the supremacy of Yahweh; Ps.89.1–18 describes the power of Yahweh and Ps.89.19–37 describes the derived power of the king. The king is the greatest ruler on earth (v.27), because Yahweh is the greatest power in heaven. The psalm shows several features of that ancient world, not least the role of national pride in the formulation of theology. The psalmist depicts heaven as a place of many holy ones; Yahweh was the greatest of these holy ones, feared in their assembly, ruler of the waters of chaos and enthroned on righteousness and justice. Yahweh is the Holy One of Israel (v.18), *one heavenly being among many.*

The Holy Ones are angel figures who appear in texts from all periods in the Old Testament. In Daniel, a late text, they are the agents of Elyon, the Watchers who bring his decrees to earth (Dan. 4.14; EV 17). Two of them discuss the fate of Jerusalem (Dan. 8.13) and the Holy Ones of Elyon are promised the kingdom (Dan. 7.18, 25, 27). They are Yahweh's entourage, for example, when he comes as King (Deut. 33.2–3). This obscure text is usually thought to represent Israel's most ancient beliefs, and yet a very similar picture of Yahweh appearing with the Holy Ones to become king is found in Zech. 14.1–9, one of the latest parts of the Old Testament. A similar text is the setting of 1 Enoch, and this is quoted in Jude 14:

> Enoch saw the vision of the Holy One in the heavens
> (...)
> And behold, he cometh with ten thousands of his holy ones
> To execute judgement upon all,
> And to destroy all the ungodly. (1 Enoch 1.2, 9)

We have to envisage an ancient kingmaking rite, known in post-exilic times and to the first Christians, when Yahweh the Holy One came to his people both as king and as judge. The imagery of this ceremony had embedded itself deeply into the memory of the people, because it persisted from the time of the monarchy at least until the late first century AD when Jude was written. If we could understand what was done we should know the significance of what is depicted in the surviving texts, and should be much nearer understanding the first formulation of Christian belief, since this expectation of the coming of the king from heaven was the basis of the early parousia expectations. In other words, the Christians expected of Jesus what had formerly been expected of Yahweh and they called him the Holy One (Mark 1.24).

In the Old Testament Yahweh himself is frequently called *the* Holy One or the Holy One of Israel, as he is in 1 Enoch 1.2. It would be very strange had this title not meant that he was regarded as the guardian angel of Israel, one of the sons of Elyon appointed to rule the nations. Habakkuk calls to 'Yahweh, my God, my Holy One' (Hab. 1.2), and he too describes how the Holy One comes for the great judgement on his enemies (Hab. 3.3). The Psalms tell of the Holy One enthroned on the praises of Israel (Ps. 22.3; 71.22). Although Yahweh is one among several Holy Ones, it comes as no surprise to discover that Israel hailed her Holy One as the greatest of the Holy Ones and so Yahweh triumphs over the other gods. In the Song of the Sea (Exod. 15), usually thought to be an ancient song incorporated into the account of the Exodus rather than a poem inspired by it, Yahweh defeats the waters and the enemies of his people. None of the gods is so powerful as Yahweh (Exod. 15.11). The prologue to Job shows a less incomparable Yahweh, a Yahweh taunted by the other sons of God, who agreed to test the loyalty of his servant Job (Job 1.6–12). Pss. 58 and 82 show Yahweh as the judge of the heavenly court. He is called upon to punish the gods (Ps. 58.1) and to condemn them to death (Ps. 82.6).

The First Isaiah is another window onto the cult of the first temple, and Holy One is one of the characteristic names of Yahweh in this text.

> They have forsaken Yahweh
> They have despised the Holy One of Israel. (Isa. 1.4)
> They have rejected the Law of Yahweh of Hosts,
> And have despised the word of the Holy One of Israel. (Isa. 5.24; cf. 10.20; 12.6; 37.23 and many more)

Yahweh the Holy One was also Yahweh of Hosts:[1]

> Yahweh of Hosts, the Mighty One of Israel (Isa. 1.24)
> My eyes have seen the King, Yahweh of Hosts (Isa. 6.5)

Note that Isaiah *saw* Yahweh, something which the Deuteronomic reformers said was impossible (Deut. 4.12). The vision of God and anthropomorphism are seen, time and again, as evidence of the older ways. Yahweh was also the Mighty One, and, as in the theophanies of Deut. 33 and Zech. 14, he was the King. He was the Judge (Isa. 2.4), and the Day of Yahweh was to be a time of horror (Isa. 2.12–19; chapters 24–7, *passim*; chapter 34. See also Hab. 3). Yahweh had a book of judgement (Isa. 34.16, cf. Exod. 32.33; Ps. 87), and a terrible sword (Isa. 34.5–6). The Messiah was the Branch of Yahweh (Isa. 4.2) on whom the Spirit of Yahweh was to rest (Isa. 11.2).

In addition, Isaiah described Elyon on his mount of assembly in the far north. The King of Babylon, or rather his heavenly counterpart, had attempted in pride to raise himself above Elyon. The prophet saw that he was cast down to Sheol. Thus when we read Isaiah we are reading texts which envisaged more than one deity; there was El Elyon the High God, there were the angels of the nations and there was Yahweh the avenging angel, protector and judge of his people. The climax of the book of Isaiah is the demise of the Assyrian army before the walls of Jerusalem. Yahweh had promised to defend his city (Isa. 37.35), and the Angel of Yahweh destroyed the army. Was this angel an agent of Yahweh, or was the angel the manifestation of Yahweh? The text is usually read as though the former were the case, but there is considerable evidence to suggest that the angel *was* Yahweh. It is this angel which is the key to recovering beliefs about Elyon and Yahweh and to the ultimate origin of Christian belief about Jesus.

There are many references in the Old Testament to the Angel of Yahweh, and of these, some would most naturally be taken to mean that the Angel of Yahweh was Yahweh's servant or emissary, his messenger. Thus the Angel of Yahweh speaks *to* Yahweh of Hosts (Zech. 1.12), Abraham said that Yahweh would send his angel to guide his servant (Gen. 24.7), and when pestilence fell on Judah after David's census, the Angel of Yahweh brought the sword of Yahweh to punish the people. The pestilence was halted when Yahweh commanded the angel to put away the sword (1 Chron. 21.27). In these examples the angel is depicted as a separate being. Included in this group must be the Exodus and wilderness narratives (Exod. 23.20, 23; 32.34; 33.2; Num. 20.16) which refer to 'my angel' and 'an angel' and especially the one of whom Yahweh said 'My name is in him' (Exod. 23.21).

The account of the census in 2 Sam. 24, however, is not so clear as to the identity of the angel figures. A careful reading shows that of the three names (Yahweh, the angel, and the Angel of Yahweh) it is by no means certain that the Angel of Yahweh was the unnamed angel. The Angel of Yahweh could have been Yahweh himself, but distinguished from the destroying angel. When the Angel of Yahweh, who is mentioned only once, appeared to David at the threshing floor,

David did not speak to *the Angel of Yahweh* but 'David spoke to Yahweh, when he saw the angel who was destroying the people' (2 Sam. 24.16–17). It is interesting that David chose to make the threshing floor where the angel appeared a holy place. In the stories of the patriarchs, altars were built where *the Lord* appeared and not just an angel (e.g. Gen. 12.7; 26.23; 35.1).

There are other texts where the Angel of Yahweh appears in isolation, and had we been told that the Angel of Yahweh was another name for Yahweh, just as Yahweh and Elohim are said to be synonyms,[2] the text would still make perfect sense.

> The Angel of Yahweh encamps around those who fear him (Ps. 34.7)
> Let them be like chaff before the wind
> with the Angel of Yahweh driving them on
> Let their way be dark and slippery
> with the Angel of Yahweh pursuing them. (Ps. 35.5–6)

The prophet Elijah was instructed by the Angel of Yahweh (2 Kings 1.3, 15); it would have excited no comment had the texts read 'Yahweh said to Elijah'. The Angel of Elohim (Exod. 14.19) could as easily have been Elohim.

Later interpretations of these angel passages, especially those concerning the Exodus, were at pains to emphasize that the mighty deeds had been done by Yahweh himself, not by an angel or a messenger. The killing of the firstborn in Egypt (Exod. 12.12) was not the work of an angel; the Exodus was Yahweh's work alone, as were vengeance and recompense (Deut. 32.35).[3] Why should there have been this emphasis when the account of the Exodus has several references to angels, as we have seen, and Judg. 2.2 actually says that it was the *Angel of Yahweh* which brought Israel up from Egypt? One possible explanation is that by the time the interpretations were made the Angel of Yahweh *had come to mean* a separate being, an emissary, when formerly it had meant Yahweh himself. 'Not by means of an angel and not by means of a messenger' would have been emphasizing the original intention of the text. These commentators would have known that the Angel of Yahweh *was* Yahweh and not another being.

A similar tendency is seen in the LXX of Eccles. 5.6, which has 'Do not say in the presence of God' where the Hebrew has 'Do not say before *the angel*', and the LXX of Isa. 63.9 which has 'Not a messenger nor an angel but he himself saved them', whereas the Hebrew has '*The angel* of his presence'. By the time the Greek translation was made it was recognized that a clear statement was necessary; 'angel' no longer meant what it had meant when the Hebrew texts were written. The translator knew that *the angel* had a special significance.

It is in the light of this possibility that we examine a third group of texts (incidentally the largest group), where Yahweh and the Angel of Yahweh seem to be interchangeable, i.e. synonymous. Zech. 12.8, one of the latest texts, has: 'The house of David shall be like Elohim, like the angel of Yahweh at their head.' Zech. 3.4–5, from the time of the restoration, describes Joshua standing before the Angel of Yahweh and Satan accusing him. The text mentions both the Angel of Yahweh and Yahweh, but it is possible that the variation was simply a matter of style. There were not two figures. The high priest stands before the Angel of Yahweh (3.1) and Satan accuses him. Yahweh speaks to Satan (3.2) and the Angel gives orders for Joshua to be vested (3.3). It is the Angel who takes away the high priest's iniquity (3.4). The speech pattern of the passage shows that no matter who is speaking, Yahweh is mentioned in the third person. Thus in 3.2 Yahweh says, 'Yahweh rebukes you, Satan', but in 3.7 it is the Angel of Yahweh who says, 'Thus says Yahweh ...' The Angel and Yahweh could be identical. Strangest of all is the role of the Angel; if the Angel and Yahweh were separate, would Satan have accused Joshua before the Angel rather than before the Lord? And would the Angel have taken away iniquity and ordered the vesting of the High Priest? The most reasonable reading of the text would make Yahweh and the Angel one and the same.

Two pieces of poetry, both thought to be ancient, also equate Yahweh and the Angel:

> The God before whom my fathers Abraham and Isaac walked
> the God who has led me all my life long to this day
> *the angel* who has redeemed me from all evil ... (Gen. 48.15–16)

> Curse Meroz, says the *Angel of Yahweh*,
> Curse bitterly its inhabitants,
> Because they came not to the help of Yahweh
> To the help of Yahweh against the mighty. (Judg. 5.23)

In the former it would be hard to distinguish between God and the angel.

Finally there are the narratives. The three who visited Abraham at Mamre were variously described as 'men', 'angels' and Yahweh. Yahweh appeared to Abraham (Gen. 18.1), three men stood before him (Gen. 18.2), Yahweh spoke to Abraham (Gen. 18.10, 13), the men set out for Sodom (Gen. 18.16), the two angels came to Sodom in the evening (Gen. 19.1). This story does not mention the Angel of Yahweh by name, but the three 'men' are clearly Yahweh and two angels, and this is how the first Christians read the passage. Note the human form of the manifestation of Yahweh.

Gideon saw the Angel of Yahweh, and this storyteller too identified Yahweh and the Angel of Yahweh. The Angel of Yahweh appeared to Gideon (Judg. 6.11–12), and introduced himself as Yahweh (Judg. 6.12). It is then as Yahweh that he speaks to Gideon (Judg. 6.14, 16). The Angel of Yahweh disappears, and Gideon realizes whom he has seen. He fears because he has seen the Angel of Yahweh face to face (Judg. 6.22) but Yahweh reassures him that he will not die (cf. Exod. 33.20, where Yahweh said 'You cannot see my face; for man shall not see *me* and live'). The parents of Samson also saw the Angel of Yahweh (Judg. 13.3). He was a man of Elohim who looked like an angel of Elohim. The couple, like Gideon, feared they would die because they had seen God (Judg. 13.22). Hagar saw the Angel of Yahweh (Gen. 16.7, 9, 10, 11) and was amazed that she had *seen God* and lived (Gen. 16.13). When Abraham encountered Yahweh in the burning bush it was the Angel of Yahweh who appeared to him (Exod. 3.2), Elohim spoke to him (Exod. 3.3) and then Yahweh spoke to him (Exod. 3.7) (LXX had *kyrios* at 3.4). Here Elohim, Yahweh and the Angel of Yahweh are three equivalent terms. It has long been assumed that Elohim and Yahweh represent the same being, even though the ancients recognized that they denoted different aspects of the divinity; why should we not understand the Angel of Yahweh in the same way? Similarly in the account of the sacrifice of Isaac (Gen. 22.12), the *Angel of Yahweh* says to Abraham 'You have not withheld your son from *me*'. Why 'me'? When Jerusalem was besieged by the Assyrians (2 Kings 19.34–5; Isa. 37.35–6), Yahweh said that *he* would defend and save Jerusalem, and then it was the Angel of Yahweh who went out to destroy the enemy camp. Was Yahweh the Angel? The story of Balaam's ass tells how Yahweh appeared to Balaam with a drawn sword, how Yahweh opened the mouth of the ass, and then he opened the eyes of Balaam so that he could recognize *the Angel of Yahweh*. This is similar to the ambiguity in the Gideon story, where Gideon recognized the Angel of Yahweh and said 'Alas Lord Yahweh, for I have seen the Angel of Yahweh.' Yahweh said, 'Peace, do not fear, you shall not die.'

What are we to make of all this, especially since scholars think that the major compilation of the Pentateuch was done by someone identifying Yahweh with El the God of the fathers and consequently altering names? The bulk of the evidence suggests that the Angel of Yahweh and Yahweh had been identical, some examples are open to either reading, and very few indeed refer clearly to two separate beings, Yahweh and the Angel. The Yahweh Angel had had the form of a man, sometimes a man with a sword (cf. Isa. 34.5–6, which describes the sword of Yahweh, and Josh. 5.13–15). He protected his people, did battle with their enemies and was their redeemer (Gen. 48.16). He was their judge and appointed the high priest (Zech. 3.4–5). Was this Yahweh, the Holy One of Israel, the son of Elyon?

In addition, the Old Testament records more elaborate visions of Yahweh. Micaiah saw Yahweh as the king on his throne, surrounded by the host of heaven. Such a vision was the source and authentication of his prophecies (1 Kings 22.19–23). Isaiah saw him as the King, Yahweh of Hosts on his throne, surrounded by seraphim. In neither case is the vision described in any detail. Only Ezekiel attempts to describe the glory of Yahweh. He saw the chariot throne, which was represented in the temple by 'the golden chariot of the cherubim that spread their wings' (1 Chron. 28.18), and on the throne he saw 'the likeness as it were of a human form' (Ezek. 1.26). The upper part of the body was of bronze and the lower part of fire. A vivid rainbow of colour surrounded him. The voice from the throne summoned Ezekiel and sent him as a prophet. In a second vision (Ezek. 8.2) the prophet saw the same figure, but this time without his throne.[4] In Ezek. 9.4 the figure is clearly named as Yahweh, who summoned the six angelic executioners to Jerusalem and sent the heavenly scribe to mark the foreheads of the faithful with the letter *tau*, the mark of Yahweh. A very similar figure, a man of fire and bronze clothed with linen and gold, appeared to Daniel (Dan. 10.5–6). Again, there was no throne. The angel figure came to reveal the future to Daniel (Dan. 10.14). He revealed himself as the angelic defender of Israel who had been helped by the archangel Michael in the battle against the prince of the kingdom of Persia. Since we know that the unnamed angel of fire and bronze, the defender of Israel, *cannot* in this passage have been Michael, was he Yahweh, Israel's most ancient defender? The angel of fire and bronze appears in many later texts, but often without a name (see chapter 5).

There is other significant information about the Angel in the Old

Testament. The four names of the Messiah, for example, are given in Isa. 9.6 as Wonderful Counsellor, Mighty God, Everlasting Father, Prince of Peace, but they are summarized in the LXX by one, 'The Angel of Great Counsel'. The Angel was fourfold. It has been suggested that the four titles of the Angel were individually represented by the four archangels and these eventually obscured the single identity of the original Angel.[5] Thus Gabriel, 'Strength of God', was Yahweh as the Mighty God, El Gibbor (Isa. 10.21); Raphael, 'Healing of God', was Yahweh as the healer (Exod. 15.26; Ps. 30.2); Phanuel, 'Presence of God' (later Uriel, 'Light of God'), was invoked in the high priestly blessing 'The Lord make his face to shine upon you' (Num. 6.25); and Michael, 'Who is like God?', was the incomparable Yahweh proclaimed by the Second Isaiah 'To whom will you compare me?' (Isa. 40.25, cf. 40.18, 43.11). In Isaiah's prophecy Wonderful Counsellor was Michael, as can be seen from the themes of Job and the Second Isaiah that Yahweh's incomparability lay in his wisdom (Job 38–9; Isa. 40, 43). Mighty God was Gabriel, Everlasting Father was Raphael and Prince of Peace was Phanuel, the Angel of the Presence and Light of God. The Great Angel was thus a figure of four aspects but these were known as late as the time of the translation of the LXX to have been four aspects of One.

The prophecies of Isaiah also show that the Angel was manifested in the child born to the royal house, and other texts confirm that Yahweh was manifested in human form in the Davidic king. I doubt that we shall ever fully understand what lies behind some of the more extraordinary statements in the Old Testament, but we can at least look at what is there. The account of Solomon's coronation says that the king sat on the throne of Yahweh and was worshipped with him. In this verse (1 Chron. 29.20) there are two objects to the one verb: *the people worshipped Yahweh and the king*. Can we justify separating the two actions as do the English translations? *The people worshipped Yahweh and did obeisance to the king* reads into the text a whole lot of things which may be obscuring what was actually said, especially as we have also been told that Solomon sat on the throne of Yahweh as king (1 Chron. 29.23), a text where there is no ambiguity at all. There is confusion, too great for us to know what happened at a coronation, but the texts do show that there was some relationship between the king and Yahweh which virtually identified them. Ps. 45 implies the same relationship. There are several possible renderings of Ps. 45.7: 'your divine throne', 'your throne is a throne of God', 'your throne O God' are the three offered by the RSV, but in a psalm addressed to the king, any of these is significant. This was noticed and used by the early Christian writers (see chapter 10). His throne in the temple must have been the throne of Yahweh, the chariot throne. Ps. 11 also describes the throne in the temple as divine:

Yahweh is in his holy Temple
Yahweh's throne is in heave. (Ps. 11.4)

There are other references, now obscured, to the divinity of the king or to his cult. Zephaniah, a prophet at the time of Josiah's reform (Zeph. 1.1) condemned those who 'bow down on the roofs to the host of the heavens, those who bow down and swear to Yahweh and yet swear by Milcom' (Zeph. 1.5). Thus the English, but the Hebrew can be read differently, as indeed it was by the translators of the LXX which has 'Those who swear by the Lord and those who swear by their king', the same pairing, suggesting that the identification of Yahweh as the king was one of the objects of the reformers' zeal. A similar condemnation is implicit in the passage inserted by a later editor at Amos 5.26, where exile is threatened, doubtless with the wisdom of hindsight. The reason for the exile is opaque in the Hebrew, but it seems that 'Sakkuth your king' should be read, as does the Greek and the quotation in the *Damascus Rule* (CD VII) 'the tabernacle or shrine of your king'. This object, together with whatever is concealed in the rest of the verse, possibly a reference to a star god, sums up the idolatry for which the people were punished with exile. Again, it is worship of the king which is the issue, and associating it with the exile does point to the time of Josiah.

The kingmaking ritual in Jerusalem has long been recognized as similar to the enthronement of Ba'al described in the Ugaritic texts, but when one compares these texts with the Old Testament material, a problem arises. Was the figure who corresponded to Ba'al in the Jerusalem ritual the Davidic king, or was it Yahweh? Or was it both, i.e. was the king thought to be divine? Is it possible that the Davidic king was seen as Yahweh, as implied by the Chronicler's description of Solomon's coronation? A key passage is the son of man vision in Dan. 7 which is thought to have had close links with Ps. 2. It may have been an imaginative elaboration of the psalm, or, as is more likely, it may have been a vision shaped by the memory of royal rituals to which the psalm alludes. If this latter is the case, then the son of man figure was the Davidic king. But Dan. 7 has also been shown to resemble closely the Ugaritic accounts of Ba'al himself ascending to El, to be installed as king and judge. 'Behind the figure of the Son of man lies Yahwe and ultimately Ba'al.'[6] Israel must have had a divinity Yahweh who corresponded in some ways to Ba'al and was represented in Dan. 7 by the Man figure, who was enthroned. The theophanies in Deut. 33.2–5, Hab. 3 and Zech. 14 were descriptions of this same installation of Yahweh as king and judge.

The vision in 2 Esd. 13, from the end of the first century AD, i.e. some two hundred and fifty years after the Daniel vision, is based on the same underlying tradition. Here the Man figure is described as a son of Elyon, i.e. as an angel. If he was a son of Elyon at the end of the first century, then presumably he was also divine in the Daniel text, and if so, who were the two divinities of the vision? Daniel, unfortunately, gives no recognizable names; there is the Ancient of Days, and there is one like a son of man. In the classic study of this vision by Emerton, it is assumed that the Ancient of Days was Yahweh, 'The Ancient of Days must, in Maccabaean times, have been understood to be Yahwe'[7] but this is not necessarily so. The deity in the Aramaic chapters of Daniel is named '*Illaya* (Elyon), and this was the ancient name for the High God, which means that the unnamed angel/son of man figure was the Holy One, Yahweh. The son of man figure certainly resembled Yahweh. One explanation offered for this is that the old Yahweh figure had somehow been divided; the High God remained Yahweh, and the functions of the warrior angel were separated off and assigned to the archangel Michael.[8] But if the High God had never been Yahweh, the vision in Daniel would record accurately the older traditions of Jerusalem.

If the king represented Yahweh in the rituals, how was it possible for Yahweh to address the king, as in Ps. 2? There is always the temptation to bring twentieth-century thinking to bear upon these texts and thus to identify some things as inconsistencies. But if the king sat on the divine throne, and Yahweh was thought to reign as king, we have to take this seriously in our attempts to reconstruct what was believed. Perhaps we read these texts much as an alien might see a celebration of the Eucharist; things are done and said which, if taken literally, seem impossible; yet to those who participate, they are profoundly significant. To begin to understand the rituals, and therefore the ways in which Yahweh was manifested to his people, we have to accept that Yahweh 'was' the king, and that the king was called Yahweh's son. No supernatural birth was envisaged, as is clear from 1 Chron. 28.6: 'It is Solomon your son who shall build my house and my courts, for I have chosen him to be my son, and I will be his father', but how this sonship was achieved is not known. Ps. 89 may be a way into the problem:

> Of old thou didst speak in a vision to thy faithful one, and say:
> 'I have set the crown upon one who is mighty,
> I have exalted one chosen from the people.' (Ps. 89.19)

'Vision' and 'exaltation' are highly significant words, especially if exaltation means 'raising up' in more than just the sense of conferring high status. There are many examples in the ancient Near East of royal figures being raised up into the presence of their gods. (For the moment we shall not ask what was meant by this, or whether there was anything to substantiate this claim rooted in royal mythology.) Emenduranki, for example, the legendary seventh king of Babylon, was summoned to the presence of the gods to learn the secrets of the creation and the divinatory techniques which were later the exclusive preserve of the kings. He became the founder of a guild of diviners. Such ascending figures were fairly common, but invariably they were royal; there were flying king cults in India, in South-East Asia and in China. These shaman figures are part of the universal experience of mankind. The ascent is always described in terms of the mythology of the shaman's own people, but all experience the sacred ascent which takes them beyond time into a world of heavenly knowledge. Their emblems are often winged or feathered. It is interesting that the emblem of royalty in Israel was a winged disc, a small indication that perhaps Israel shared in this world of the royal ascent. The heavenly journey reinforced the belief that the ordinary world of human existence and the upper world of their mythology were once in a harmony which had been destroyed by the action of evil forces. The shaman had to repel these forces and thus restore the cosmic harmony. As a result of his initiation he had enhanced powers of vision and hearing; he could see into the very nature of things and understand the processes of life itself. Thus he became a healer. The commonest way to induce the experience of ascent was by fasting, lightening the body so that the soul could fly. Once the shaman figure had ascended to the heavenly places and knew the secrets of the creation, he enjoyed a life which had already passed through death, and he became a being from another world.

We do not know the mythology of Israel, but it is more than likely that the interpretation of the royal ascent experience was in terms of this lost mythology. In addition, our own predisposition prevents our recognizing this underlying mythology, and from reading familiar texts in an unfamiliar way. M. Eliade made this point very strongly in his *Myths, Dreams and Mysteries*, although not speaking of the Old Testament:

All too often the occidental allows himself to be impressed by the manifestation of an ideology, when he is ignorant of the one thing it is important above all other to know: the ideology itself, that is, the myths ... In a number of different contexts ... we find complementary but structurally indissoluble meanings which fall into a pattern ... Furthermore, we do not manage to decipher everything that such a pattern presents ... until ... we take the trouble to integrate them into a whole.[9]

The starting point for reconstructing the royal mythology must be Dan. 7, if only because it describes how 'dominion, glory and kingdom' are bestowed by the Ancient of Days (Dan. 7.14). This text describes an ascent to heaven as the preliminary to the installation of a royal figure, but it is an external account of the process, an enthronement *observed* by the visionary rather than one in which he participates. Several later texts describe the ascent experience from within, so to speak, and tell how the visionary ascends to the presence of God and is thereby transformed. There are also very ancient texts in which this experience is implied.

Two passages in the Old Testament suggest that Israel's mythology did include a belief that the king 'ascended' into the presence of God. The first is from the eighth century, Isaiah's oracle against Babylon (Isa. 14). The King of Babylon (Isa. 14.4) was also Day Star, son of Dawn, (Isa. 14.12) who had climbed too high in the heavenly places. Because he had attempted to set himself above Elyon, he was thrown down 'like a loathed branch' (Isa. 14.19) and left to die. Presumably the King of Babylon was thought to have had a heavenly counterpart whose demise both symbolized and caused his own. The king's heavenly aspect was the Day Star, whom we know from the Ugaritic texts to have been one of the sons of El,[10] in other words he was a god. When he was thrown down as punishment for his pride, he became mortal. The second is Ezekiel's royal oracle against the King of Tyre (Ezek. 28.12–19), who had been in Eden, the garden of God on the holy mountain, and had been driven out for corrupting his wisdom. An earlier oracle (Ezek. 28.2–10) had condemned the Prince of Tyre for thinking that he was a god, in strange contrast to this later oracle where he – or his heavenly self – was clearly divine. The jewels which covered him were his sanctuary, and when this was profaned, he was destroyed along with the city and people of which he was the patron. The judgement was executed by the Lord Yahweh.[11]

These descriptions of the kings of Babylon and Tyre fit exactly with the situation depicted in Ps. 82, where the gods, the sons of Elyon, are judged and condemned to die like men. Note too that the King of Babylon is a despised branch, *netser*, a word used only of people, just as the royal prince of the house of Jesse is called the *branch* from his root (Isa. 11.1), and the *branch* in Dan. 11.7 is Ptolemy III Euergetes. Once only is the word used of a non-royal person, and then it is Isaiah's description of Israel, the people whom Yahweh has planted (Isa. 60.21). If 'branch' can be used to describe a Davidic prince as well as the King of Babylon, and if the fall of the sons of Elyon also underlies Ps. 82, it is possible that the other aspects of this myth were applied to the Davidic kings. Did they, like the kings of Babylon and Tyre, have a divine counterpart, their star, their son of Elyon on the mountain of God? If so, it would explain the curious line in Matt. 2.2: 'Where is he who is born king of the Jews? *For we have seen his star* …' The Second Isaiah democratized this royal theology, and applied it to the people as a whole. He used this same imagery of casting down when he applied the royal titles to Israel: 'You are my Servant, I have chosen you and not cast you off' (Isa. 41.9), and this suggests, as does Ps. 2, that the king was raised up onto the holy mountain, perhaps in a mystical ascent, and certainly in the royal mythology which supported the monarchy.

We see in these oracles the remnants of Israel's royal mythology. The Davidic kings ascended to the garden of God and sat in the divine council as did the rulers of Babylon and Tyre. The Second Isaiah explained the destruction of Jerusalem as the casting out of Israel's princes: 'Therefore I profaned the princes of the sanctuary, I delivered Jacob to utter destruction and Israel to reviling' (Isa. 43.28). Who could the princes of the sanctuary have been if they were *profaned*? This verb *ḥll* was also used to describe the fate of the King of Tyre, the demise of a divinity. The princes of Jerusalem's sanctuary had had a similar fate (cf. 'He has cast down from heaven to earth the splendour of Israel', Lam. 2.1). If these princes had been the visible manifestation of Yahweh to his people, then the reputation of Yahweh as a god was bound up with their fate. Yahweh was tested along with the loyalty of his servants under stress, as is so vividly depicted in Job, and the prosperity of his people reflected his power. Thus Ezekiel explained that the people would be restored to their land for the sake of Yahweh's reputation among the nations (Ezek. 36.22–3). Our reading of the Second Isaiah is, however, complicated by the fact that he identified El and Yahweh and thus confused the earlier picture of Yahweh as the judge. The events of history seemed to have shown that Yahweh himself had been judged and thrown from his city, but this was clearly impossible. It was proclaimed that Yahweh had punished his city and this is how the impossible had happened: 'Yahweh is in the right, for I have rebelled against his word' (Lam. 1.18).

Almost contemporary with Dan. 7 is the *Exodus* of Ezekiel the Dramatist which gives a good indication of how the son of man vision might have been understood at the time. *Exodus* depicts Moses exalted into the presence of God where he is made God and King:

Methought upon Mount Sinai's brow I saw
A mighty throne that reached to heaven's high vault,
Whereon there sat a man of noblest mien
Wearing a royal crown; and his right to me
Made sign, and I stood forth before the throne.
He gave me then the sceptre and the crown,
And bade me sit upon the royal throne,
From which himself removed. Thence I looked forth
Upon the earth's wide circle, and beneath
The earth itself, and high above the heaven.
Then at my feet, behold! a thousand stars
Began to fall, and I their number told,
As they passed by me like an armed host:
And I in terror started up from sleep.[12]

Later, at the burning bush, God addresses him as his faithful servant and son. Moses here is installed in heaven with royal status; *he is given the crown of God and the throne*. The imagery is the same as that of Daniel's vision and of Ps. 110, but Ezekiel shows that the figure who went up to heaven was mortal, an earthly leader who was transformed into a heavenly king as the result of his ascent to heaven. He reigned on God's behalf. Was Ezekiel the Dramatist using ideas drawn from contemporary Hellenistic views about the nature of kingship, or was he drawing on the more ancient beliefs about the Davidic kings?[13] Daniel's vision was for a people whose religion and traditions were threatened by the claims of Hellenistic rulers; it is not likely that *he* would have adopted those same pagan views as the basis for his message. Daniel was drawing on the traditions of his own people whose kings had ascended to the presence of God and received from him their power and authority. They had sat upon the divine throne, and reigned as God's agent. The crowning of Moses shows that this belief survived into the second century BC.

Two centuries later, Philo's *Life of Moses* has a similar picture of the role and status of Moses:

Did [Moses] not also enjoy an even greater partnership with the Father and Maker of the universe, being deemed worthy of the same title? For he was named God and King of the whole nation. And he was said to have entered into the darkness where God was, that is, into the formless and invisible and incorporeal archetypal essence of existing things, perceiving things invisible to mortal nature. (*Life of Moses* I.155–8)

Philo shows that Moses' great status was based on his mystic vision, and he identifies this with his ascent of Mount Sinai. In other words, we have here another example of the ascent of the mountain of God, the vision and the transformed status of a human being, just as is implied by the cryptic words of Ps. 89.

One of the most curious of the functions attributed to Yahweh in the Old Testament was that of the high priest as described in Deut. 32.43. Yahweh came to his people; his Day was the moment when all in heaven and earth bowed down to him and he avenged the blood of his servants. He was king and judge, but he also made expiation/atonement for the land of his people as the high priest. The lines of the song of Moses which describe this vengeance and expiation have survived in two versions which are significantly different. The Hebrew of the MT has:

Praise his people, O you nations;
for he avenges the blood of his servants,
and takes vengeance on his adversaries,
and makes expiation for the land of his people. (Deut. 32.43)

The Greek of the LXX has:

Rejoice with him, heavens.
Bow down to him, sons of God,
rejoice with his people, nations,
confirm him, all you angels of God,
because he will avenge the blood of his sons,
he will take vengeance upon his adversaries,
he will repay those who hate him,
and will.purify the land of his people.

The reading of 4Q Deut q has 'the blood of his sons' like the LXX, and 'bow down to him gods, the sons of El', which is closer to the Greek than to the MT. There is the suspicion, therefore, that this is another text dealing with the angels and the sons of God which later transmitters of the Hebrew Scriptures have seen fit to modify, since the Greek agrees with a Hebrew text known to be at least as early as the first century, and thus earlier than the MT. This modification has removed the heavenly warrior priest from his context among the sons of God.

The expiation rite was probably a part of the great Day of Yahweh ritual which celebrated the day of his enthronement and the judgement on his enemies. We can only speculate as to how 'Yahweh' performed this rite of expiation, especially as it was expiation for the *land* of his people. The pattern of festivals for the month Tishri in the period of the second Temple suggests that the three (New Year, Day of Atonement, Tabernacles) were the separated parts of what had formerly been the one great festival. By the first century AD the three festivals had many messianic and eschatological features, all part of the ritual renewal and restoration of the land. Central to them all was the blood rite of the Day of Atonement. Its meaning as described in Lev. 16 is not clear; a young bull and two goats made atonement. The blood of the bull made atonement for the high priest and his house, the blood of one of the goats made atonement for the holy place, the tent of meeting, the altar and the assembly of Israel. Atonement was for places as well as for people. One of the two goats was for Yahweh and the other was for Azazel.

Three later writings are based on this pattern of vengeance and expiation. The Assumption of Moses, thought to date originally from the time of Antiochus Epiphanes, is a rewriting or expansion of Deut. 31–4. Unlike either of the Hebrew versions of the text, the Assumption of Moses describes the destruction of Satan, 'and sorrow shall depart with him' (Ass. Mos. 10.1). The Heavenly One appears for the judgement, the whole creation is disordered and dissolved into chaos, and then Israel rises up to see the end of its enemies (see chapter 5). Older than the Assumption of Moses in the oldest stratum of 1 Enoch is the account of the fallen angels (1 Enoch 6–11). The pattern of the book as a whole shows that this section is set in the dramatic scene described in the first chapter; when the Great Holy One comes for the judgement, the creation dissolves before him and the righteous have peace and prosperity. The judgement is a judgement on the fallen angels who have oppressed the righteous and corrupted the earth.

The bloodshed they have caused has cried out to heaven (1 Enoch 8.4). When the judgement begins Azazel is bound and cast into a deep pit in the desert. 'Make an opening in the desert which is in Dudael and cast him therein' (1 Enoch 10.5), is clearly referring to the same place as the Targum *Pseudo-Jonathan* on the Day of Atonement, recording ancient Palestinian tradition from the time of the second temple, which says that the scapegoat was sent to Beth Chaduda (Mishnah has Beth Hororo, *Yoma* 6.8). 1 Enoch knew the same tradition, even though the name has become somewhat garbled in the course of transmission and translation. The third writing is the Melchizedek text from Qumran, 11QMelch, which describes the role of Melchizedek on the Day of Judgement. The high priest is to be the appointed judge, the Elohim of Ps. 82, and he is to be proclaimed as the king mentioned in Isa. 52.7: 'Your Elohim reigns'. The Day on which this happens will be the Day of Atonement at the end of the tenth Jubilee, when Melchizedek/Elohim will free the people from the hand of Satan (see chapter 5).

These three texts show that the destruction of Satan/the banishment of Azazel were part of the old judgement tradition, and the Targum and 11QMelch associated these with the Day of Atonement. What will have represented Azazel in the Atonement rituals? When the scapegoat went out into the desert we are told that he carried the sins of the people (Lev. 16.22). Was the goat an offering to Azazel, or did the animal actually represent the banished leader of the angels, driven out into the desert to die as a preliminary to the restoration of the creation? Did the lot fall on the animal *for* Azazel or *as* Azazel? Both are a possible translation of the preposition *l*, and what we have in this text is an example of how we cannot render the text into English until we know what it means, because the sense of the text has to determine our choice between two possible English words with very different meanings. Alas, we do not know what the original text of Leviticus meant at this point, and so the possibility must remain that to translate 'for Azazel' might be reading into it a meaning not actually there. If one goat *represented* Azazel banished into the desert, then the other *represented* Yahweh, which would fit well with what is implied in Deut. 32.43: he made expiation for the land of his people. Was it this blood representing Yahweh, which was taken into the Holy of Holies to effect atonement and restore the creation? Later traditions show how closely the blood rite was associated with the restoration and healing of the creation. The judgement and restoration pattern discernible in the earliest theophany texts was the basis of the later Tishri festivals and of the hope expressed in 11QMelch of a final Day of Atonement. This hope became the basis of Hebrews, where the heavenly high priest offers his own blood and of Revelation, when Jesus is Yahweh, the heavenly judge and redeemer.

The evidence of the Old Testament must be allowed to speak for itself and we must be prepared to read it as its first users did. It is customary to bring certain presuppositions to our reading of the Old Testament such as 'Israel was monotheistic' or 'Yahweh and the Angel of Yahweh are separate figures' or 'Yahweh and Elohim are synonymous, a sign only of different scribal traditions'. The original readers of the Old Testament knew none of this. They knew that Yahweh was but one of the sons of Elyon; they knew that Yahweh and the Angel had been identical, even though that understanding had become lost and Yahweh's own presence at the Exodus needed to be emphasized; and they knew that Yahweh and Elohim were not identical but had represented different aspects of the second deity (see chapter 7). They knew that Yahweh was manifested in human form as high priest, king and judge. In the centuries between the exile and the Christian era both fusion and confusion occurred. Yahweh was identified with Elyon and his Angel acquired a separate existence but no name. Anthropomorphism and the vision of God were suppressed. The original distinction between Yahweh and Elohim was lost as is apparent from the various ways in which Philo and the rabbis explained it (see chapters 7 and 8). They were obviously remembering something, but *what* was left to the needs of the moment. The corrupted Hebrew text of Deut. 32.43 which describes Yahweh as judge and expiator lost its original context when it lost its 'sons of God'. The Greek however, which kept the sons of God and presumably a knowledge of the original meaning of the verse, appears in Heb. 1.6 as a part of the description of Jesus, another indication that the first Christians saw in Jesus Yahweh coming as judge and high priest.

Notes to chapter three

1 Is this how we are to read the name? If Yahweh means 'He who causes to be' then 'Yahweh of Hosts' must mean 'He who creates the Hosts'. See W.H. Brownlee, 'The Ineffable Name of God', BASOR 226 (1977), pp.30–45.

2 Even though Philo and the early rabbis said that the names denoted different aspects of God, they were not synonyms. See chapters 7 and 8.

3 Examples of this emphasis on the work of Yahweh alone have been collected in J. Goldin, 'Not by means of an Angel and not by means of a Messenger' in J. Neusner, ed., *Religions in Antiquity; Essays in memory of E.R. Goodenough*, Leiden 1970, pp.412–24. See also Celsus's allegation that the Jews worship angels (Origen, *Against Celsus*, I.26 and V.6).

4 On the importance of this separation see C.C. Rowland, *The Open Heaven*, London 1982, pp.95–7.

5 G.H. Dix, 'The Seven Archangels and the Seven Spirits', JTS 28 (1927).

6 J.A. Emerton, 'The Origin of the Son of Man Imagery', JTS New Series ix (1958), p.242.

7 Ibid., p.239.

8 First suggested by N. Schmidt, JBL xix (1900), p.22. One might compare here Vawter's remark in JBL 99 (1980), p.206, that Sirach 24, an approximately contemporary composition, *seems to identify Yahweh with El Elyon* and to transform the *persona* of Wisdom into Torah.

9 M. Eliade, *Myths, Dreams and Mysteries*, London 1960, pp.70, 119.

10 F.M. Cross, *Canaanite Myth and Hebrew Epic*, Cambridge, Mass. and London 1973, p.22.

11 See my *The Older Testament*, pp.235–8.

12 E.H. Gifford, *Eusebii Pamphilii Evang Praep*, Oxford 1903, vol.III/I, p.407.

13 W.A. Meeks, 'Moses as God and King' in Neusner, op.cit.

Chapter four The Evidence of Wisdom

If the Old Testament is less monotheistic than is often assumed, a further question presents itself. What are we to make of the female figure who appears so often just beyond the reach of certainty, as a shadow across many texts and as an obvious gap in others? In the post-exilic period there appeared an unnamed Great Angel and a female figure called Wisdom, and it is remarkable how many of the roles of the ancient Yahweh are attributed by these later texts both to the Angel and to Wisdom. Various explanations have been offered for the appearance of the Wisdom figure, for example that she was the Egyptian Ma'at or Isis; but more likely, in view of her prominence and her similarity to Yahweh, is that both Angel and Wisdom were survivals from the older cult in which Yahweh had had several aspects, male and female. The angels and archangels of the post-exilic period were also remnants of the older ways, but they arouse less hostility than the possibility of a 'goddess' (not a good word to use, but the only one there is) in ancient Israel. The most cursory reading in the field reveals it to be a minefield of prejudices and assumptions which take precedence even over the archaeological evidence.

In the middle of the first century AD, Philo described a second God who had two aspects represented by the two cherubim of the temple. Both cherubim, he said, represented the divine mediator and a study of their roles shows that what they represented was the two aspects of the God of Israel, the son of El Elyon. (Here I anticipate the conclusions of chapter 7.) Philo assumes that one was male and one female; the creation was the work of both, and the mother figure was called either Knowledge of Wisdom.[1] Philo, as I shall show, drew his theology from the most ancient traditions of Israel and not from an amalgam of hellenized Judaism and contemporary Greek philosophy, as is so often suggested. He demythologized what he had inherited, it is true, but one of the myths he drew upon was that of a composite male and female divinity, recognizable as Yahweh. The Babylonian Talmud also knew of a male-and-female Yahweh who created a male-and-female Adam in his image: 'Male and female he created him. But he did not write created them' (b. *Megillah* 3a). Compare *Genesis Rabbah* 8.1: 'When the Holy One, Blessed be He, created Adam, he created him an hermaphrodite'. The Jewish Christian *Pseudo-Clementine Homilies* knew that Adam had been both male and female (Hom. III 54.2), whereas Philo seems to have criticized the idea of the hermaphrodite Adam even though he kept to the male-and-female Yahweh. He wrote that God made male and female and created *them*, plural, after his image (*Who is the Heir of the Divine Things?* 164). Patai has shown how this male-and-female tradition of the cherubim was remembered, how the two statues were intertwined with one another as man and wife, and how, when the Gentiles entered the temple and desecrated it, the statues were paraded through the streets as proof that the Jews had been idolaters. He quotes too from a fourth-century Babylonian teacher, Rabba bar Rab Shila, who had read his text of 1 Kings 7.36 rather differently. Instead of describing the cherubim, lions and palm trees 'according to the space of each with wreaths round about' he read that they were 'like a man intertwined with his wife'.[2] Ezekiel *implies* that the figures of lion and cherub were joined since he mentions only cherubim and palms on the temple walls, but says that the cherubim had two heads, one of a lion and the other of a man, facing in opposite directions (Ezek. 41.18). Such a representation does invite the conclusion that the cherub was twofold.

In addition there is the otherwise inexplicable feminine imagery used of Yahweh in Deuteronomy and the Second Isaiah. Yahweh was the one who gave birth to his people and watched over them as an eagle watches over its young (Deut. 32.11, 18). 'To give birth' is by far the commonest meaning of the verb used here, *yld*. Occasionally, as in the genealogy of Gen. 10, it means to beget, and so there must remain the possibility that that is how it is to be understood here in Deut. 32.18 and also in Num. 11.12, where Moses implies that the people are not his responsibility as he did not 'bear' them. There is the same verb in Ps. 2.7, where the king, according to the English version, is *begotten* by Yahweh at his coronation (even though there was a Christian tradition that when the words were spoken at Jesus's baptism, they were spoken by Wisdom, *his mother*; see below and also chapter 10); and in Ps. 110.3 where the English versions give 'your youth', the LXX reads the ambiguous Hebrew as 'I begot you'. The commonest meaning, however, was 'to give birth', the woman's role, and there must have been some reason for ascribing this to Yahweh. In Isa. 42

Yahweh has both male and female roles; first he is a mighty warrior (Isa. 42.13) and then a woman in labour (Isa. 42.14). The people are condemned for questioning the ways of Yahweh and compared to one who says to his father 'What are you begetting?' and to his mother 'With what are you in labour?' (Isa. 45.9–11). Yahweh is even more mindful than a mother who cannot forget her child (Isa. 49.14–15) and Yahweh comforts Zion as a man *is comforted by his mother* (Isa. 66.13). The simplest explanation of this imagery is that there had been a feminine aspect to Yahweh which must not be thought of as a separate goddess but rather as part of a manifold deity who had several aspects and manifestations.

It was the Deuteronomists who claimed to have brought into one cult all the ''*elohim*' and made them one Yahweh (Deut. 6.4) when they centralized worship in Jerusalem and purified it of all that was not to their taste. Before their time there had been local Yahwehs; there had been a Yahweh in Hebron to whom Absalom had made a vow whilst he was in Geshur (2 Sam. 15.7), and there had been a Yahweh in Zion whom the psalmist extolled (Ps. 99.2). A Yahweh in Samaria and a Yahweh in Teman are mentioned in eighth-century inscriptions which also seem to mention a female deity, presumably his consort.[3] All the traditions of the loss of a female deity from Israel, by whatever name she is remembered, point to this period of reform as the time when she was expelled. As Wisdom she appears in the Enochic texts which recall how she was forsaken at this time. The *Apocalypse of Weeks*, an undateable text now incorporated into the fifth section of 1 Enoch, tells the history of Israel in cryptic form as a series of ten weeks, of which the sixth is clearly the period of the late monarchy. In this sixth week, those who lived in the temple became blind and godlessly forsook Wisdom. At the end of that week the temple was destroyed by fire and the people scattered. The generation of the seventh week, the period of the second temple, was apostate (1 Enoch 93.8–9). Another Enochic history says that the bread of the rebuilt temple was polluted and not pure (1 Enoch 98.73). Enoch's admonitions for the future warned against sinners who would tempt men to think Wisdom evil 'so that no place may be found for her' (1 Enoch 94.5). The picture is clear; Wisdom was abandoned not when the temple was destroyed, but by blinded people just *before* the time of the destruction, and those who restored Jerusalem were not true to the tradition because they found no place for Wisdom. It was the Deuteronomists who had made no place for Wisdom; they had offered the Law as a substitute (Deut. 4.6). The Book of Baruch hints at something similar. Set in the exile, it records the people's lament at their fate and concludes by recalling them to Wisdom (Bar. 3.12). The text understands wisdom as the Law, 'She is the book of the commandments of God and the Law that endures forever' (Bar. 4.1), but some of the imagery hints at earlier ways:

> [he] gave her to Jacob his servant
> and to Israel whom he loved.
> Afterwards she appeared upon earth
> and lived among men. (Bar. 3.36–7)

The Wisdom figure can be detected in some gnostic texts which also had their roots in ancient Israel. The greatest of these texts is the *Pistis Sophia* which contains several laments uttered by the forsaken Wisdom who had been cast out and rejected (see chapter 9). Similarly there is a rejected female figure in the writings of the Kabbalists, the earliest survivals of which come from twelfth-century Provence. They express Judaism in mythological terms, but the symbols and concepts can be traced back through the gnostic writings to Philo and, I suspect, into an even earlier period. These Kabbalists taught that there was a female element within God, Shekinah, and they dwelt much upon the theme of her exile. This, they said, showed that a part of God had been exiled from God, and redemption would come when the two were reunited.[4]

Jeremiah, or rather his editor, gives a contemporary account of the rejection of the female divinity; he calls her the Queen of Heaven. The prophet confronted the people of Jerusalem and threatened them with great evil. They had turned the logic of the Deuteronomic reformers to their own advantage and had been saying that the destruction of Jerusalem was punishment not for forsaking the Law of Yahweh and not for the guilt inherited from Manasseh, but for *abandoning the worship of the Queen of Heaven*. The women of Jerusalem made it clear that this had been an established cult in Jerusalem (Jer. 44.17–18). It would appear, then, that the figure whom the Enochic writers and the gnostics remembered as Wisdom and the Kabbalists as Shekinah, the figure abandoned at the time of Josiah's reform, has been known to her worshippers as the Queen of Heaven, and so deep were her roots in Israel's religion that her loss was never forgotten; on the contrary, her restoration was to be the sign of redemption.

venus

vs

moon = Eve

51

It was suggested long ago by Dix that the Queen of Heaven was a Wisdom figure. He concluded that she had been imported from Babylon and had influenced the ideas of the prophets. Marduk had been the son of Damkina-Ishtar the Assyrian goddess of wisdom and she it was 'who appears to have suggested the imagery which the later Jewish Hakamim used to describe the figure of the heavenly Wisdom, the mother of the divine Logos'. Thus, he said, Isaiah saw *the young woman* who was to give birth to Immanuel (Isa. 7.14) and Micah saw *the one who bears* giving birth to the bringer of peace (Mic. 5.3). After discussing the titles of the Assyrian goddess, he concluded that they were similar to those of *the young woman* and *the one who bears*:

> We conclude, therefore, that both Isaiah and Micah knew this mother goddess full well, as did their contemporaries also. It would have been pointless to describe the mother in terms which were literal translations of the titles for this goddess of wisdom unless those who read the predictions were familiar with her figure and knew the terms under which she was described. It seems probable, that both prophets made use of terms which had become current in Judah and that their contemporaries were wont so to describe the Assyrian goddess of wisdom whom they knew as 'the Queen of Heaven' ... The Hebrew prophets gave her no name.[5]

Need the lady have been foreign? If there had been expectations of an angelic ruler, a 'son' of Yahweh (Immanuel, God With Us) to occupy the throne of David, would he have had a foreign goddess for his mother? It is more likely that the Queen of Heaven rejected by the reformers had been consort to the one whom Isaiah described as 'The King, the Lord of Hosts' (Isa. 6.5), presumably the one who appears in a contemporary inscription as Yahweh's Asherah.

We have now three figures with which to work: Wisdom, Asherah and the Queen of Heaven. I suspect that they are one and the same, and that archaeological evidence for the worship of Asherah is evidence not of a separate goddess in Israel but rather of a twofold aspect of Yahweh. Those who made Yahweh One also removed Asherah and all associated with her. It is a curious fact that Asherah is only associated with Ba'al in texts influenced by the Deuteronomic reformers; in the extra-biblical Hebrew evidence, such as it is, Asherah is always linked with Yahweh, and in Canaanite texts of the first millenium she is never linked to Ba'al. This has led some scholars to suggest that the Deuteronomists linked Asherah and Ba'al in order to discredit both together.[6]

It is perhaps worth pondering at this point the other biblical evidence for a female figure having been abandoned at the time of the exile. The great remaker of Israel's traditions at that time was the Second Isaiah. He it was who began the reinterpretation and democratization of the older cult mythology.[7] The great liturgical dramas of the temple were the framework of his theology, with the Servant figure derived from the divine king of the temple rites, sharing his destiny with his people.[8] Equally prominent in the prophecies but almost totally neglected in modern commentaries on them, is a rejected female figure whose destiny was also that of the people. The sufferings of this figure are very similar to those of the servant.[9] She is also the herald of good tidings to Zion and Jerusalem; in Isa. 40.9 $m^e ba\check{s}\check{s}eret$, 'herald', is the feminine form of the world whereas in Isa. 52.7 the herald is masculine, $m^e ba\check{s}\check{s}er$. The herald of Isa. 61.1-4, 'I have been anointed to bring good tidings', could have been either male or female. Although this female figure came to be identified with the city or with the people (Isa. 54.7 'I will bring you home again'), the fact that at the beginning of the prophecies she brings news to the city shows that she did have another identity before becoming the city. The fate of the city is explained in terms of the fate of the female figure, the repeated assertion being that she has been abandoned by her husband (Isa. 49.14) and deprived of her children (Isa. 54.1). Even though the woman as city has come to dominate our reading of the texts, the memory of the original woman persisted; the new Jerusalem of John's vision was the Bride of the Lamb (Rev. 21.9-14) and the woman in labour (Isa. 66.7) became the woman clothed with the sun (Rev. 12.1-6), which must surely indicate that John envisaged her as a divinity. She was later identified with Mary, the mother of the Son of God. Similarly Yahweh in his city was read as prefiguring the incarnation in his mother (Zeph. 3.16-17; Zech. 2.10-11 came to be read in this way).[10] The woman who appears as the Bride of the Lamb and the bearer of the heavenly child is evidence that even as late as the first century the Christian visionaries were in touch with the 'goddess' of the ancient cult who 'was' her city and was also the bride of its God and the mother of its king. Presumably they were not the only ones with this knowledge.

The work of the reformers has resulted in a distorted assessment of the evidence for Asherah's role and importance; modern scholars tend to read with the eyes of those reformers, and even though it is widely recognized that there had been a goddess known as Asherah in Israel's pre-exilic religion, it is implied that she had no rightful place there. She was 'associated with *some forms* of the cult of Yahweh'; she had 'special importance in as least one form of *popular* Yahwism'.[11] The evidence, however, suggests that Asherah had had a long association not just with one or two forms of crude popular religion but with the temple itself. The reformers eliminated the local cults of Yahweh and also removed the Asherah from the temple where the women had woven hangings for it (2 Kings 23.6-7). The Asherah, whatever it was, was important; during the reign of Asa, another reformer, 'an abominable image for Asherah' was removed and burnt (1 Kings 15.13); during the reign of Hezekiah the Asherah was cut down (2 Kings 18.4); during the reign of Manasseh the image of Asherah was set in the temple (2 Kings 21.7). In the northern kingdom, the prophets of Asherah were listed among the enemies of Elijah (1 Kings 18.19) but they are thought to be a later insertion into the narrative since they play no further part in the story and are not killed along with the prophets of Ba'al (1 Kings 18.40). The Asherah was not removed during Jehu's purge of Ba'al worship; it was still in Samaria during his son's reign (2 Kings 13.6) Even after the account of Josiah's removing the Asherah from the temple in Jerusalem (2 Kings 23.6) Ezekiel 'saw' the image on his visionary journey to Jerusalem.

Scholars long doubted that this Asherah could have been a female deity in the Old Testament; the Asherah, it was said, had been a cult object mistakenly personified after its proscription when later writers no longer knew what the word meant. Then the Ugaritic literature was discovered at Ras Shamra which mentioned one Lady Aṭirat of the sea, the consort of El and the creatress of the gods, *qaniyati'ilima* (CTA 4.1 23; 4.3. 26; 4.3 35 and *passim*).[12] The resemblance to Ezekiel's 'image of jealousy' is striking. This customary translation makes little sense; it is more likely that what he saw was not *sml hqn'h* but *sml hqnh*, the image of the creatress, the title of Aṭirat. (She would have been the consort of *'l qnh*, the creator of heaven and earth, the God of Jerusalem mentioned in Gen. 14.9 and the 'image of jealousy' would have been no more than the customary wordplay to avoid mentioning the unmentionable.) Aṭirat at Ugarit was also named Elat, the feminine form of El, (CTA 4.4.48) and she was the mother of seventy sons (CTA 4.6. 46), an unmistakable link to the older tradition of Israel which mentions the sons of El but not their mother, nor their number (Deut. 32.8).[13] These sons appear later as the seventy angels of the nations, one of whom was Yahweh, the angel of Israel. Even as late as the gnostic texts (e.g. *Apocryphon of John* CG. II.1.10) this great angel was remembered as *the son of Wisdom*. The goddess at Ugarit was also *qdš* (CTA 14.4.197), perhaps the name of a goddess, Qudshu, but also recognizable as the Hebrew *qdš*, a holy one.[14]

Once the Lady Aṭirat had been recovered from oblivion and had been recognized as a familiar figure, the fact of a goddess in ancient Israel had to be faced; yet there still persisted a refusal to acknowledge that she had any right to be there. The testimony of the apocalyptists, the gnostics and many later traditions was ignored in favour of the Deuteronomists' picture, even in the face of a vast amount of archaeological evidence, all of which had to be explained away:

Yet the very fact of *the necessity* for reform in ancient Israel reminds us that the worship of Asherah, the 'Mother Goddess', sometimes personified as the consort of Yahweh, was popular until the end of the Monarchy. The archaeological record has preserved for us an *alternate version of events* as portrayed in the received text ...[15]

The 'archaeological record' mentioned here, which is at variance with the canonical account, is the discovery at Kuntillet 'Ajrud of inscriptions which mention Asherah alongside Yahweh. Two buildings were excavated; on the walls of one was found writing in Phoenician script and in a side chamber were several large storage jars, decorated and inscribed with Hebrew letters. In each case there was a blessing of the type 'Blessed be **** to Yahweh and to his Asherah'. There are problems over the meaning of Asherah here; it is unlikely to be a personal name since Hebrew does not attach the possessive suffix to a name. Asherah must have been something which represented the goddess. It is possible that it was something wooden, perhaps a tree or the representation of a tree since it could be planted (Deut. 16.21), reformers could cut it down (Deut. 7.5), or burn it (Deut. 12.3). The Asherah was erected near or under a tree (1 Kings 14.23; 2 Kings 17.10). It was *made* (1 Kings 14.15; 16.33; 2 Kings 17.16). The LXX could translate the word either by 'tree' as at Isa. 17.8 and 27.9 or, more frequently, by 'grove' as at 1 Kings 16.23, where Ahab made a *grove*. Jewish tradition recorded in the Mishnah remembered that an Asherah could be either a sacred tree or a tree under which was an idol (*Abodah Zarah* 3.5–10).

In addition to Kuntillet 'Ajrud there is an inscription at Khirbet-el-Qom which seems to invoke the blessing of Yahweh and his Asherah and there is a cultic stand recovered in 1968 from the site of ancient

Taanach which has two 'Asherah' scenes and two Yahweh scenes. None of the identifications is beyond dispute; the Asherah scenes depict a lady between two lions, and a sacred tree between two lions, and the Yahweh scenes have a 'sun horse' between two pillars and an empty space between two cherubim, since Yahweh was the unseen God who spoke from between the cherubim.[16]

Beyond all dispute is the fact of huge numbers of female figurines found at Israelite sites, which are seen as 'indisputable evidence of widespread syncretism, verging on polytheism, among *the common people*. They probably owned them, however, not so much for theological as for magical reasons, using them as good luck charms'[17] (*my emphases*). There is no basis for this judgement of syncretism beyond the fact that we have been told what Israel's religion was like and are therefore obliged to interpret the actual facts in the light of this. Excavations at Ramath Rachel have uncovered female figurines even in a royal palace, which caused some surprise to the excavators. G.W. Ahlström spoke for many when he said, 'we can only hope that the argument from evidence which [certain scholars] and others have not hitherto understood, may be accorded more attention and objective appreciation.'[18]

Commenting on the discovery of a number of female figurines and miniature horses, some with 'sun discs' on their heads, which she dated about 700 BC, Dame Kathleen Kenyon said:

A reasonable interpretation of the deposits in the two caves is that they are derived from a sanctuary, or possibly two sanctuaries, of a cult associated with fertility worship and with the allied worship of the sun ... It is a salutary lesson that the centuries long struggles of supporters of the pure worship of Yahweh were so far from establishing a national religion that such a cult centre should exist almost within a stone's throw, at least within three hundred metres, from the south east corner of the enclosure of Yahweh's temple.[19]

Three generations or so before the time of the reformers the cult of the mother goddess had been flourishing in Jerusalem; these figurines must have represented the Queen of Heaven, the protectress of Jerusalem whose neglect was to be the cause of its downfall.

There are other female deities associated with Israel. Fifth-century texts from the Jewish community at Elephantine in southern Egypt mention one 'Anath-Yahu,[20] presumably Israel's version of the Canaanite goddess Anath who was a complex deity, both wife and sister of Ba'al, a virgin and a mother figure, the goddess of love and war. A third goddess may underlie one of the later archangels mentioned in 1 Enoch 10.1, the passage where an archangel is sent to warn Noah about the flood. Two versions of this text exist in Greek (apart from the Ethiopic), of which the Greek found in a Christian grave at Akhmim (Gg) names the archangel as Istrael. The other Greek version has Uriel and the Ethiopic is not clear. It has been suggested that Istrael, in the semitic original, will have been Ishtarel, and Ishtar, as we have seen, was the goddess of wisdom. In the Babylonian version of the flood story, the *Epic of Gilgamesh*, it was this goddess Ishtar who was especially concerned with the fate of mankind at the great flood and her lament is recorded:

Then Ishtar the sweet-voiced Queen of heaven cried out like a woman in travail: 'Alas the days of old are turned to dust because I commanded evil; why did I command this evil in the council of the gods? I commanded wars to destroy the people, but are they not my people whom I brought forth? Now like the spawn of fish they float in the ocean.'[21]

What could have led to the association of Ishtar and Uriel? It is thought that the Gg text was carelessly written, possibly in haste, but nevertheless there must have been some reason for making what is, after all, a complete change in the name. Uriel and Ishtarel are not simply variants made by a hasty scribe. Were there some who remembered Wisdom under this name, as an angel and as Ishtar?

The three goddesses, Asherah, 'Anath and Ishtar (Astarte in Canaan), were never clearly defined. There is a frustrating fluidity about their roles and functions that has led some to suggest that all three were no more than aspects of one female deity, the Mother Goddess. 'At Ugarit, as in the Hellenistic world and beyond, each goddess retained her distinct identity, yet could be worshipped with her sisters as one.'[22] All of them can be detected at the edges of our knowledge, in the shadows created by the bright light of seventh-century reformers. The fact that no complete correspondence can be found between the Israelite deity and any other known goddess argues for her being native to Israel rather than an import from Egypt or the imposition of Assyrian overlords.[23] My purpose here, however, is not to study the goddess as such but to show just how many fragments of the older cult do survive, and how the ancient goddess was indistinguishable from Yahweh, being simply the female aspect.

We begin with the two certainties: she was known as the Queen of Heaven, and she was associated with a tree symbol. Her enforced association with Ba'al has led to her being called a fertility goddess, but she was in fact the consort-creatress. 'Fertility goddess' is a pejorative term, and should be used only by those prepared to use the term 'fertility God of heaven and earth' at the beginning of the Creeds. Being the creatress-consort and having the tree symbol are in themselves sufficient to link her to the later Wisdom figure who is described in just this way. Wisdom is the consort of Yahweh who:

> ... glorifies her noble birth by living with God,
> and the Lord of all loves her.
> For she is an initiate in the knowledge of God
> and an associate in all his works ... (Wisd. 8.3–4)

She shares the throne or sits beside it:

> ... give me the Wisdom that sits by thy throne (Wisd. 9.4)
> ... and from the throne of thy glory send her (Wisd. 9.10)
> Wisdom departs not from the place of thy throne. (1 Enoch 84.3)

In a 'monotheistic' religion, the allusion to a consort is in itself striking and demands explanation. She is also the tree of life:

> She is the tree of life to those who lay hold of her
> and those who hold her fast are called happy. (Prov. 3.18)[24]

Sir. 24.13–22 has an even more elaborate picture of Wisdom as the tree, planted in Jerusalem and unlike any other tree in beauty and height. It is perfumed with the incense of the holy of holies and its fruit is for all to eat, 'and those who work with my help will not sin' (Sir. 24.22). The latter is presumably a reference to the sin of Adam and Eve when they took their fruit. Her other queenly attributes were that she permitted kings to rule (Prov. 8.15–16), a role which is elsewhere that of Yahweh, and she gave her devotees a garland and a crown (Prov. 4.9).

The tree symbol was one of the significant transformations in the wake of the reform. The trees of the garden of Eden, I suggest, had once been those of the older cult, just as the garden had itself formerly been the heavenly garden of the gods.[25] The fruit of the tree (originally there had been but one) gave knowledge and life, and the serpent spoke well to Eve when he said that the fruit would open their eyes and make them like the *'elohim* (Gen. 3.5). This was the original role of the heavenly knowledge; it transformed the human into the divine and thus gave 'life' which was not subject to mortality. The Yahweh of the reformers evicted the dangerous pair from the garden once they had acquired knowledge, so that they would not also acquire life, and thus the heart of the older belief was destroyed. Humankind could not become divine just as the divine could not become human. Separation was the key to true religion, and knowledge, said the new men, did not transform the wise into gods, but rather drove the disobedient from the presence of God. The Wisdom writings remembered older ways; Wisdom *did* give life – 'he who finds me finds life' (Prov. 8.35) – and this was immortality: 'Because of her I shall have immortality' (Wisd. 8.13), or the life to be restored to the faithful at their resurrection:

> And the righteous shall arise from their sleep,
> And Wisdom shall arise and be given unto them. (1 Enoch 91.10)

Those who corrupted Wisdom were punished with mortality, the fate of the prince of Tyre (Ezek. 28.17–19) who had had great wisdom and understanding and had used it to accumulate great wealth. The wealth was not condemned but the pride it engendered caused his downfall (cf. Isa. 10.13ff; 47.10) and he was subject to death. Thus the gift of wisdom and immortality could be lost through pride:

> And then there shall be bestowed upon the elect Wisdom
> and they shall all live and never again sin
> Either through ungodliness or through pride,
> But they who are wise shall be humble. (1 Enoch 5.8)

Given the correspondence between the roles of the ancient goddess and wisdom, I suggest that the so-called personification of Wisdom in later texts is better regarded as a memory of the goddess and that the vivid images in these writings can enable us to reconstruct something of her original self.

In the time of the restoration, Wisdom is still trying to keep her place in Jerusalem, but the reformers have driven her out. The picture at the beginning of Proverbs is that of the goddess calling to her people. She haunts her old territory and calls her children back to her. Jerusalem is the strange woman who opposes the lady Wisdom and lures away the young. There are, it is true, examples in Egyptian wisdom literature of young men being warned against the wiles of foreign harlots, and these are thought to have been the models for the warnings in Proverbs against the strange woman and her ways. One need hardly go into great detail, as is often done, to show that Proverbs here must be dependent on outside sources. Young men have always been warned against foreign harlots; it is not an insight whose pedigree needs tracing through the ancient Near East. A more likely clue as to the identity of the strange woman of Proverbs is to be found in the Third Isaiah, who describes the restored city of Jerusalem in no uncertain terms as a harlot (Isa. 57.7–10).

The language of the prophet is very similar to that of Proverbs. The prophet tells of the harlot's envoys sent down to Sheol, Proverbs of the harlot's path leading down to the shades (Prov. 2.19), her steps to Sheol (Prov. 5.5). Her house is the way to Sheol (Prov. 7.27). The foreign woman in Proverbs is a rival to Wisdom; she has left her husband and, significantly, the covenant of her God (Prov. 2.17). The prophet says much the same; the harlot has made a covenant with others (Isa. 57.8: RSV 'bargain'). Jerusalem as the harlot city is a common motif. The harlot has offered sacrifices and paid vows (Prov. 7.14) before coming to entice the unwary to her couch (Prov. 7.15–18) This was no ordinary harlot!

There is much in Prov. 1–9 which suggests that once it (or that a part of it) had addressed the situation which the Third Isaiah also addressed. The restored Jerusalem with its Persian money and new post-Deuteronomic ways confronted and excluded Yahweh's more ancient worshippers who had never experienced the exile. Compare, for example, the descriptions of corruption in Isa. 59.1–8 with those of Prov. 1.16; 2.12–15; 4.16–19; 6.16–19. There are no exact quotations, but the similarities are unmistakable. The sequence in Prov. 6.16–19, doubtless proverbial, could have been the basis of Isa. 59.1–8:

a lying tongue and hands that shed innocent blood (Prov. 6.17, cf. Isa. 59.3);
a heart that devises wicked plans (Prov. 6.18, cf. Isa. 59.4);
feet that make haste to run to evil (Prov. 6.18, cf. Isa. 59.7);
a false witness who breathes out lies (Prov. 6.19, cf. Isa. 59.4);
a man who sows discord among brothers (Prov. 6.19, cf. Isa. 66.5).

The wise man, the devotee of the older Wisdom, warns against the new ways; he knows the claims of the Deuteronomists that the upright man would inherit the land (Prov. 2.20–3) but *he* says that those who keep to Wisdom are the upright. There are several other points of contact with the Deuteronomists.[26]

The Teachings of Wisdom are like the Torah of the Deuteronomists:

Let not loyalty and faithfulness forsake you;
bind them about your neck,

write them upon the tablet of your heart. (Prov. 3.3)
My son, keep your father's commandment,
and forsake not your mother's teaching.
Bind them upon your heart always;
tie them about your neck.
When you walk they will lead you;
when you lie down they will watch over you;
and when you awake they will talk with you. (Prov. 6.20–2)

With this one should compare the injunctions of Deuteronomy about the commandments:

... you shall talk of them when you sit in your house, and when you walk by the way, and when you lie down and when you rise. And you shall bind them as a sign upon your hand, and they shall be as frontlets between your eyes. (Deut. 6.6–9; cf. Deut. 11.18–21)

The Torah was offered as a replacement for Wisdom (Deut. 4.6). Such a degree of correspondence makes it very likely indeed that the older Lady Wisdom was calling to the people who had neglected her, those whom the Enochic tradition remembered as impure and blinded. Wisdom was calling out to people who would not listen to her (Prov. 1.24), just as Yahweh called out to his people (Isa. 65.1–2). To ignore Wisdom brought calamity (Prov. 1.24–31) just as happened to those who ignored the words of Yahweh.

The Wisdom figure of Prov. 1–9 cries out in the streets and at the city gates (Prov. 1.20–1; 8.3). Why there in particular? It has been suggested that the streets and gates of the city were where the wise man searched for students(!).[27] It is more likely that these were the places where she had been worshipped. Jeremiah does not mention any special temple or cult place where the women of the city went, but implies that she was worshipped in the streets of the city (Jer. 7.17; 44.17, 21).

Job was also written at this time and it shows how the new role of wisdom was evolving. Henceforth it would not be a creative power but simply a body of teaching and accumulated observations. The speeches of Yahweh (Job 38–41) which finally bring Job to submission, demonstrate the power of Yahweh to create, and this power to create is his Wisdom (e.g. 39.26 'Is it by your wisdom ...?'). This creative power was remembered in later tradition as *something distinct*, one of the two primary manifestations of the second God (see chapter 7). Job admits that he does not possess such wisdom, i.e. wisdom to create, yet the wise men whom we meet in non-biblical texts claimed, by implication, to have had exactly this knowledge which the Yahweh of Job said was not for mankind.[28] Here was the crux; was wisdom simply a body of teaching, or was there given with that knowledge a godlike power to create?[29]

Later texts show that Wisdom had virtually all the characteristics of the Spirit of Yahweh. She was present at the creation and was the first creature brought forth and begotten by Yahweh. Those who feel unhappy with 'begotten' argue that *qnh* should be translated 'acquire' but the overall context of Prov. 8.22–31 does make 'begot' or 'created' the more likely meaning, especially as *qnh* is the verb used to describe the creative activity of both El and Atirat. Yahweh as the creator of Wisdom, rather than as her spouse, suggests that here, as in Sir. 24, we see the results of the post-exilic fusion of El and Yahweh.[30] Perhaps the early Christians remembered well when they compared the origin of Wisdom to the origin of Eve, taken from the side of Adam, not as his child but as his consort,[31] the separation, one assumes, of the male and female natures previously one in the Adam who had been made in Yahweh's image. Wisdom was beside Yahweh in the work of creation, a 'master workman'.[32] It is the Second Isaiah who comes closest to Proverbs in describing the process of creation; Isa. 40.12–17 and 28–31 is very similar to Prov. 8.25–9 and yet the emphasis is very different. Exactly what acts are envisaged is less important than comparing these emphases. Proverbs says that Wisdom was beside Yahweh in his great work, whereas Isaiah is emphatic that Yahweh worked alone. Isaiah was contradicting an existing belief that there had been someone with Yahweh in the work of the creation since such a figure would have been quite inconsistent with his proclamation of absolute monotheism.

Elsewhere in the Old Testament the creative power is not Wisdom but the Spirit of God moving on the face of the waters (Gen. 1.2), or the Spirit of God which made man (Job 33.4, cf. Job 27.3 where the Spirit of God is the breath of life). It was the spirit that transformed dust into living beings (Job. 34.14; the Hebrew is obscure here but the Greek is clear enough). When Yahweh sent forth his Spirit all things were created (Ps. 104.30) or they were recreated (Isa. 32.15). This was the breath of God, yet Sirach 24 says *Wisdom* was the breath of Elyon and describes her as the creator in language reminiscent of Isaiah:

> I came forth from the mouth of the Most High
> and covered the earth like a mist.

I dwelt in high places
and my throne was in a pillar of cloud.
Alone I made the circuit of the vault of heaven
and have walked in the depths of the abyss. (Sir. 24.4–6)

She had formed everything: 'for Wisdom, the fashioner of all things, taught me' (Wisd. 7.22). The power to create or to control and order the creation was intimately bound up with knowledge of the creation. It was this issue of creative power which lay at the heart of the crisis in Israel's Wisdom tradition. Knowledge of the natural order gave power over the creation and thus gave to the wise man a godlike status. The serpent in Eden had spoken well about the effect of knowledge. When Job was addressed from the whirlwind it was the power of Yahweh's creative wisdom that confronted him. Job's wisdom was not of that kind; he did not have access to the secrets of the creation. He could only observe but not create. Those secrets, however, were known to the people who handed on the apocalypses and fragments of their lists of revealed wisdom have survived.[33] These were the secrets known to Solomon, the secrets of the healing arts, astronomy and so forth, the secrets which the fallen angels had betrayed and thus corrupted the creation.

Wisdom also empowered and inspired the kings and prophets. Solomon was given the Spirit of Wisdom:

Therefore I prayed and understanding was given to me;
I called upon God and the spirit of Wisdom came upon me. (Wisd. 7.7)

Elsewhere this was understood to be the Holy Spirit (Wisd. 9.17, cf. Prov. 8.15–16). The Spirit of Wisdom would also dwell in the heavenly counterpart of the king, in the Elect One who was to be ruler and judge;

... the Elect One standeth before the Lord of Spirits
And in him dwells the Spirit of Wisdom
And the Spirit which gives insight
And the spirit of understanding and of might,
And the spirit of those who have fallen asleep in righteousness. (1 Enoch 49.2–3)

The Wisdom of God had been seen in Solomon because of his wise judgements (1 Kings 3.28; cf. 2 Sam. 14.20, where David was wise like one of the 'elohim). The Spirit of Yahweh, the spirit of Wisdom and Understanding, the spirit of Counsel and Might, the spirit of Knowledge and the fear of Yahweh were to be in the royal figure (Isa. 11.2). The familiarity of these words must not blind us to their strangeness. The spirit of Yahweh *was* the spirit of Wisdom and the spirit of the fear of Yahweh. How the Spirit of Yahweh could be both is not easy to imagine, but this pattern of plurality meets us at every turn. The kings in whom wisdom was present (I do not say they possessed it since this implies that wisdom was less than personal) were believed, as we have seen, to be the presence of Yahweh with his people and to be the vehicle of the sevenfold spirit. Wisdom could also enter holy souls in every generation and transform them:

> In every generation she passes into holy souls
> and makes them friends of God and prophets. (Wisd. 7.27)

This corresponds to the gift of the Spirit of Yahweh in Old Testament texts. The Spirit was put on the seventy elders (Num. 11.26, 29) and they prophesied. The spirit gave warnings through the prophets (Neh. 9.30) but had been ignored (Zech. 7.12). The spirit entered Ezekiel (Ezek. 2.2) and transported him in visions (Ezek. 11.2, 4). The spirit was upon the anointed one who prophesied in Isa. 61.1 and the spirit inspired Balaam (Num. 24.2) and Saul (1 Sam. 10.10).

Wisdom is frequently described in imagery drawn from the older cult, but in roles usually associated only with Yahweh. *She* was the one allotted to Israel as its guardian angel, *she* acted as the mediating figure, the priest, in the sanctuary in Jerusalem, and she, the consort of the King, was driven out and returned to heaven among the angels:

> And he said, 'Make your dwelling in Jacob,
> and in Israel receive your inheritance.'
> In the holy tabernacle I ministered before him,
> and so I was established in Zion. (Sir. 24.8, 10)

This text is clearly the same as Deut. 32.9, but there Elyon allots Israel not to Wisdom but to *Yahweh* for his inheritance, and it is Yahweh who has the high priestly role in Deut. 32.43, where he makes expiation for the land and the people (the text is not entirely clear, but the key word 'expiate' is not in dispute). In view of the exact duplication of roles, there must have been some ancient memory of a ministering patron angel, like the ministering angels of the heavenly temple described in the *Songs of the Sabbath Sacrifice*, but the priestly guardian was remembered equally as Yahweh and as Wisdom.

The definition of Wisdom and the possession of Wisdom must have been a source of disagreement in the time of the second temple. Those who condemned the Jerusalem cultus said that Wisdom no longer dwelt there. If we read only the psalms and the prophets, we should think it had been Yahweh alone who 'dwelt' in the temple, which brings us back to the question of the two cherubim. According to later tradition (e.g. in *Numbers Rabbah* 15.10) there had been no cherubim in the second temple. Five things were hidden away when the first temple was destroyed which were to be restored when the Lord rebuilt the temple and the holy place. These five were the fire, the ark, the *menorah*, the spirit and the cherubim. The saying must have had meaning beyond its face value, since there *was* a *menorah* in the second temple. Perhaps it meant that the original significance of those objects would be restored. Whatever the truth of the matter, the cherubim and whatever they stood for, like the oil for anointing the high priest, were remembered as a feature of the first temple and not of the second. Traditions about the male and the female must have come from the time of the first temple, the time when Wisdom had been an angelic minister there along with her consort:

> Wisdom went forth to make her dwelling place among the children of men,
> And found no dwelling place:
> Wisdom returned to her place,
> And took her seat among the angels. (1 Enoch 42.2)

Enoch had foreseen the evil ways of sinners who would give no place to Wisdom;

> For I know that sinners will tempt men to make Wisdom evil,
> So that no place may be found for her ... (1 Enoch 94.5)

So central a figure/concept is not likely to have been a foreign import into Israel's tradition, a mere fusion of various elements from the pagan goddesses such as Isis and Ishtar. What, then, could have been meant by a Wisdom who ministered in the tabernacle on Zion (Sir. 24.8–12) or, on the alternative view, had been forsaken just before the destruction of the first temple (1 Enoch 93.8)? Wisdom must have been one of the ministering spirits whom we meet elsewhere in the visionary texts, part of the heavenly hierarchy, rather than a later personification of the teaching of the wise men.

From her place by the divine throne (1 Enoch 84.3) she flows out as the water of life. The Similitudes describe Wisdom flowing from fountains in heaven (1 Enoch 48.1; 49.1). Sirach compares Wisdom to the four rivers flowing from Eden (Sir. 24.25–7; cf. Gen. 2.10–14), a similar image to Enoch's when one remembers that the place of the divine throne was the heavenly garden of Eden. Enoch's fountains are Sirach's river. She has and gives foreknowledge of signs and wonders 'and of the outcome of seasons and times' (Wisd. 8.8). If Wisdom also conferred divine status, then knowledge of the future must have been a sign of divinity and the logic of the Second Isaiah's argument against the gods of the nations becomes clear. They had been challenged to reveal the future and they could not, which was proof that they were no gods (Isa. 41.23). The only God was Yahweh who could *create* all things including the future.

Finally, Wisdom was the one who guided Israel's history. Whereas the Pentateuch had seen the mighty hand and outstretched arm of Yahweh throughout Israel's history, the Wisdom of Solomon attributed this guidance and protection to Wisdom. *She* had saved Noah, guided Jacob, protected Joseph, delivered the slaves from Egypt by entering into Moses and so on:

A holy people and blameless race
she delivered from a nation of oppressors.
She entered the soul of servant of the Lord,
and withstood dread kings with wonders and signs.
She brought them over the Red Sea
and led them through deep waters;
but she drowned their enemies,
and cast them up from the depth of the sea. (Wisd. 15.16, 18)

From this brief outline it can be seen that Wisdom or the spirit of Wisdom was identical in many of its functions with the spirit of Yahweh and, we must assume, with Yahweh (e.g. Wisd. 9.17). All were aspects of, or ways of talking about, the power which created the world, guided Israel's history, empowered kings to uphold the divine order with their just rule and gave immortality to those whom they possessed. Yahweh/Wisdom was manifested in the prophets and above all in the kings. As late as the Wisdom of Solomon this identification of Yahweh and Wisdom was remembered: 'For it is [God] who gave me unerring knowledge of what exists, to know the structure of the world and the activity of the elements' (Wisd. 7.17). Compare: 'I learned both what is secret and what is manifest, for Wisdom the fashioner of all things taught me' (Wisd. 7.22). It is now widely recognized that the name 'Yahweh' must have meant 'He causes to be, he creates' rather than 'I am', and this brings the ancient Yahweh even closer to the creating Wisdom of the later texts.[34]

The expulsion of Wisdom and her corruption was seen by the apocalyptists as the key to understanding the evils of their age.

1 Enoch 6–10 describes the angels seizing the heavenly knowledge for themselves and bringing it to earth where it became the cause of corruption and bloodshed. Suter's study of the fallen ones shows how this myth indicates a situation where there is 'rebellion from within rather than sin or evil imposed from without'.[35] He argues that the Enochic writer saw the fallen ones as the priests of the second temple. If he is correct, then their attitude to Wisdom, taking it for themselves in order to rule the earth, fits well with two other positions adopted by the Enochic writer: that Wisdom was driven out before the exile and that the cult of the second temple was not pure.

Wisdom was not forgotten; the female aspect of Yahweh was known to the first Christians. Paul described Jesus as the Power of God and the Wisdom of God, a twofold incarnation (1 Cor. 1.24). In Rom. 10.6–10 he takes words which in Deut. 30.12–14 are said of the Law and in Bar. 3.29–30 of Wisdom, yet he applies them to Christ. In each case there was something or someone who was not inaccessible in heaven or far away but on earth and near at hand. The evangelists imply Jesus spoke as Wisdom; the words which Matt. 23.34 attributes to Jesus, Luke 11.49 attributes to Wisdom.[36] The Ebionites, an early Jewish Christian group, told of a vision of a *pair* of great angels who were the Son of God and the Holy Spirit, male and female. Several gnostic writings describe twofold angels with a male and a female aspect. Some early Christian writers, especially in the Eastern Church, perpetuated in their teachings about the Holy Spirit the mothering and creative roles of the Lady Wisdom. Their greatest church in Byzantium was dedicated to her: Hagia Sophia, the Holy Wisdom. It is only by recognizing this double aspect of the ancient Yahweh that we can begin to understand the writings of the first Christian centuries with their trinity of El Elyon, Yahweh and Wisdom.

Notes to chapter four

1 Philo, *On Drunkenness*, 8.30; 9.33.

2 R. Patai, *The Hebrew Goddess*, New York 1967, pp.121–5.

3 See, for example, J.A. Emerton, 'New Light on Israelite Religion', ZAW 94 (1982). Also G.W. Ahlström, *Aspects of Syncretism in Israelite Religion*, Horae Soederblomianae V, Lund 1963, pp.52–3,

4   G.G. Scholem, *On the Kabbalah and its Symbolism*, tr. R. Mannheim, London 1965, pp.107–8.

5   G.H. Dix, 'The Influence of Babylonian Ideas on Jewish Messianism' JTS 26 (1925), p.243.

6   S.M. Olyan, 'Some Observations concerning the Queen of Heaven' Ugarit-Forschungen 19 (1987), especially p.171 n.60, and also *Asherah and the Cult of Yahweh in Israel*, SBL Monograph 34, Atlanta 1988.

7   See my *The Older Testament*, chapter 9.

8   J. Eaton, *Liturgical Drama in Deutero-Isaiah*, London 1979.

9   J.F.A. Sawyer, 'The Daughter of Zion and the Servant of the Lord in Isaiah: a Comparison', JSOT 44 (1989).

10 Sawyer, ibid., cites in n.21 M. Thurian, *Marie. Mère du Seigneur, Figure de l'Eglise*, Taizé 1962.

11 Emerton, op.cit., p.18.

12 CTA is A. Herdner, *Corpus de Tablettes en Cunéiformes alphabétiques découvertes à Ras Shamra-Ugarit de 1929 à 1939.*

13 J. Day, 'Asherah in the Hebrew Bible and North West Semitic Literature', JBL 105 (1986) is the best short survey of the Asherah debate.

14 See Olyan, op.cit., pp.163–4, and notes.

15 W.G. Dever, 'Asherah, Consort of Yahweh', BASOR 255 (1984), p.31.

16 W.A. Maier, *Aserah, Extra Biblical Evidence*, HSM 37 Atlanta 1986, p.168. The original report by P.W. Lapp is in BASOR 1969. The figure at the top of the stand is now thought to be equine not bovine, see Glock 'Taanach' in IDB Supplement.

17 G.E. Wright, *Biblical Archaeology*, London 1957, p.117.

18 Ahlström, op.cit., p.52.

19 K. Kenyon, *Digging up Jerusalem*, London 1974, p.142.

20 B. Porten, *Archives from Elephantine*, Berkeley, 1968.

21 Quoted from *The Epic of Gilgamesh*, tr. N.K. Sanders, Penguin 1960, p.108.

22 R.A. Oden, 'The Persistence of Canaanite Religion', Biblical Archaeologist 39 (1976), p.36.

23 Olyan, op.cit., n.7. Other views are that the figure was Ma'at or Isis, or that she was like Anat in the Ugaritic Aqht legend, see R.J. Clifford, 'Proverbs IX: a suggested Ugaritic Parallel', Vetus Testamentum xxv, 1975. N. Whybray, *Wisdom in Proverbs*, London 1965, pp.87–92 found Wisdom to be originally and

primarily an Israelite personification of an attribute of Yahweh. He sets himself firmly against mythology; of Prov. 8 he says: 'The terms used to describe wisdom's origin are metaphorical not mythological', p.103. How does he know? To borrow from Job 38.4, 'Were you there when I laid the foundation of the earth?'

24 Is it coincidence that happy and Asherah are from the same root?

25 See my *The Older Testament*, chapter 9.

26 W. McKane, *Proverbs*, London 1970, p.279.

27 Ibid., 273.

28 See my *The Older Testament*, chapter 12.

29 Wisdom was to play a prominent role in later magical practices and it may be that this was one of the reasons for its prohibition.

30 B. Vawter, 'Prov 8.22: Wisdom and Creation', JBL 99 (1980), tries hard to show that *qnh* means only 'acquire' or 'possess', but he does not succeed.

31 R. Murray, *Symbols of Church and Kingdom*, Cambridge 1975, p.318.

32 'Master workman' is a disputed translation; another possibility is 'nursling'. For discussion see Whybray, op.cit., pp.101-3, where he chooses every possible option against there having been a Wisdom figure.

33 M. Stone, 'Lists of Revealed Things in Apocalyptic Literature', in *Magnalia Dei: the Mighty Acts of God. Essays in Memory of G.E. Wright*, New York 1976.

34 Cf. Wisd. 7.7. Brownlee, op.cit., ch.3, n.1, shows how 'creating' was the original meaning of the name Yahweh.

35 D. Suter, 'Fallen Angel, Fallen Priest: The Problem of Family Purity in 1 Enoch 6-16', HUCA 50 (1979).

36 J.D.G. Dunn, *Christology in the Making*, London 1980, pp.196-206.

Chapter five

The Evidence of the Angels

The Angel of Yahweh has no obvious heir in later texts. Although the so-called inter-testamental writings are full of angels, they are new angels with names. They have, apparently, no antecedents and, apart from a brief appearance in Daniel, the great archangels are not mentioned at all in the Old Testament. The lack of continuity between the Old Testament and later writings is usually explained by saying that the angels developed only when there was a need for mediators between the people and God who had become more distant. This is a half-truth. After the reforms of the exilic period when Yahweh was fused with El-Elyon, he certainly did become a more distant God, but angels were not 'invented' to fill the gap. The angels were those heavenly beings who had formerly been the sons of Elyon, the kin of Yahweh the Holy One. When Yahweh became Elyon, his roles were filled by other angels. Ideas about the angels were refined and elaborated over the centuries but in their essentials they remained the same.

Several crucial texts in the Hebrew Bible which mention angels have become obscure; at other places the Greek, which was thought to have introduced newly fashionable angels into the text, has been shown to have kept to an earlier Hebrew now recovered at Qumran. The problem now is to account for the disappearance of the angels not for their appearance. It seems that their demise was one of the results of the development of monotheism. Tradition has it that the names of the angels were brought back from Babylon, which is usually interpreted as meaning that angels were 'invented' at that time. The context of the tradition, however, suggests that it was the *names* of the angels, like the names of the months, which had been altered in Babylon, not that angels as such had been invented there. The passages are never said to suggest that there had been no calendar before the exile, only that the months had acquired new names. The case with the angels was similar. Discussing the fixing of New Year on the first of Tishri and the other Babylonian names for the months, the Jerusalem Talmud says: 'R.Shim'on b.Laqish said: The names of the

70

angels were also introduced by the Jews in this way, at the return from Babylon' (j. *Rosh Ha-Shanah* 1.2). Elsewhere, the names of the archangels only are mentioned: 'R. Hanina said: The names of the months came up with us from Babylon. R. Simeon b. Lakish said: Also the names of the archangels Michael, Rafael, and Gabriel' (Gen. Rab. 48.9).

It is significant that the fourth archangel is not named here. He appears in other texts as Phanuel, as Sariel and as Uriel and he is thought to have represented the pre-exilic angel of the presence.[1] This was not a simple one-to-one correspondence, however, since all the archangels in the later texts seem to have represented aspects of the ancient Yahweh. The great confusion over the archangels' names in the post-exilic period has been caused by the fact that only one group within Israel had accepted the fusion of El Elyon and Yahweh. The returned exiles, influenced by the monotheism of the Second Isaiah and the Deuteronomists' blueprint for the restored nation, recognized that Yahweh was El, but they did not abandon the idea of a patron angel for Israel. He acquired a new name and appeared mainly as Michael, the Prince of Israel, pre-eminently a warrior as Yahweh had been. The roles of Yahweh were divided among all the archangels, who had formerly been known as the seven eyes of Yahweh (Zech. 4.10) or the four presences (Ezek. 1.1, 5). It is interesting that both these pieces of information about the pre-exilic angels come from prophets who were also priests, and therefore presumably acquainted with the traditions of the temple. Those who had not accepted the new monotheism had had no need to rename their patron angel. For them, El Elyon remained El Elyon and the Angel remained the Angel. Sometimes he was unnamed, sometimes he had a secret name, which must have been the sacred name, and sometimes he had a name formed from Yahweh. With this in mind the confusion of the texts begins to clear a little and patterns emerge which show that the angels did have antecedents in the Old Testament. The roles of the unnamed Angel are those of Yahweh: he is manifested in human form, enthroned, a warrior and a high priest. His servants ascend to his presence and are transformed into his angelic agents.

The reform of Israel's religion was like a great shipwreck; fragments of the older ways surfaced in later literature for centuries, and it is only the earlier beliefs about the manifold presence of Yahweh the second God which can explain the diversity but consistency in later texts. Over the centuries the two systems began to mingle; perhaps they had never clearly separated in the minds of the less sophisticated. Yahweh was known both as the High God and as the Angel and his manifold presence was variously named.

The memory of the Great Angel survived for centuries, a sure sign that this was an important belief and not the deviation of a minor sect. A letter written in Provence in 1230 on the subject of the Kabbalah said:

And with regard to the tenth sefirah (power) they received a tradition that it was identical with what our teachers named in one place the Prince of the Divine Countenance and in other places the Prince of the World and it is he who appeared to the prophets.[2]

The Angel of the Presence was reckoned to have been the one who appeared in the Old Testament. An identical belief is attested two centuries earlier in the writings of al-Qirqisani, a tenth-century Karaite scholar who compiled an account of Jewish sects. He described one known as Magharians, so called because their sacred books were found in a cave. They had appeared before the time of the Christians. Whether or not this identifies them with the Dead Sea sect is a matter for speculation but they were certainly pre-Christian. He quotes Daud ibn Marwan al-Muqammis to the effect that the Magharians did not take literally the anthropomorphic descriptions of God in the Old Testament: '[They] assert instead that these descriptions refer to one of the angels, namely the one who created the world.'

Another Karaite scholar, Benjamin al-Nahawandi, is reported to have held similar views:

... that the creator created nothing but a single angel and that it was this angel who created the entire world, sent out prophets and commissioned the messengers, performed miracles and issued orders and prohibitions; and that it is he who causes everything in the world to happen, without (the interference of) the original creator.

Shahrastani, who had corrupted the name Magharian to Makariban, said:

One part of the Makaribans believe that God spoke to the prophets through an angel whom he had chosen and placed above all creatures and whom he had appointed as his proxy over them. He who addresses Moses with spoken words is that angel ...

and it was this angel who was spoken of as God in the anthropo-morphical passages of the Hebrew Bible.[3]

72

Several centuries earlier again, and an inscription in Jewish Aramaic on an incantation bowl (usually dated between the fourth and sixth centuries AD) mentions 'YYY the Great, the angel who has eleven names'.[4] Five other bowls have been found with similar inscriptions, from which it is possible to recover the eleven names which belonged to Yahweh the Great, Yahweh the Angel.

Origen, writing early in the third century, quoted from *The Prayer of Joseph*, which had originally been a substantial Jewish work.[5] Little of it has survived and one can only guess its date and milieu, but what does survive shows that angels were believed to take human form and that certain human beings had angelic selves. There was one angel who was chief captain of the heavenly host and first minister before God, but he was also Jacob:

If one accepts from the apocrypha presently in use among the Hebrews the one entitled 'The Prayer of Joseph' he will derive from it exactly this teaching ... that those who have something distinctive from the Beginning when compared to men, being much better than other beings, have descended from the angelic to human nature. Jacob, at any rate, says: 'I, Jacob, who am speaking to you, am also Israel, an angel of God and a ruling spirit. Abraham and Isaac were created before any work. But I, Jacob, whom men call Jacob but whose name is Israel, am he whom God called Israel, a man seeing God, because I am the first born of every living thing to whom God gives life.

[Am I not] Israel, the archangel of the power of the Lord and the chief captain among the sons of God? Am I not Israel, the first minister before the Face of God? (...)

We have made a lengthy digression to render more credible the belief concerning John the Baptist ... [that he] being an angel took a body in order to bear witness to the light. (*On John* II.31)

The Prayer of Joseph also bears witness to belief in the Great Angel. Jacob the man was also Israel the Angel and Israel meant 'the man who sees God'. He had been in the presence of God and thus he had become an angel. An untitled gnostic text (usually known as *On the Origin of the World* [OOW]) expressed a similar belief about Jesus; there were, it said, angelic beings around the heavenly throne, 'and a first born called Israel, i.e. the man who sees God' and also having another name 'Jesus the Christ' which is like the Saviour ... sits at his right hand upon an excellent throne' (OOW.CG II.5.105). Here the man who saw God and became the angel was Jesus.

These late texts bear witness to belief in a Great Angel who was the creator, the God manifested in human form in the Old Testament, an angel enthroned as vicegerent, chief captain of the heavenly host and chief minister of the heavenly liturgy. In several earlier texts the Great Angel also appears but he is unnamed. Since these texts cannot be dated with certainty it is not possible to trace the development of the Angel in more than a broad outline. What is remarkable is not how the Angel changed but the way in which the very earliest characteristics persisted for centuries, even after the name had changed.

The Book of Daniel in its present form dates from the mid-second century BC and shows the Angel at this period. In Dan. 8 the little horn sets itself against an unnamed Prince of the Host who then loses his continual burnt offering, and his sanctuary is overthrown. Since the sanctuary and offerings are those of the temple in Jerusalem the Prince of the Host must have been Yahweh who was worshipped there. Then there is reference to an unnamed Prince of Princes, presumably the same figure; a bold king would come against him and be broken by 'no human hand'. Daniel also saw the angel of fire and bronze (Dan. 10.5–6), the same figure as Ezekiel had seen as the man on the throne and whom he knew as Yahweh. In Daniel he had been fighting with the Prince of Persia (Dan. 10.13) but Michael had come to help him, an important detail since it shows that the unnamed angel in Daniel cannot have been Michael.

2 Maccabees is approximately contemporary with Daniel and it too has a description of the unnamed angel warrior. When Heliodorus went to Jerusalem to rob the temple treasury, 'the Lord of Spirits and all power made a great manifestation' (2 Macc. 4.24). A horseman with armour and weapons of gold, attended by two glorious young men, appeared to punish and repel the thief. We are not told whom the bystanders thought they had seen but the text suggests that it was a manifestation of the Lord of Spirits, coming as of old to defend his temple. A troop of golden horsemen appeared over Jerusalem at another time of crisis (2 Macc. 5.1–4). Were these the Hosts? These accounts show the beliefs and expectations in the second century BC; the heavenly host and the heavenly warrior to defend Jerusalem were very real to people at that time. It is impossible that the angel of Yahweh who came to defend Jerusalem in Isaiah's time, Yahweh who set an ambush for Jehoshaphat's enemies in the wilderness of Tekoa (2 Chron. 20.22) and the golden horseman of Maccabaean times were not connected.[6]

The Assumption of Moses, although reworked later, was probably written at this time, and it too depicts the unnamed Angel:

And then his kingdom shall appear throughout all his creation
And then Satan shall be no more
And sorrow shall depart with him
Then the hands of the Angel shall be filled
Who has been appointed chief
And he shall henceforth avenge them of their enemies
For the heavenly one will arise from his royal throne
And He will go forth from his holy habitation
With indignation and wrath on account of his sons. (Ass. Mos. 10.1–3)

The Angel here is a warrior (he shall avenge them) and a priest (his hands shall be filled). He has been appointed the chief, presumably of the angels, he has a kingdom with a royal throne and he has sons. It is customary to read this text as though the angel and the heavenly one are two separate figures, the angel being Michael.[7] This is not so; they are one. Both the chief angel (v.2) and the heavenly one (v.3) take vengeance on the enemies of Israel. The chief angel, the warrior priest whose kingdom is imminent, is also the heavenly one leaving his holy place. In the Old Testament the one who left his place to come for vengeance was Yahweh:

For behold Yahweh is coming forth out of his place
to punish the inhabitants of the earth for their iniquity,
and the earth will disclose the blood shed upon her
and will no more cover her slain. (Isa. 26.21)

Mic. 1.3 is similar. This identification of the Angel as Yahweh is confirmed by a comparison with Deut. 32.43. The Assumption of Moses is based upon (or without prejudging the issue we should perhaps say 'deals with the same events as') Deut. 32–3. On this basis, Deut. 32.43 corresponds to Ass. Mos. 10, but there is no Angel. *Yahweh* is the one who comes to avenge the blood of his servants and make expiation for the land of his people. The Hebrew text here has been significantly corrupted (see chapter 3), and the angels of its context obscured as a result, but there can be no doubt that the writer of The Assumption of Moses would have described Yahweh as an angel.

The warrior angel appears in Revelation, but here it is implied that he is Jesus. The King of Kings and Lord of Lords who leads the host of heaven is called the Word of God and he has a name inscribed on his crown which none knows but himself. The secret name was the sacred name Yahweh and since those who had it inscribed on their crowns were the high priests (see chapter 7), the warrior angel must have been the heavenly high priest. John also saw the angel of fire and bronze who introduced himself with the titles of Yahweh (see chapter 10). The earliest Christian apocalypse, then, not only knew the Great Angel but knew him as Jesus. Others also knew that the Angel was Jesus; there is a magical text from fourth-century Egypt which even invokes 'Jesus the god of the Hebrews'.[8]

In the Testaments of the Twelve Patriarchs an unnamed Angel appears who is warrior and mediator. The Testament of Levi describes two figures in his vision, one of whom is the Most High on the throne in the heavenly temple and the other an angel who reveals himself to Levi as both intercessor for, and defender of, Israel. Again the heavenly warrior priest is unnamed:

And thereupon the angel opened to me the gates of heaven, and I saw the holy temple, and upon the throne of Glory the Most High ...
And [the angel] said: I am the angel who intercedeth for the nation of Israel that they may not be smitten utterly, for every evil spirit attacketh it. (Test. Levi 5.1, 6)

The angel is said to have been Michael,[9] but the only evidence for this is the fact that Michael has these roles elsewhere where he is named. Test. Dan. describes an angel who intercedes for Israel and defends them: 'Draw near unto God and unto the angel that intercedeth for you, for he is mediator between God and man, and for the peace of Israel he shall stand up against the kingdom of the enemy' (Test. Dan. 6.1). The role of this mediator angel is exactly that of Jesus in 1 Tim. 2.5, the 'one mediator between God and men'. We do not need to ask if the writer of the Testament drew on 1 Tim. or vice versa, a question which implies that the mediating angel was a minor figure known only in a few texts. Both 1 Tim. and the Testaments were drawing on a common tradition of the Angel and the Christians identified him as Jesus.

Test. Dan. says more about the Angel: 'For the very Angel of Peace shall strengthen Israel that it fall not into the extremity of evil' (Test. Dan. (6.5). The Angel of Peace is another name for the Great Angel;[10] in the Old Testament he was called the Prince of Peace (Isa. 9.6), and he was the one of the two angels who waited for the souls of the dead. The other was the angel of Satan: 'The angel of peace leadeth them into eternal life' (Test. Asher 6.6); 'The inclination of the good man is not in the power of the deceit of the spirit of Beliar, for the angel of peace guideth his soul' (Test. Benjamin 6.1). The Angel of Peace was

Enoch's guide in the heavenly places (1 Enoch 40.8; 52.5), but he was also known as Uriel (1 Enoch 21.9). This overlapping of names shows how the Great Angel appeared as any of the archangels. Here he is Uriel; elsewhere he is Michael or Gabriel.

In Joseph and Aseneth there is an unnamed Angel, introduced as 'commander of the whole host of the Most High' (J. and A., 14.7). He is described as a man of fire, shining like molten iron, with a robe, a crown and a staff. He has heard the prayer of Aseneth and has himself written her name in the book of life (15.3–4). When Aseneth asks the Angel his name she is told that his name is the first of those written in the book of the Most High, none of which can be spoken or known in this world.

Among references to an unnamed Great Angel must be included all those which mention a son of man. 'Son of man' may not in itself have been a significant phrase since it probably meant no more than 'a human being' or 'a man', but in the apocalypses a man always meant an angel (as in 'the *man* Gabriel', Dan. 9.21, or a '*man's* hand', Rev. 21.17) and so 'son of man' must also have meant an angel. In the son of man visions outside the New Testament (Dan. 7; 2 Esd. 2.42–8; 13.1–13; and The Similitudes of Enoch), the appearance of the figure is not described. We are told only that a stream of fire came from his mouth (2 Esd. 3.10) and he had 'the appearance of a man, and his face was full of graciousness, like one of the holy angels' (1 Enoch 46.1). It is not until Revelation that John describes a son of man, and it becomes clear that this was not just a phrase for an ordinary human being. The son of man figure in Rev. 1.13–16 is the angel of fire and bronze, the same as the man in Ezek. 1.26–8. Since Dan. 7, the earliest known son of man text which uses that particular phrase, has already been seen to be a description of Israel's second God, other son of man passages should be read in this light. Son of man, or man, was a way of describing an angelic being, the chief of whom was Yahweh, and so the New Testament passages which refer to the coming of the son of man in fact refer to the Day of the Lord (e.g. Matt. 24.27–31) which is just how the first Christians described it (1 Thess. 5.2; see chapter 10). It is not necessary to speculate how the day of Yahweh expectations were transferred by the Christians to the Son of Man texts; Yahweh was the Man.

In other texts the Great Angel has his own name. He is Jaoel, Yahoel or Joel, all of which are formed from the sacred name and *el*.[11] In the Apocalypse of Abraham, usually dated to the end of the first century AD, Abraham was commanded to leave his father's idolatrous household. He fasted forty days, prepared a sacrifice and then received a revelation. The Angel sent to guide him on his heavenly ascent (Ap. Abr. 10–11) was Jaoel who had 'the likeness of a man' (Ap. Abr. 10.4) and distinguished himself from Michael: 'And with me Michael blesses you forever' (Ap. Abr. 10.17). He was robed in purple with a turban of rainbow around his head, he carried a golden sceptre, his hair was white and his body like sapphire. He was a high priest because he wore a turban, the kidaris, the head-dress of the high priests (Exod. 28.37; 39.28; Zech. 3.5). He lived in the seventh heaven and revealed to Abraham the whole history of his people. Both in Daniel and in this Apocalypse, the Great Angel is *sent*, sent to Daniel to reveal the future to him (Dan. 10.11–14) and sent to Abraham to strengthen him for his ascent to heaven. Daniel does not say who the Angel's master was, but the Apocalypse does. He was sent by the Eternal One.

In the Slavonic Life of Adam and Eve there is an angel named Joel who, again, is distinguished from Michael: 'We heard Michael the archangel and Joe praying for us' (Life, 31). The Apocalypse of Moses, a very similar text, also mentions the archangel Joel (Ap. Mos. 43.5).

In 3 Enoch there are more angel names derived from Yahweh. The great angel in this text is named Metatron and he meets Rabbi Ishmael on his ascent to heaven (see below). The Angel has many names, of which the first are Yahoel Yah and Yahoel. Metatron the archangel reveals that in his earthly life he had been Enoch who had been taken up to heaven (3 Enoch 4.3). Once there he had been given the title 'The Little Yahweh' (3 Enoch 12.5). 3 Enoch is a difficult text to handle, compiled as it is from many older sources, and probably reaching its present form in Babylon between the fifth and ninth centuries AD. Even at this date the Great Angel is still important, and he has his earlier characteristics: he bears the sacred name, he reigns as vicegerent and he had formerly been human.

Another text identifies Metatron and Yahweh. Metatron is mentioned in b. *Sanhedrin* 38b, a passage attributed to R. Nahman,[12] who told of R. Idi in dispute with a heretic over the meaning of Exod. 24.1: 'And he said to Moses "Come up to Yahweh".' The heretic said the verse implied two deities, since it would otherwise have said 'Come up to me'. The rabbi replied that Yahweh at this point meant not Yahweh but Metatron since he was the angel of whom it was said 'For my name is in him' (Exod. 23.21). This passage shows several things: that there was a dispute over the identity of the Angel; that those who said the angel of Yahweh was different from Yahweh named that angel Metatron; that others believed there were *two* deities, the second of which was named Yahweh; and that the rabbis thought such beliefs heresy. Since most of the texts on which we depend for our knowledge of early Judaism have been collected and transmitted through channels which believed the Angel to be a heresy, we begin to see what happened to him.

The belief that a human being could be transformed into an angel when he experienced the presence of God is one of the characteristics of texts which retained the patterns of the royal cult. What had been the ascent of the king became the ascent of the mystic to contemplate the throne. The ascent transformed him. Later texts describe the experience from within, and several show that important figures 'became' the Great Angel. Thus, as we have seen, *The Prayer of Joseph* shows that Jacob was also 'the man who sees God', i.e. the angel Israel, and Moses, according to Ezekiel the Dramatist, had been made God and King when he ascended and saw the heavenly throne.

The earliest known account of participating in the ascent experience from within, so to speak, is in 1 Enoch 14, where Enoch in a priestly role is carried to heaven and sees a wall of crystal surrounded by fire, a crystal house with a starry ceiling, and then a larger house of fire. In this second house is a throne set upon streams of fire and on the throne is the Great Glory surrounded by a host of holy ones. The visionary has travelled into the heavenly temple, the reality which lay beyond the building in Jerusalem, just as the heavenly patron angel was beyond the king and the ministering angels beyond the priests.[13] Enoch enters the presence of the Great Glory as a priest interceding for the fallen angels. He is instructed to take them a message of judgement.

Enoch also describes how human beings could be transformed into angels. Since it was the custom of the apocalyptists to describe human beings as animals and angels as men, when the Enochic histories describe the transformation of an animal into a man, they indicate that a human being has become an angel. In the Book of Dreams, Noah is born a bull and becomes a man (1 Enoch 89.1) and Moses is a sheep who becomes a man (1 Enoch 89.36). In the Apocalypse of Weeks, three 'men' are the key figures; Noah, Abraham and Elijah

(1 Enoch 93.4, 5, 8). Most remarkable of all is the description at the end of the Similitudes where Enoch is transformed into a son of man and describes the experience:

> And I fell on my face,
> And my whole body became relaxed,
> And my spirit was transfigured,
> And I cried with a loud voice,
> ... with the spirit of power,
> And blessed and glorified and extolled. (1 Enoch 71.11)

The merkabah mystics in Palestine and later in Babylonia also record the experience. One of their writings, *The Greater Hekhalot*, probably compiled in the third or fourth century AD, describes vividly the experience of ascent and transformation:

Whoever looks upon him is instantly torn; whoever glimpses his beauty immediately melts away. Those who serve him today no longer serve him afterwards: for their strength fails and their faces are charred, their hearts reel and their eyes grow dim at the splendour and radiance of their king's beauty. No eyes are able to behold it, neither the eyes of flesh and blood nor the eyes of his servants. Whoever beholds it, whoever glimpses and sees it, his eyeballs are seized by balls of fire, his eyeballs discharge fiery torches which burn him and consume him. For the very fire that springs out of the man beholding the garment of Yahweh burns him and consumes him.[14]

3 Enoch also described the process of transformation. When R. Ishmael ascended to heaven in a vision, the Holy One sent Metatron to protect him from the hostile angels. Metatron was the servant of the Holy One, an angel, a Prince of the Presence, and he strengthened the terrified Ishmael. Metatron had seventy names, but the King called him Na'ar, the youth.[15] He revealed that he had been Enoch, the scribe who recorded the wickedness of his own generation. This must have been built on the tradition in the Similitudes where Enoch was transformed into a son of man; here the heavenly being is not just an unnamed son of man but is identified as Metatron. The Holy One (3 Enoch 10.1) made a throne for him like the throne of Glory, and placed it at the door of the seventh palace. A herald was sent out to proclaim that this was Metatron who had been appointed as ruler over all but eight of the princes. He had the power to speak and act in the name of the Holy One (3 Enoch 10.5). The Holy One revealed to him all the secrets of the creation (3 Enoch 11.1). Metatron was robed in the robe of glory (3 Enoch 12.1), crowned, and then named 'The Little Yahweh'. On the crown were written the letters by which heaven

and earth had been created (see chapter 6). Enoch was transformed into Metatron by being changed into fire (3 Enoch 15). It would not be hard to imagine that this was derived from the coronation ritual of the ancient kings. They too had spoken in the name of Yahweh and had sat on a throne which was both in heaven and on earth. As high priests they would have worn the sacred name on their crown.

Most interesting of all is the possibility that Jesus himself described the mystical experience. Several of the sayings attributed to him can be best understood in this setting, for example: 'I speak of what I have seen with the Father' (John 8.38) and 'I saw Satan fall like lightning from heaven' (Luke 10.18),[16] as can the early hymn quoted in Philippians: 'Therefore God has highly exalted him and bestowed upon him the name which is above every other name, that at the name of Jesus every knee should bow ... and every tongue confess that Jesus Christ is Lord' (Phil. 2.9–11). The word used here for Lord, *kyrios*, is the word used to translate the sacred name in the Greek Old Testament (see chapter 11); the first Christians identified Jesus as the *Kyrios* of their native Judaism.

The fusion of Yahweh and El Elyon led to the widely attested tradition of the two Yahwehs, where both High God and Angel had the same name. In the Apocalypse of Abraham, the guardian angel is Jaoel, but this is also one of the names for God. In the song of praise which Abraham was instructed to sing before the fiery presence of God, among the names of God are 'El, El, Jaoel' (Ap. Abr. 17.13). In the Apocalypse of Moses there is the archangel Joel (Ap. Mos. 43.5) and Jael is one of the names for God (Ap. Mos. 29.4). Metatron was known as the Little Yahweh, implying that there was a Greater Yahweh, but this seems to have been more of a title than a name, conferring a certain status when he was enthroned. Something similar had been said of Moses by Philo: 'He was named God and King' (*Life of Moses*, I.158), although he used *theos* implying that the original had been *'elohim*, rather than *kyrios* which would have indicated the title Yahweh. Other texts also mentioned both a Greater and a Lesser Yahweh:

The titles ... functioned independently of the Metatron traditions. Thus we encounter the Great Jao and the Little Jao in the third century Christian gnostic work *Pistis Sophia* and in the gnostic *Book of Jeu*. In the Syriac *Gannat Bussame* (Garden of Delights) we find listed among deities worshipped by unbelievers 'Adonai katon the general of Adonai gadol, who are reverenced by the Israelites'.[17]

There is also the mysterious reference in Sir. 51.10: 'I appealed to the Lord (*kyrios*), the Father of my Lord (*kyrios*), not to forsake me in the days of affliction', which is the earliest use of the two Lords I have found.

The Ascension of Isaiah is an Apocalypse expanded by Christians at the end of the first century; it has two Yahwehs: 'And I saw how my LORD and the angel of the Holy Spirit worshipped and both together praised the LORD' (Asc. Isa. 9.40). This implies that for the first Christians both Father and Son were known as Yahweh, since there follows this: 'And I heard the voice of the Most High, the Father of my LORD as he said to my LORD Christ who will be called Jesus 'Go out and descend through all the heavens' (Asc. Isa. 10.7).[18]

Eusebius, writing in the early fourth century, shows that Christians remembered the tradition of the two LORDS, two Yahwehs:

First, then, Moses expressly speaks of two divine lords in the passage where he says 'Then the LORD rained from the LORD fire and brimstone upon the city of the ungodly' where he applied to both the like combination of Hebrew letters in the usual way and this combination is the mention of God expressed in the four letters which is with them unutterable.

In accordance with him David also, another prophet, as well as king of the Hebrews, says, 'The LORD said unto my Lord, sit thou on right hand' indicating the Most High God by the first LORD and the second to him by the second title.

This is he whom the same prophet in other places clearly distinguished as the Word of the Father.[19]

Yahweh was a manifold deity; the Great Angel had many names. Philo (see chapter 7) and the rabbis (see chapter 8) knew of the plurality and distinguished between the different aspects. Philo, as we shall see, knew the Angel as the Logos, and it is his usage which offers a way into the complex subject of the archangels. Philo's Logos was a plural entity; his name was the name of the powers (*Who is the Heir?* 103). There were six of these powers and he was their head. Elsewhere the powers were defined as the glory which surrounded God; they were, in fact, the angels, suggesting that the angels were all a part of the one whole since they were all manifestations of the second God. It is often observed that 'Lord', *kyrios*, is a form by which a certain class of angels was known and addressed. Paul spoke of many Gods and many Lords (1 Cor. 8.5) but said that for Christians there could be only one God and one Lord. The *Songs of the Sabbath Sacrifice* have shown that there were beings called gods within Judaism; they were the angels of the heavenly temple. Similarly, there were, I suggest, lords, the archangels who manifested the second God, those heavenly beings whom Philo had called the powers. The Deuteronomists had emphasized the unity of Yahweh, 'our *'elohim* is One' because they were trying to eradicate the older angels, but it is interesting that the mediaeval Kabbalists interpreted the verse differently. For them it spoke of the unity of God in all his powers (*sefiroth*): 'From the outset the Kabbalists made every effort to prove that this formula, so all-important in the liturgy, refers to nothing other than the process in which the ten sefiroth are manifested as the living and effective unity of God.'[20] Col. 1.19 makes it clear that all the powers, the whole *pleroma* (translated in the English versions as 'the fullness of God') were present in Jesus but Paul, whilst proclaiming that Jesus manifested all the powers, was careful to distinguish the One Lord from the One God, the Father (1 Cor. 8.6).

The plurality of the second God was variously expressed. The archangels were sometimes four and sometimes seven which may account for the magical text which knew that Yahweh had eleven names. Eleven is not one of the usual symbolic numbers. The seven archangels are implicit in the Old Testament. Zechariah the prophet has seen the seven eyes of Yahweh which were the seven lamps of the *menorah*. The eyes ranged through the whole earth (Zech. 4.10). Since the lamp represented the presence of Yahweh with his people,[21] its sevenfold form, the eyes, was his sevenfold presence. At the climax of his Revelation, John saw the new Jerusalem which had no need of sun or moon because the Lamb, the risen Lord, was its lamp (Rev. 21.23). Now the Lamb in Revelation had many of the roles of Yahweh (see chapter 10), and at the climax of the vision, the two symbols of Lamb and Lamp were fused. Earlier in the vision John had seen the Lamb with seven eyes which were the seven spirits of God sent out into all the earth (Rev. 5.6). These seven spirits or eyes of Yahweh became the seven archangels, all of whom were 'present' in the Messiah because he manifested the LORD in his entirety. Even as early as Isa. 11.2 the sevenfold spirit had been associated with the Davidic king. The sevenfold presence can be traced through into the gnostic texts (see chapter 9) and into the early Christian writings (see chapter 10).

The archangels as a group had several functions: they were priestly figures, they brought the judgement, they defended Israel and they revealed knowledge. Raphael explained to Tobit that he was 'one of the seven holy angels who present the prayers of the saints and enter

83

into the presence of the glory of the Holy One' (Tobit 12.15, cf. Rev. 8.3–4). They were warriors, as can be seen from the role they played in the battle plans of the Qumran Community; the names of the archangels were written on the 'towers' and 'the King of Glory is with us together with the Holy Ones. Valiant [warriors] of the angelic host are among our numbered men, and the Hero of war is with our congregation; the host of his spirits is with our foot soldiers and horsemen' (1QM XII). The archangels also brought the judgement; on the day of Yahweh the archangels acted. Ezekiel had seen the Lord summon six men with weapons for slaughter and a seventh to mark the elect with the sign of Yahweh (Ezek. 9.2–3). Enoch saw seven men in white as the agents of the judgement (1 Enoch 87; 88), one of whom was the scribe (1 Enoch 90.21). There were seven angels in John's vision (Rev. 8.2) and they too brought judgement.

The seven archangels are named in 1 Enoch and their duties listed; other texts show that these roles were by no means fixed, and that the archangels were often interchangeable:

And these are the names of the angels who watch. Uriel, one of the holy angels, who is over the world and over Tartarus. Raphael, one of the holy angels, who is over the spirits of men. Raguel, one of the holy angels who takes vengeance on the world of the luminaries. Michael, one of the holy angels ... is set over the best part of mankind and over chaos. Saraqael, one of the holy angels, who is set over the spirits, who sin in the spirit. Gabriel, one of the holy angels, who is over paradise and the serpents and the cherubim. Remiel, one of the holy angels, whom God set over those who rise. (1 Enoch 20)

In addition, Uriel revealed secrets to Enoch (1 Enoch 19.1; 21.9; 72.1) and answered Ezra's questions before sending him as a 'messenger to my people' (2 Esd. 2.48; 4.1).

Raphael revealed secrets to Enoch (1 Enoch 22.3; 32.6) and he took human form to help Tobit in his struggle against the demon Asmodeus (Tobit 3.17; 5.4; 6.6–7). Michael was the great warrior and priest, the Prince of Israel (see below). Saraqael is not known elsewhere under that name, but the Greek version of 1 Enoch has Sariel here and he appears in the Qumran texts in place of Uriel. Gabriel reveals the history of Israel to Daniel (Dan. 8.16; 9.21) and he, like Uriel, guides Enoch through the heavens (2 Enoch 21.3). He sits at the left of the heavenly throne (2 Enoch 24.1). Remiel is probably the Jeremiel who speaks to Ezra (2 Esd. 4.36). He also appears in the Apocalypse of Zephaniah as 'the great angel Eremiel, who is over the abyss and Hades', the familiar figure of fire and bronze, shining like the sun. He is also known as Ramiel, the angel of true visions (2 Bar. 55.3), and the angel who destroyed the Assyrian army at the walls of Jerusalem (2 Bar. 63.6). The roles of the archangels were interchangeable; Enoch was guided by Uriel, by Gabriel, and also by the Angel of Peace (1 Enoch 40.8; 52.5). Gabriel was the angel in charge of Paradise, and yet it was Raphael who explained to Enoch about the tree of knowledge (1 Enoch 32.6).

In other traditions there were only four archangels, but there were several versions of their names. They were Michael, Gabriel, Raphael, and then either Phanuel, Sariel or Uriel. It is thought that the three names all belonged to the same angel but at different periods. The four had originally been the four living creatures who were a part of the fiery throne in Ezekiel's vision: 'And from the midst of [the throne] came the likeness of four living creatures. And this was their appearance; they had the form of men, but each had four faces and each of them had four wings' (Ezek. 1.5–6). Enoch knew similar beings: 'those who were there were like flaming fire and when they wished they appeared as men' (1 Enoch 17.1), but by his time the four were known as the presences: 'And on the four sides of the Lord of Spirits I saw four presences' (1 Enoch 40.2).

These were the fourfold form of the older 'Angel of the Presence' which was rendered in the Greek of Isaiah 63.9 as 'not a messenger nor an angel but he himself' and are thought also to underlie the four throne names of the messianic child rendered into Greek by the one name: 'The Angel of Great Counsel'.[22] According to Jubilees these angels of the presence were created on the first day of the creation (Jub. 2.2). Jubilees, although it stands in the reformed tradition and distinguishes between Yahweh and the angels, nevertheless shows several things about them. It was the unnamed Angel of the Presence who revealed the history of Israel to Moses (Jub. 2.1), whereas elsewhere the revealer has been Uriel, Raphael, Gabriel and the Angel of Peace. The Angel of the Presence appeared to Abraham at Mamre. Jubilees distinguishes him from the Lord; presumably he was one of the men who accompanied him. 'We appeared to Abraham', says the Angel of the Presence, 'and the Lord executed his judgements on Sodom' (Jub. 16.15). In the account of the binding of Isaac there are three divine beings involved; the Angel of the Presence, the Prince Mastema and the Lord (Jub. 18.9). It is the Angel of the Presence who calls to Abraham the first time, whereas in Gen. 22.10 it is the angel of Yahweh. His speech does not make clear who is involved: 'For now I have shown that thou fearest the Lord and hast not withheld thy son, thy first born son, from me' (Jub. 18.12). Most curious of all is the account of the Exodus. The Angel of the Presence reminds Moses of what happened: it was Prince Mastema who tried to kill Moses on the way back to Egypt (Exod. 4.24 says it was Yahweh); it was the Lord who brought the plagues; but it was the Angel of the Presence who stood between Israel and the Egyptians at the Red Sea. The biblical account is ambiguous: it was the Lord who went before them in the pillar of cloud (Exod. 13.21), but he was also described as the angel of God (Exod. 14.19). In the Qumran *Hymns* there are the Angels of the Face (1QH VI) among whom the men of the covenant hope to stand, with no need of a mediator or a messenger to make reply; an interesting comment on the role of these angels. One version of the Testament of Levi says that Levi, when he was travelling through the heavens, saw the Angels of the Presence 'who minister and make propitiation to the Lord for all the sins of ignorance of the righteous' (Test. Levi 3.5). The Angel of Peace tells Enoch the names of the four archangels:

This first is Michael, the merciful and long-suffering: and the second, who is set over all the diseases and all the wounds of the children of men, is Raphael: and the third, who is set over all the powers, is Gabriel: and the fourth, who is set over the repentance unto hope of those who inherit eternal life, is named Phanuel. And these are the four angels of the Lord of Spirits ... (1 Enoch 40.9–10)

Enoch saw the four of them going in and out of the heavenly temple (1 Enoch 71.8). These texts in the Similitudes name the fourth archangel Phanuel. Elsewhere in 1 Enoch he is Uriel.

The four archangels are the mediators: 'Then Michael, Uriel, Raphael and Gabriel looked down from heaven and saw much blood being shed on the earth (...) And now to you, the holy ones of heaven, the souls of men make their suit saying "Bring our cause before the Most High"' (1 Enoch 9.1–3). The four were then commissioned to bring the judgement: Uriel was sent to warn Noah, Raphael to bind Azazel, Gabriel to destroy the children of the fallen angels, and Michael to destroy Semjaza, one of their leaders. In the War Scroll they are named as the guardians of the towers: 'On the first Michael [on the second Gabriel, on the third] Sariel and on the fourth Raphael, Michael and Gabriel' (1QM IX). By the time of John's vision the four living creatures of Ezekiel's vision had altered somewhat, and instead of having four heads each they were four single-headed creatures, but they were still by the throne, the presences. As with the seven, so too the pattern of the four archangels being one, separate manifestations of the second God, persisted into the gnostic and early Christian writings. A Jewish mystical text, *The Greater Hekhalot*, has many names for Yahweh, most frequently Tootrusea-Yahweh. One explanation for this name is that 'it is composed of the Greek word for "four" – *tetra* (referring to the four letter name of God, YHVH ...) plus the Greek word for "essence" or "being" – *ousion*. It is thus a compound word meaning "the essence of the four (lettered name)".'[23] Whilst there is little doubt that the name derived from the words for 'four' and 'being', it seems likely that it referred to the fourfold nature of Yahweh as represented by the four presences.

The Great Angel came to have several names; fragmentary texts from Qumran show that he was known there by such names as the Prince of Light, which would have been equivalent to Uriel, the Light of God: 'And the Prince of light thou hast appointed from ancient times to come to our support ... and all the spirits of truth are under his dominion' (1QM XIII). This is obviously the chief angel, the Lord of the hosts: 'All the children of light are ruled by the Prince of Light and walk in the ways of Light, but the children of falsehood are ruled by the Angel of darkness and walk in the ways of darkness' (1QS III). The Prince of Light is also the Angel of Truth: 'The God of Israel and his angel of truth will succour all the sons of light' (1QS III). The *Testament of Amram* (4Q Amram) suggests that the Prince of Light and his enemy the Prince of Darkness each had three names. Unfortunately the text is in a poor state, but comparing 4Q Amram and other fragments (4Q 286–7, 280–2) it seems that the other names of the evil angel were Satan and Melchiresa' (i.e. the king of evil), and the other names of the Prince of Light were Michael and Melchizedek.

Michael appears in other texts as the warrior and high priest, the guide of the mystic on his ascent and the chief of the angels, exactly the roles of the unnamed Angel: 'And the chief captain, Michael, led me before the face of the Lord' (2 Enoch 22.6); 'And I will give thee, Enoch, my intercessor the chief captain Michael' (2 Enoch 33.10). It is as the warrior that he appears in Rev. 12.7 fighting with his angels against the dragon. As the Great Prince of Israel (Dan. 10.21; 12.1), he was to lead the heavenly hosts in the final battle against evil and thus establish his kingdom:

This is the day appointed by him for the defeat and overthrow of the Prince of the kingdom of wickedness and he will send succour to the company of his redeemed by the might of the princely Angel of the kingdom of Michael ... He will raise up the kingdom of Michael in the midst of the gods. (1QM XVII)

Michael was the angel who ruled: 'And the great and glorious angel is Michael who has power over this people and governs them; for this is he who put the law into the hearts of those who believe' (Hermas *Similitudes* viii.3.3). Again, we see the roles of Yahweh as lawgiver and ruler. He held the keys of the kingdom of heaven (Greek Baruch 14.2) and he was one of the angels who opened the grave on Easter morning (Asc. Is. 3.16). Michael was also a priestly figure. He interceded for Israel, presented the merits of men to God (Greek Baruch 14.2) and carried them in an enormous vessel (Greek Baruch 12.8; cf. Rev. 5.8 where the angels offer golden bowls full of prayers). He served in the heavenly temple and offered sacrifice there. In the fourth of the seven heavens 'in which (the heavenly) Jerusalem and the temple and the altar are built, Michael the great Prince stands and offers up thereon an offering' (b. *Hagigah* 12b).

In The Life of Adam and Eve Michael is depicted as the angel who instructed the devil to worship Adam because he had been made in the image of God. When the devil and his angels refused, they were driven from heaven (Life 12–17). He was the 'archangel, the messenger of God' (Life 25.3); he brought seeds to Adam from Paradise and showed him how to till the ground (Life 22.2).

The Great Angel was also Melchizedek. There were some groups in the early church who regarded Melchizedek as an angel. Origen, for example, regarded him thus, although later writers such as Jerome rejected the idea.[24] The intricacies of this debate need not concern us; what is important is that the idea of Melchizedek as an angel had even been considered. The silence of the Pentateuch about his origins may have given rise to the tradition that he had no ancestors and must have been an angel; he has no genealogy and as a priest he should have had one.[25] Or the tradition of his being an angel may have derived from the pre-Christian beliefs about him.

Two things only are said about Melchizedek in the Old Testament. First, he was the priest of El Elyon in Jerusalem who met Abraham and blessed him. Gen. 14 records accurately the ancient titles of El Elyon now confirmed by archaeological evidence: 'Procreator of heaven and earth' (Gen. 14.19). When Abram swears his oath the name is changed to Yahweh El Elyon (Gen. 14.22), but this Yahweh is thought to be a later insertion since it does not appear in the LXX, the Peshitta or the Aramaic of the *Genesis Apocryphon*. In all probability, then, Melchizedek represented the priesthood of El Elyon as distinguished from that of Yahweh. Second, Melchizedek was associated with the royal house. Whatever the confused text of Ps. 110 means, it *does* show that the kings in Jerusalem were regarded as priests like Melchizedek; in other words, as priests of El Elyon. For the purpose of this enquiry the date of Ps. 110 is not important; were it from the period of the first temple it would show that the Elyon cult was practised in Jerusalem at that time: and if it were a composition from the time of the Maccabees who adopted the title *priests of El Elyon*, it would testify to the survival of the cult of El Elyon at least until the second century and to its association with the royal house.[26] Both Gen. 14 and Ps. 110 show Melchizedek as a priest.

11QMelch gives a very different picture. Thirteen small fragments in a poor state of preservation were discovered in 1956, and the Melchizedek they depict is an angel figure. A whole series of Old Testament texts has been strung together to describe him and his role, and the question which cannot be answered with any certainty is: Is this a traditional association of texts, or was it the original choice of the author of 11QMelch, decking new ideas decently with Scripture? Were these Old Testament texts, which we read in a very different way, being understood in the way that was normal for the time? The texts link various attributes and functions of Old Testament 'figures' which were also linked and applied to Jesus. If the 11QMelch associations were traditional, then the Christian use of these texts would not have been original, not creative theologizing on their part, but rather the fulfilment of an existing pattern of expectation derived from the Old Testament. The Melchizedek of 11QMelch is the agent of God's judgement in a Jubilee year which was no ordinary Jubilee but, it would seem, the Jubilee which marked the great release of the last judgement. It was associated with the Day of Atonement, presumably also the preliminary to the last judgement, the time when expiation was made for 'the sons of (light), (the l)ot of Mel(ch)izedek'. Ps. 82.1 was applied to him; it was not *'elohim* but Melchizedek who was the judge in the council of the gods, to wreak vengeance on Belial and his spirits. Melchizedek was the one heralded in Isa. 52.7, the one anointed by the spirit, possibly a reference to the proclaimer of Isa. 61.1ff. Melchizedek was not a warrior, but he had Yahweh's other roles of judge, high priest and reigning *'elohim*.

A third name by which the Angel came to be known was Metatron, only found in much later texts but attached to a familiar figure and in fact identified with the angel of Yahweh in the Talmud (b. *Sanhedrin* 38b). It is easy to forget, when making comparisons and tracing developments, that a century in the ancient Near East was just as long as it is today, and that texts separated by three or four centuries really were very widely spaced. Any apparent continuity must be significant and what is recovered must be the way in which the angel of Yahweh was known even at that relatively late period.

The most detailed description of Metatron is not found until 3 Enoch, a mystical text composed in Babylonia no earlier than the fifth century AD, although its roots almost certainly lay in the apocalypticism of pre-Christian Palestine.[27] Metatron, as we have seen, was the angel enthroned as ruler at the door of the seventh heaven and given the name 'The Lesser Yahweh'. To him had been revealed all the secrets of the creation. His name was thus a name of power and it appears in spells inscribed on bowls.[28] Nobody knows the origin and significance of the name Metatron; it may have derived from *ntr*, 'guard, protect'; it may be from the Latin *metator*, 'precursor, preparer' (even though there is no agreement as to the exact meaning of the Latin word); it may have been connected with Mithras; it may have come from μεταθρονον, 'the one next to the ruler', or from μετατυρραvον, 'the co-occupant of the divine throne'; or it may have been contrived so as to give a gematrical value equal to that of Shaddai, the divine name. Such uncertainty is not confined to the name Metatron; there are few angel names whose meanings are beyond dispute, and even when we know which elements have formed the name we are no closer to knowing what it actually meant. Thus Gabriel is clearly derived from 'strength' and *El*, 'God', but in what sense Gabriel represented or was the strength of God we do not know.

The role and function of Metatron has to be deduced from the few scattered references to him, and even here there is no agreement as to when an angel figure is intended and when a simple noun. The earliest occurence of the word is in *Sifre Deut*. 32.49, an early third-century work[29] from Palestine: 'With his finger God was a metatron to Moses and showed him the whole land of Israel.' Metatron was explained as a 'guide'. Similarly Gen. Rab. 5.4 (on Gen. 1.9): 'The voice of God was made a metatron over the waters.' The voice of God guided them.[30] In these examples Metatron seems to have been a function rather than simply a name, but when dealing with angel names it is hard to draw the line between these two. Yahweh was probably a function, as indeed was Gabriel or Uriel.

Later midrashim mention Metatron weeping after the Shekinah had left the temple (*Lamentations Rab.* Intro. 24) and ministering in the heavenly tabernacle which was called the tabernacle of the Na'ar. Metatron offered the souls of the pious before God as an expiation for Israel at the time of the exile when the earthly sanctuary was destroyed. He was the high priest.[31] In b. *Abodah Zarah* 3b Metatron instructs in heaven the children who have died too young to learn Torah,[37] and in b. *Hagigah* 15a it is reported that Elisha b. Abuya ascended to the presence of God and there saw that Metatron was allowed to sit in the divine presence and write down the merits of Israel. He thought that Metatron was a second deity (see chapter 8). The tone of the passage makes it clear that Elisha b. Abuya was mistaken; he was a heretic, and Metatron was punished with sixty fiery lashes for giving the wrong impression.

The role of Metatron as the heavenly scribe bears further investigation since it is one of the lesser known aspects of Yahweh. Yahweh had been the heavenly scribe in whose book were recorded the details of the judgement (Exod. 32.32–3; Ps. 56.8; Isa. 34.16). He wrote down the names of the elect (Ps. 87.6). Enoch too had recorded the deeds of the evil angels (1 Enoch 12.4; 15.1) and been taken to Eden to record the 'condemnation and judgement of the world and all the wickedness of the children of men' (Jub. 4.2). Enoch had also been a priest in Eden; he burned incense there before the Lord (Jub. 2.25). Once transformed into the angel Metatron he continued to function as the great scribe of the judgement.

Metatron was also one of the four archangels; he was identified with Michael in *The Visions of Ezekiel*, a composite work whose earliest stratum probably dates from the fourth century. It describes the seven heavens more or less as they appear in b. *Hagigah* 12b. The fourth heaven, Zebul, is the place of Michael, the great prince. In *The Visions* the Prince dwells in Zebul, and several rabbis reveal his secret names. Eleazar Nadwadaya said one of them was 'Metatron, like the name of the divine dynamis', and yet Enoch was transformed into Metatron by being changed into fire (3 Enoch 15).

The references to Metatron under that name are not earlier than the fourth century, but since the figure of the Great Angel under other names had been known for many centuries, to what extent can Metatron be said to be 'compounded of diverse elements'?[33] Is it not equally possible that 3 Enoch gives a very detailed description of the role of the Great Angel?

Closely linked to Metatron/Enoch's enthronement as Yahweh is 1 Enoch 71, where Enoch is named as Son of Man. Just as Enoch/Metatron had been transformed into fire (3 Enoch 15), so Enoch had been transfigured (1 Enoch 71.11). The visions of the Son of Man figure in the Similitudes of Enoch have much in common with the Enoch/Metatron visions, but since there are several traditions combined in the Similitudes describing the Elect One/Son of Man, comparisons cannot be straightforward:

Enoch/Metatron sits on a throne (3 Enoch 10.1; 48C5) as does the Elect One/Son of Man (e.g. 1 Enoch 45.3; 55.4; 61.8);
Enoch/Metatron was ruler over all but eight of the princes (3 Enoch 10); The Elect One is enthroned by the Lord of Spirits to act as judge (1 Enoch 61.8; 62.2);
Enoch/Metatron was given all the secrets of the creation (3 Enoch 11.1; 48C7); The Elect One has the Spirit of Wisdom and insight and knows all secrets (1 Enoch 49.2–4; 51.3);[34]
Enoch/Metatron judges the heavenly household (3 Enoch 48C8) and the Elect One judges the heavenly beings (1 Enoch 61.8);
Enoch/Metatron has written upon his crown the letters by which heaven and earth were made; originally these would have been the letters of the sacred name (3 Enoch 13.1). The Cosmic oath which sustains the creation is revealed as the name of the Son of Man (1 Enoch 61.13).[35]

Metatron and the Enochic Son of Man are the same figure at different stages in its development; it is interesting that the earliest known depiction of a son of man figure is that of Dan. 7 which, as we have seen, is thought to have been based on *a tradition of two deities*, with Yahweh as the son of man figure.

In all these texts which, at the most modest estimate, range from the second century BC to the fifth century AD, there is a discernible theme. There is a second figure who has, or achieves, divine status. The imagery is always that of enthronement rather than that of any other form of initiation ceremony. The resulting divine being is the agent of judgement, sometimes as warrior, sometimes as high priest, sometimes as judge. A theme which persisted for so long must have been central; the problem of names and details only shows that it was widely used, adapted and interpreted.

Perhaps the most curious and the most telling survival can be found in the writings of medieval Jews, the Hasidim of Germany and the earliest Kabbalists of Provence. The latter distinguished between an unknown God, the Cause of Causes and a second divine being, the Creator,[36] whilst the former described a cherub on the heavenly throne, through whom they prayed. The manifested divinity, they taught, was manifold, the ten sefiroth, and these ten formed a great tree:

The mythical character of Kabbalistic theology is most clearly manifested in the doctrine of the ten sefiroth, the potencies and modes of activities of the living God ...

The Kabbalists' doctrine of the dynamic unity of God ... describes a theogonic process in which God emerges from his hiddenness and ineffable being to stand before us as the Creator ...

This theogonic process is none other than the ancient sons of Elyon in a new guise: 'Mythical structures reappear, no longer in the persons of the old gods ... but concentrated in a new and often unique way in the one world ... of the tree of the sefiroth.'[37] The sons of Elyon here have retained their ancient symbol of the seven-branched lamp, the tree of Life: 'God appears in his potencies in the trunk and branches of the theogonic and cosmogonic tree, extending his energy to wider and wider spheres.'[38] Further, the manifestation was in human form; the symbolism depicts the God of the sefiroth as primordial Man, and the great Name Yahweh was shown by Gematria to be the same as Adam.[39] As ever, this anthropomorphism was a problem, and the debate between Maimonides and Abraham ben David (known as Rabad) has a certain familiarity:

When Maimonides says that whoever believes the Creator has a body is a heretic, and Rabad, in a celebrated gloss, objects that 'many, and his betters' have believed just that, it seems clear to me that behind this criticism stands the doctrine of the Jewish mystics in France concerning the cherub who is the demiurge.[40]

Anti-Christian writing attributed teaching about the Trinity to a misunderstanding of Kabbalah. Profiat Duran, a Spanish scholar writing in 1397, claimed to have heard in his youth many Kabbalists teaching that Jesus and his disciples were Kabbalists who did not perfectly understand and made mistakes.[41] There is no smoke without fire; this late polemic points to something very important, namely that those most intimately acquainted with the Kabbalah sense that a version of this system was the foundation of Christian theology. Beneath the sefiroth of the mediaeval Kabbalists we glimpse the ancient powers of Yahweh, complete with their Eden and temple setting.

The angels are, and will doubtless remain, elusive. Angel texts must not be read in isolation, nor must they be set in a false context. The later kabbalists may have drawn on ideas found in the gnostic texts, and these in turn have affinities with Philo. Ultimately, however, we are driven back to the tradition which must have been the root of them all, and this has been largely obscured due to the way in which the Old Testament has been transmitted and then read. A line must therefore be drawn from the later understanding back through the 'Angel' texts and into the Old Testament whence, ultimately, they sprang. The original understanding of the Old Testament and the 'Angel' texts will have been what determined their use in later periods; in other words, the latest position will have been determined by the earlier ones. There is a certain perversity in assuming that, because we read the Old Testament in a way which differs from that of the ancients, it is they who must have been using a fanciful exegesis for their own ends. In order to recover the original understanding of the Angel in the Old Testament, it is necessary to retroject from the later positions. The manifold nature of the second Deity is abundantly clear in the Christian, Gnostic and later Jewish texts, as is the name of that second deity. Only the first stage is obscured. What is consistent throughout is the pattern of royal/temple imagery associated with the second deity, and his characteristic roles. Over two millennia he was the Angel, the warrior, the high priest, the scribe, the enthroned one and the one manifested in human form.

Notes to chapter five

1 G.H. Dix, 'The Seven Archangels and the Seven Spirits', JTS 28 (1927).

2 G.G. Scholem, *Origins of the Kabbalah*, ET Princeton 1987, p.225.

3 L. Nemoy, 'Al-Qirqisani's Account of the Jewish Sects', HUCA 7 (1930).

4 J. Naveh and S. Shaked, *Amulets and Magic Bowls*, Jerusalem/Leiden 1985, p.135.

5 J.Z. Smith, 'The Prayer of Joseph', in J. Neusner, ed., *Religions in Antiquity*, Leiden 1970.

6 The angelic horsemen appear again in the tradition; Zechariah saw them (Zech. 1.8) as did John (Rev. 6.1–8) who knew that

their leader, the rider of the white horse, was Yahweh (Rev. 19.11–16; see also chapter 10). The horse seems to have been a symbol of Yahweh; many small figurines of horses, some with solar discs on their heads, have been found in Jerusalem, not far from the temple site. They have been dated to about 700 BC and possibly illustrate the sun horses removed by Josiah from the temple (2 Kings 23.11). Similar horses have been found at Hazor and Lachish. A horse bearing a solar disc is also thought to represent Yahweh on the cultic stand found at Taanach.

7 For example R.H. Charles in APOT II, p.421.

8 H-D. Betz, ed., *The Greek Magical Papyri in Translation*, Chicago 1986, p.96.

9 For example R.H. Charles in APOT II, p.307.

10 See Dix, op.cit., who uses the term Messianic Angel.

11 Iao and Yahu were both forms of the sacred name.

12 A.F. Segal, *Two Powers in Heaven*, Leiden 1978, p.168.

13 As depicted in the *Songs of the Sabbath Sacrifice.*

14 From *The Penguin Book of Hebrew Verse*, p.199.

15 Or 'servant'. Is this a vestige of the king as the servant of the Lord?

16 See my *The Gate of Heaven*, chapter 4.

17 P.S. Alexander, 'The Historical Setting of the Hebrew Book of Enoch', JJS 28 (1977), p.162.

18 Knibb's translation in J.H. Charlesworth, ed., *The Old Testament Pseudepigrapha*, vol.1, New York and London 1983. In the note to Asc.Is. 1.7 he says that he has rendered by LORD the Ethiopic word which commonly translates the Hebrew Yahweh to distinguish it from other titles.

19 F.H. Gifford, *Eusebii Pamphilii Evang Praep*, Oxford 1903, vol.XI, xiv.

20 G.G. Scholem, *On the Kabbalah and its Symbolism*, tr. R. Mannheim, London 1965, p.131.

21 See my *The Older Testament*, chapter 9.

22 Dix. op.cit., p.239.

23 D.R. Blumenthal, *Understanding Jewish Mysticism*, New York 1978, p.62.

24 F.L. Horton, *The Melchizedek Tradition*, Cambridge 1976; M. De Jonge, and A.S. Van der Woude, '11Q Melchizedek and the New Testament', NTS 12, 1966.

25 J.D.G. Dunn, *Christology in the Making*, London 1980, p.20.

26 J.J. Petuchowski, 'The Controversial Figure of Melchizedek', HUCA xxviii (1957).

27 H. Odeberg, *3 Enoch or the Hebrew Book of Enoch*, Cambridge 1928, reprinted New York 1973, p.37; G.G. Scholem, *Jewish Gnosticism, Merkabah Mysticism and the Talmudic Tradition*, New York 1960.

28 These incantation texts show how close were the worlds of mystic and magician, and how important the angels were in both.

29 G.F. Moore, 'Intermediaries in Jewish Theology', HTR xv (1922), p.72ff.

30 Odeberg, op.cit., p.94.

31 L. Ginzberg, *Legends of the Jews* 7 vols. Philadelphia 1909–38: vol.3, p.185.

32 3 Enoch 48C 12 says he teaches stillborn children.

33 Alexander, op.cit., p.161.

34 3 Enoch never actually sets Enoch/Metatron on the divine throne but there are grounds for thinking that some material in 3 Enoch has been toned down; see Alexander, op.cit.

35 There are various suggestions as to what these letters were. See Odeberg, op.cit., p.34, and below chapter 6.

36 Scholem, *Origins of the Kabbalah*, p.210.

37 Scholem, *On the Kabbalah and its Symbolism*, p.100.

38 Ibid., p.102.

39 Ibid., p.104.

40 Scholem, *Origins of the Kabbalah*, p.211.

41 Ibid., p.354.

Chapter six The Evidence of the Name

The Deuteronomists and their heirs reformed and reformulated the ancient cult. One of the clearest examples of this process can be seen in their characteristic 'Name' theology, although exactly what was meant by 'the Name' before and after their influence is not entirely clear. Only the broadest of outlines can be sketched, but even this is enough to show how crucial this concept is for understanding the nature of the second God. The temple, said the Deuteronomists, was no longer the dwelling place of Yahweh himself as it had been in the time of the kings who had represented him. It became simply the place of his Name:

The Deuteronomic theologumenon of the name of Jahveh clearly holds a polemic element, or, to put it better, is a theological corrective. It is not Jahveh himself who is present at the shrine, but only his name as the guarantee of his will to save; to it and it only Israel has to hold fast as the sufficient form in which Jahveh reveals himself. Deuteronomy is replacing the old crude idea of Jahveh's presence and dwelling at the shrine by a theologically sublimated idea.[1]

Their polemic was against belief in the actual presence of Yahweh, and since the Deuteronomists are known to have been opposed to the monarchy as they had known it, this must have been polemic against the royal cult.

Older texts suggest that before the reform the Name had been simply a synonym for the presence of Yahweh, and not a substitute. There are several examples of this:

Behold the Name of Yahweh comes from far,
burning with his anger and in thick rising smoke;
his lips are full of indignation
and his tongue is like a devouring fire. (Isa. 30.27)

This is a fire theophany in anthropomorphic terms. Similarly we find in the Hebrew of Ps. 75.5 'Your Name draws near'. In Ps. 20.1–2 Yahweh, the Name, dwells in the sanctuary:

> Yahweh answer you in the day of trouble!
> The Name of the God of Jacob protect you!
> May he send you help from the sanctuary,
> And give you support from Zion.

With this we might compare 'the dwelling place of thy name' (Ps. 74.7); or 'Go now to my place that was in Shiloh, where I made my Name dwell at first' (Jer. 7.12); cf. 'Yahweh is in his holy temple' (Ps. 11.4) and 'Is not Yahweh in Zion?' (Jer. 8.19). Throughout Ps. 118.10–13 Yahweh and the Name of Yahweh seem to be synonymous, and even though other instances are less clear, lines such as these from the psalms still suggest that Name meant something other than what we might mean by it:

> ... how majestic is thy Name in all the earth. (Ps. 8.1)
> Through thee we push down our foes
> Through thy Name we tread down our assailants. (Ps. 44.5)
> Save me, O God, by thy Name
> Vindicate me by thy might. (Ps. 54.1)

The Name was the presence and power of Yahweh. It could be manifested in human form in two ways: it could be 'in' someone, as exemplified by the angel of whom Yahweh said 'My Name is in him' (Exod. 23.20–1) or it could 'clothe' someone. These two apparently contradictory ways of describing the presence derive from the original temple setting and can be seen at their clearest in Philo, who says that the Logos, second God, was the heavenly high priest. He passed through the temple veil and *clothed* himself in it as he did so, thus taking material form. This suggests that complementary imagery was used of the earthly high priest, namely that he was the one *in* whom the second God was present (see chapter 7). The Name was also worn by the high priest on his turban; the account in Exodus says that the golden plate bore the words 'Holy to Yahweh', but Philo reveals another tradition. He says that the golden plate was inscribed with the four letters of the Name, in other words he wore the sacred name. There is a great deal in later tradition to suggest that the high priest when he wore the Name actually represented Yahweh, especially when he performed the atonement rituals. Since the king had also been a manifestation of Yahweh, it is easy to see how vesting and crowning with the Name came to be used of certain figures who had been recognized as Yahweh's vicegerents.

The Old Testament also described the Spirit of the Lord as clothing human beings as though the Spirit and the Name were synonyms:

Gideon was *clothed* with the Spirit (Judg. 6.34) as was Zechariah, the son of Jehoiadah the priest (2 Chron. 24.20) and Amasai when he uttered his words of loyalty to David (1 Chron. 12.18). The tradition of clothing persisted well into the Christian era; a fourth-century Samaritan book about Moses said frequently that he had been vested with the Name of Yahweh, for example: 'He said: "Moses, Moses," revealing that he would be vested with prophethood and the Divine name' (*Memar Marqa* I.1); 'I have vested you with my Name' (*Memar Marqa* I.9); 'Exalted is the great prophet Moses whom the Lord vested with his Name' (*Memar Marqa* II.12).[2] Moses was also vested with the Image which Adam had cast away in Eden (*Memar Marqa* V.4) and 'Image', like 'Name', was one of the titles of the second God. When Moses came down from Sinai, even in the biblical account, his face was radiant, indicating that he had been transformed and become angelic. Later tradition said that this encounter with the Lord was the time when Moses had himself become God and King (Philo, *Life of Moses* I.155–8). Vesting with the Name, then, must have originated in the royal ceremonial which was perpetuated in the high priesthood. Wearing the Name meant bearing both divine and royal state. Metatron enthroned was named as the Lesser Yahweh and wore the Name on his crown (3 Enoch 13). The crown bearing the sacred name eventually became a substitute for the Name itself. There is a curious saying of Hillel recorded in the Mishnah: 'He that makes worldly use of the crown shall perish' (*Aboth* 1.13), which may be early (first century AD) evidence for the practice. Later interpretation added by way of explanation: 'Whoever makes use of the Ineffable Name has no share in the world to come',[3] may explain why the first and highest of the Kabbalists' *sefiroth* (powers) was named *keter* which means 'the crown'.

A theurgic ritual from mediaeval Germany described how the Name was literally 'put on'. Several manuscripts exist of a 'Book of the Putting on and Fashioning of the Mantle of Righteousness', which describe how a garment has to be made like the high priest's ephod on which the secret names of God have to be written. The adept has to fast and purify himself for seven days and then go at night to water. Here he calls out the Name over the water. If he sees a green form above it, he is impure and has to repeat the purification, but if he sees a red form he can enter the water, put on the Name and invoke the angels.[4]

The Deuteronomists suppressed the anthropomorphism of the

older tradition and any idea of the visible presence of God was abandoned. There were two reasons for this: they were the heirs to the monotheism of the Second Isaiah who had identified El Elyon and Yahweh and therefore 'relocated' Yahweh in heaven rather than in the temple in Jerusalem; and they were constructing from the ruins of the monarchy a faith for Israel which no longer had the king at its centre and therefore no longer had his presence as a visible sign of Yahweh with his people. The old concept of a human form present in the temple was no longer tenable, and the ancient descriptions of theophanies derived from temple ceremonial were no longer acceptable. The Deuteronomists rewrote the tradition: 'Then Yahweh spoke to you out of the midst of the fire; you heard the sound of the words but saw no form; there was only a voice' (Deut. 4.12). With this one should compare the contemporary Ezekiel, a temple priest who was able to describe 'one like a man' on the fiery throne (Ezek. 1.26), or the tradition that Moses was permitted to see the 'form' of the Lord (Num. 12.8). T.N.D. Mettinger has explored this transformation in detail in his book *The Dethronement of Sabaoth*, and his conclusions are important:

The concept of God advocated by the Deuteronomistic theology is strikingly abstract. *The throne concept has vanished and the anthropomorprhic characteristics of God are on the way to oblivion.* Thus the form of God plays no part in the depiction in the D work of the Sinai theophany. (Deut. 4.12)[5]

This warns us more clearly than anything else that the traditions which emphasized the throne of God, e.g. those of Dan. 7, Matt. 25.31–46, and Revelation must be understood in the light of something other than the Deuteronomic point of view which has come to dominate our reading of the Old Testament. The vital tradition of anthropomorphism, where the Name was in an angel, or a chosen human being was vested and crowned with the Name, was the older tradition and it survived together with a great deal of the older theology. The early Christians drew upon it: 'Therefore God has highly exalted him and bestowed upon him the Name which is above every other name' (Phil. 2.9).

The clearest evidence for its survival, however, is in the widespread tradition of interpreting words for 'man' as references to the Messiah, or of designating the Messiah simply as 'the man'.[6] This can best be seen by examining the various translations of the Balaam oracles, which were believed to predict the Messiah (Num. 24.3–9; 15–24).

Thus Num. 24.7a, where the Hebrew has the curious lines: 'Water shall flow from his buckets ... and he shall rule over many nations' became in the LXX: 'And there shall come *a man* out of his seed and he shall rule over many nations', while both the *Fragment* and *Pseudo-Jonathan* Targums have: '*Their king* shall rise from among them and *their saviour* shall be from out of them.'

Philo quotes the lines as messianic prophecy: 'There shall come forth from you one day *a man* and he shall rule over many nations' (*Life of Moses* 1.290). The unanimity of both translation and Targums suggests strongly that the Hebrew may once have said something other than 'water shall flow from his buckets'. What that was we shall never know, but it is important to note that where the Greek has 'the man' the Targum specifically names the Messiah and that these two very similar understandings of the verse represent the tradition of Egyptian and Palestinian communities separated in time by several centuries.

The same is true of the interpretation of Num. 24.17b, where the Hebrew gives 'A star shall come forth out of Jacob, and a sceptre shall rise out of Israel.' 'Son of a Star' (*Bar Kochbar*) was to become an important messianic title in the second century and the translations again show that 'man' had a particular significance. The LXX has: 'A star shall rise from Jacob and there shall arise *a man* from Israel.' The Targums give Messiah (*Onkelos*), Saviour and Ruler (*Fragment*) and Messiah, Great Sceptre of Israel (*Pseudo-Jonathan*). *The Blessing of the Prince of the Congregation* (1QSb) alludes to the verse: 'God has established you as a sceptre ... and he shall strengthen you with his Name'. Note the role of the Name. *The Damascus Rule* is similar: 'The sceptre is the Prince of the whole congregation' (CD VII).

Zech. 6.12 '*The man* whose name is the Branch' was read as a messianic oracle and there are 'royal' texts where *the man* clearly refers to the king: 'The man who was raised on high, the anointed (messiah) of the God of Jacob' (2 Sam. 23.1). It may be that there is more than first meets the eye in the promise to the Davidic house: 'There shall not fail you *a man* on the throne of Israel' (1 Kings 2.4; 8.25; 9.5; Jer. 33.17). The meaning of 'the Man' was not lost to the first Christians. Luke attributes to Paul the line 'he has fixed a day on which he will judge the world in righteousness by *a man* whom he has appointed' (Acts 17.31), and John attributes to Pilate 'Behold *the Man*' (John 19.5).

When the reformers denied that Yahweh could himself be present in the temple and said that he had a voice but no form, they cut away from their tradition what was to become the taproot of Christian theology, namely belief in incarnation. The temple was left, so to speak, empty. Solomon's prayer at the dedication of the temple is the classic expression of this new theology, and shows how the older ways were taken over and criticized by the new. There must have been some tradition of what Solomon had said at the dedication of the temple but that is now lost; it has been replaced by the Deuteronomists' criticism: 'But will God indeed dwell on earth? Behold heaven and the highest heaven cannot contain thee; how much less this house which I have built (1 Kings 8.27; cf. 1 Kings 8.16–20, 29, 44, 48). Nathan's prophecy is another place where the new theology shows through: 'Would you build a house for me to dwell in? [Your son] shall build a house for my Name' (2 Sam. 7.5, 13). In each case the older ways are assumed and rejected. In each case the literal presence of Yahweh is denied and the temple is said to be for his Name. Thus the Name came to be a substitute for the presence of Yahweh whereas formerly it had been synonymous with his presence. Mettinger concluded: 'In the Name theology, not only the Sabaoth designation but also the cherubim throne have disappeared. God himself is no longer present in the temple, but only in heaven. However, he is represented in the temple by his Name'.[7] When Yahweh was no longer Yahweh Sabaoth, the host of heaven also disappeared and thus we see how the three vital strands of the older cult, the angels, the presence and the human form, were suppressed.

An important result of this transformation was that the temple became only a house of prayer: 'Hearken to the prayer which thy servant offers towards this place' (1 Kings 8.29; also vv.30, 38, 42, 44, 48). The whole of Solomon's dedication prayer describes the temple as the place *towards which* the faithful can pray, suggesting that it, and the Deuteronomic viewpoint it represents, were written in the exile by people who were far away.

Among those for whom the Name continued to denote the visible presence of Yahweh, it is interesting that this presence is described in the old way as the Son of God. *The Gospel of Truth*, thought to be a Valentinian gnostic meditation on the significance of Christ, contains the statement 'The Name of the Father is the Son'. Like all gnostic writings the text is dense and obscure, but there does seem to lie behind this passage a belief that 'the Name' was a separate being rather than just a name in our sense of the word, and that the Name was that aspect of God which could be perceived and known:

Now the Name of the Father is the Son. It is he who first gave a name to the one who came forth from him, who was himself, and he begot him as a son. He gave him his name which belonged to him; he is the one to whom belongs all that exists around him, the Father. His is the Name, his is the Son. It is impossible for him to be seen. But the Name is invisible because it alone is the mystery of the invisible which comes to ears that are completely filled with it. For indeed the Father's Name is not spoken, but is apparent through a Son. Since the Father is unengendered, he alone is the one who begot a Name for himself before he brought forth the aeons in order that the Name of the Father should be over their head as lord, that is, the Name in truth which is firm in his command through perfect power. For the Name is not from (mere) words, nor does his Name consist of appellations, but it is invisible. He gave a Name to himself, since he sees himself, he alone having the power to give himself a Name. For he who does not exist has no Name. For what name is given to him who does not exist? But the one who exists exists also with his Name, and he knows himself. And to give himself a Name is [the prerogative of] the Father. The Son is his Name. He did not therefore hide it in the work, but the Son existed; he alone was given the Name. The Name therefore is that of the Father as the Name of the Father is the Son. (*Gospel of Truth* 38–9)

The Name in its visible aspect is the Son and the role of the Name/Son is to rule the heavenly powers. The Father cannot be known in himself, i.e. in essence, but his existence can be known through the Name. The original picture of Elyon and his sons has here been clothed with later ideas of existence and essence, but the gist remains recognizable. There was the High God whose sons could be manifested in the created order and one Son in particular was deemed to be their ruler. This must have been Yahweh, here described as the Son and the Name. Another gnostic text preserved by Clement of Alexandria says that Jesus's invisible part was 'the Name which is the only begotten Son' (*Excerpts from Theodotus* 26.1).

The *Gospel of Philip* also contains a speculation on the Name using the image of the robing;

One single Name is not uttered in the world, the Name which the Father gave to the Son, the Name above all things; the Name of the Father. For the Son would not become the Father unless he wears the Name of the Father. (*Gospel of Philip* 54)

Some medieval Jews seem to have kept the memory that the Name was the second God, but the evidence for this is indirect. The Kabbalists regarded the Torah as a living being,[8] but the way they spoke of it and the role they gave to it shows that they attributed to the Torah many of those things which formerly had been attributed to the Name. The Torah was even identified with the Name and said to be the expression of God's power as this was concentrated in the Name. Like the Name, the Torah had been created two thousand years before the creation of the world (Gen.Rab. 8.2): 'For the Kabbalist, this "creation of the Torah" was the process by which the divine Name or the divine Sefiroth ... emanated from God's hidden essence.'[9] The name itself 'was not only the tetragrammaton Yahweh but the totality of manifestations of divine power'.[10] In other words, they knew that *plurality* was associated with the sacred name. Some also held that the Torah was Wisdom, pointing right back to the Deuteronomists' attempt to replace Wisdom by Torah. Apart from changing Name/Wisdom to Torah, the older theology remained intact. Wisdom had been the emanation of God's glory, pervading and ordering all creation, (Wisd. 7.22–6) and so too the Torah was said to be the expression of 'that part of [God's] being which can be revealed to Creation and through Creation'. For the Kabbalists the Torah/Name 'contains power, but at the same time embraces the secret laws and harmonious order which pervade and govern all existence'.[11] To our ways of thinking, the idea of God's Torah being a part of the natural laws and harmonies of the universe is easier to grasp than the older mythological idea of the Name as ordering and sustaining the creation. But once the Torah is treated as a living being, we are pointed back to the other view of the creation where the Name creates and sustains everything. The oldest evidence for the role of the Name is exactly this, and this evidence for the Name as the means whereby creation is established and maintained provides the most remarkable thread linking the ancient religion of Israel to the esoteric tradition of medieval Judaism.

The role of creator is seen in the sacred name itself; Yahweh probably meant 'He who causes to happen'. Scholars have suggested several possible meanings but the most likely is that it derived from a causative form of the verb 'to be': 'This understanding of the ineffable Name may be directly related to a host of passages in the Hebrew prophets, especially in contexts of threats and promises, where "I am Yahweh" may appropriately mean "I am He who makes things happen."'[12] The LXX does not attempt to translate the meaning of the Name but renders it by *kyrios*, the Lord. Some Greek versions, however, leave the four Hebrew letters standing in the Greek text, perhaps an early indication that the letters themselves were important, as they were for the later magicians and mystics. The traditional translation 'I AM' is only appropriate for Exod. 3.14, the self-revelation of the Lord at the burning bush, where the Name is not YAHWEH but 'EHYEH. When the Lord reveals his own name, he uses 'I cause to be' rather than 'He who causes to be', the name by which his worshippers refer to him. The Palestinian Targums agree in their interpretation of this name 'Ehyeh. 'He who spake to the world, Be, and it was; and who will speak to it, Be, and it will be' and 'He who spoke and the world was from the beginning and is to say again to it: Be and it will be' are how the *Fragment* and *Neofiti* Targums render Exod. 3.14. Thus bringing into being, *creating*, is the root concept associated with the Name and it is interesting that creating is the activity most particularly associated with the Angel whom the Magharians said had appeared in human form in the Old Testament.

The tradition is ambiguous as to how the Name was involved in the creative process; sometimes the Name was treated as just a set of letters, a magical seal with great power; sometimes it was depicted as a great bond and at others it was clearly a heavenly being. How, for example, are we to understand the process of creation described in the Prayer of Manasseh?

> Thou who hast made the heaven and the earth with all their order;
> who hast shackled the sea by thy *word of command*,
> who hast confined the deep
> and sealed it with *thy terrible and glorious name*.

To shackle the sea with a word of command in no way suggests that 'word' was anything more than we should mean by it, and sealing the deeps with a name could be no more than an allusion to the use of inscribed seals. But the process of creation is not that described in Gen. 1. Here it is the binding and sealing of powers like the work of a great magician, and the power which binds is the Name and the Word. Parallel lines of poetry suggest that the *Word of command* and the *Name* were equivalent. Both Philo and the Targums show that Word was as much a designation of Yahweh as Name (see chapters 7 and 8).

Jubilees associates the Name with a great oath which is binding in the sense that it binds the natural order together. Isaac requires his sons to swear an oath: 'There is no oath greater than it by the Name glorious and honoured and great and splendid and wonderful and mighty, which created the heavens and the earth and all things together' (Jub. 36.7). There are stories in the Talmuds with a similar tradition: 'When David dug the pits, the Deep arose and threatened to submerge the world ... (David) thereupon inscribed the (Ineffable) Name upon a sherd, cast it into the Deep and it subsided sixteen thousand cubits' (b.*Sukkah* 53a). 'When David came to dig the foundations of the temple he dug fifteen hundred cubits and did not reach the Deeps. At length he came upon a potsherd and wished to raise it. (It) said to him, "You cannot (lift me up)." "Why?" he asked. "Because I am here to suppress the Tehom," replied the potsherd' (j *Sanhedrin* 10). Both these stories are attributed to rabbis of the third centuty AD, but they are believed to have been much older. In the talmudic examples it was a written name which bound the forces of chaos, but in the Prayer of Manasseh this is not clear.

The sacred name, both written and spoken, became an important part both of magical practices and of speculation about the processes of creation and there was a considerable 'Jewish' element even in the practices of pagan magicians. Both creation and magic were closely related, since the role of the magician was to control the creation and alter it to his will. (In the passages which follow page references are to Betz, *Greek Magical Papyri in Translation*.[13] Although they may be garbled, the formulae of the magicians testify to several of the characteristics of Yahweh. One of the commoner names for him in the texts was ARBATHIAO, meaning the fourfold Yahweh (pp.57, 65, 67, 123), a memory of the four archangels who 'were' Yahweh. Several of the Hebrew titles survived in recognizable form: YAHO, ADONAI, ELOAI, SABAOTH (p.39) and even the curious form PIPI (p.33), which was what happened to the divine name Yahweh when the shapes of its Hebrew letters were given their nearest equivalent in the Greek alphabet, resulting in the form πιπι. The sevenfold nature was recognized in the invocation of seven angels, variously but recognizably named as The One (p.70). The sevenfold lamp was imitated in a charm using a lamp with seven wicks, each of which bore a name. Five of the names are familiar: IAO, ADONAI, SABAOTH, IAEO, MICHAEL; the other two are not: PAGOURE, MARMOROUTH (p.135). Another formula ran: 'I conjure thee by the God Iao, the God Abaoth, the God Adonai, the God Michael, the God Suriel, the God Gabriel and the God Raphael'.[14] The Great Name was known to be in Jerusalem (p.194) and the magicians knew a 'sacred, hidden book of Moses called eighth or holy ... the ritual using the Name that encompasses all things' (p. 182). The more detailed formulae incorporate the names of pagan gods alongside the Jewish tradition but the original is, nonetheless, clear:

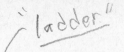
"ladder"

You are the holy and powerful name considered sacred by all the angels ... I invoke your hundred lettered Name which extends from the sky to the depths of the earth; save me for you are always ever rejoicing in saving those who are yours ...

I call upon you ... before whom the unquenchable lamp continually burns ... the great God, the one who shone on the whole world, who is radiant at Jerusalem ... (p.61)

'in-dwelling' 'present' - ziwa

The original of this, in that the lamp still burns, must have antedated the fall of the temple in AD 70. Yahweh the scribe was also remembered in the figure of Jeu, the scribe who appears in the papyri (p.103), and also in the gnostic texts (see chapter 9).

For our purposes, the most revealing of the papyri are those which identify Jesus as the God of the Hebrews, i.e. as Yahweh. A Coptic formula ran: 'Hail God of Abraham; hail, God of Isaac; hail, God of Jacob; Jesus Chrestos, the Holy Spirit, the son of the Father who is above (or below) the Seven/ who is within the Seven. Bring Iao Sabaoth; may your power issue forth from him' (p.62). A Greek charm against demons ran:

'70'

I conjure you by the God of the Hebrews, Jesus ...
I conjure you by the one who appeared to Osrael [i.e. Israel] in a shining pillar and a cloud by day ...
because I conjure you by the seal which Solomon placed on the tongue of Jeremiah ...
I conjure you by the great God Sabaoth through whom the river Jordan drew back ...
I conjure you by the holy one in Jerusalem before whom the unquenchable fire burned for all time ... (pp.96–7)

These spells came from Egypt and were written in Greek but such magic was not confined to pagan societies where Jews had settled. Many amulets and bowls have been found inscribed in Hebrew and Aramaic which also work magic with forms of the Name, including the form *'Ehyeh 'Asher 'Ehyeh*, 'I Am Who I Am'. It is one of these which describes Yahweh as 'the Great Angel with Eleven Names'.[15]

Magical use of the Name had long been forbidden. The fact that the Decalogues of Exod. 20 and Deut. 5 both forbid taking the Name in vain suggest that the problem was ancient. The more restrained Judaism of such groups as the Pharisees would not permit the sacred Name even to be uttered; other titles such as 'Lord' were substituted. The Mishnah warns that any who utter magical charms over a wound or who pronounce the Name with its proper letters will have no place in the world to come (*Sanhedrin* 10.1). It is interesting that this prohibition is coupled with one against the reading of forbidden books. The Qumran community expelled those who uttered the Name for any reason whatsoever (1QS VII). According to the Mishnah the Name was only pronounced by the high priest on the Day of Atonement (*Yoma* 3.8): 'And when the priests and the people which stood in the Temple Court heard the Expressed Name, they used to kneel and bow themselves and fall down on their faces and say, "Blessed be the name of the glory of his kingdom for ever and ever!" ' (*Yoma* 6.2). The sound of the Name, it was said, could be heard as far away as Jericho (*Tamid*. 3.8).

Shofar

The uttering of the Name and its prohibition were inseparable from the idea of possessing divine power whether this took the form of magic or the related high priestly functions of making atonement. The Name was Yahweh the creator and renewer made present. It is with good reason that Urbach concluded thus his discussion of the Power of the Divine Name: '... the discontinuance of the enunciation and mention of the Name was intended to prevent the blurring of the distance between God and Man and the use of the Name for magical purposes'.[16]

The mystical writings, which continued to 'blur the distinction' emphasized the vision of God and the possibility of human beings approaching the throne and acquiring the status of an angel, even of the Great Angel. They continued to use the Name in many forms, primarily as the key to understanding the secrets of the creation and to the power that this unleashed. The earliest of these writings, even though it cannot be dated with certainty, must be the Similitudes of Enoch which describes visions of the throne and the great judgement. The passage showing the role of the Name in the creation is not entirely clear, but the gist of it is that Michael knows the Name which has to be spoken in the 'oath' to bind together the whole of the natural order. Through the power of this 'oath' the heaven was suspended before the creation of the earth, the mountains and the seas were created and the heavenly bodies bound to their orbits:

> And this oath is mighty over them
> And through it [they are preserved and] their paths are preserved,
> And their course is not destroyed. (1 Enoch 69.25)

The Name in question was that of 'that Son of Man' and there was great joy that it had been revealed (1 Enoch 69.26). The judgement began after the Son of Man had taken his place on the throne and 'the

Word of that Son of Man' went forth in strength as part of the judgement (1 Enoch 69.27–9). Since Name and Word were virtually synonymous, the judgement and the renewing of the creation are here shown to be the same process, and we find ourselves very near to the description of the second God in Philo, namely that the two names by which he was designated in the Old Testament, Yahweh and Elohim, denoted respectively his two aspects as ruler and creator. At the very end of the Similitudes, Enoch himself is designated Son of Man (1 Enoch 71.14–17), an outstanding testimony to the ancient belief that the king/high priest was recognized as the agent or manifestation of the Lord. Enoch had originally entered the presence of the throne as *a priest* in order to intercede for sinners (1 Enoch 15.2) but had been told to take them a message of judgement.

In 3 Enoch we see the tradition at a later stage, although again there is no certainty as to the date of composition nor of the age of any of the source material incorporated in it. By the time of R. Ishmael's vision which this text records, Enoch had been taken to heaven and transformed into the Great Angel Metatron; we may presumably see in Metatron the earlier Son of Man figure. Enoch/Metatron had been crowned with the letters which formed the creation; presumably these were the letters of the sacred Name since they were inscribed on the crown as they had been on the crown of the high priest:

> He wrote with his finger, as with a pen of flame, upon the crown which was on my head,
> the letters by which heaven and earth were created;
> the letters by which seas and rivers were created;
> the letters by which mountains and hills were created;
> the letters by which stars and constellations, lightning and wind, thunder and thunderclaps, snow and hail, hurricane and tempest were created;
> the letters by which all the necessities of the world and all the orders of creation were created. (3 Enoch 13.3. Enoch 41 is a fuller account of these letters of creation)

Metatron then showed Rabbi Ishmael the secrets of the creation, and how the various names of the Yahweh effected various aspects of it; this must be the equivalent of the great 'oath' in 1 Enoch:

I saw water suspended from the height of the heaven of Arabot through the power of the name Yah, I am that I am ...
I saw fire, snow, and hailstones enclosed one within the other without one destroying the other, through the power of the name 'A Consuming Fire' as it is written 'For YHWH your God is a consuming fire ...' (3 Enoch 42.2–3)

Other names are shown to perform other miracles within the natural order. The opposing powers and elements within the creation were kept in order and separated by the power of the Name, so that the creation did not revert into chaos:

I saw rivers of fire in the midst of rivers of water and rivers of water in the midst of rivers of fire, through the power of the Name 'He keeps the peace' as it is written 'He keeps the Peace in his heights'. He keeps peace between fire and water ... (3 Enoch 42.7).

Another mystical text, *The Lesser Hekhaloth*, tells of a great spell which unfortunately is no longer preserved:

This the spell and the seal
By which the earth is bound
And by which the heavens are bound
And the earth flees from it
And the universe trembles before it.[17]

There is a uniformity in the tradition which suggests that it was deeply rooted; targums, magical texts and mystical writings all agree that it was the Name, whether uttered or invoked or written, which sustained the creation.

The gnostics knew this tradition; *Pistis Sophia* 136 describes how Jesus stood by the altar and called out IAO to the four corners of the earth. Strange movements in the created order followed this command. It is interesting that the command was associated with the altar, i.e. that it had a temple setting, and that the divine name was the command which moved the creation. J. Fossum has collected together a considerable body of evidence from Samaritan sources showing how the Name as the means of creation came to be the letters of the tetragrammaton used in increasingly complex and quasi-magical ways. One fourth-century text in particular deserves attention; Marqa is describing the promise to Moses that he would deliver the Israelites from Egypt:

I will reveal to you my Great Name YHWH. I did not reveal it to the righteous of the world. El-Shaddai was the Name by which I revealed myself to Abraham, Isaac and Jacob; but this great Name I did not reveal to them. It is a Glorious Name that fills the whole of creation. By it the world is bound together; and all the covenants of the righteous are bound by it forever. I shall not forget it as long as the world exists. Since you are found to be in the hands of the Most High of the whole world, I have revealed to you my Great Name. (*Memar Marqa* 1.4)[18]

This text implies a belief about the Name similar to that in the *Gospel of Truth*, namely that the Father (here the Most High) has a Son/Name (here the Great Name that binds together the creation) whom he reveals and will not forget.

This use of the Name is also found in early Christian texts (see chapter 10). In a cryptic ode describing the baptism of Jesus as a time when the powers of the underworld were defeated, the themes of baptism and creation are interwoven. The abysses are sealed with the seal of the Lord almost as though the Lord himself fulfilled the role which elsewhere was given to the magical sherd bearing the divine Name (*Odes of Solomon* 24). J.H. Bernard in his notes offers as a parallel the Coptic baptismal office: 'qui in unum locum aquas congregasti ac mare coercuisti abyssosque obserasti easque sancto et gloriosissimo nomine obsignasti'.[19]

There is a similar tradition in *The Shepherd of Hermas* where the *Name of the Son of God* and *Son of God* are synonymous; both support the whole creation: '... the Name of the Son of God is great and incomprehensible, and supports the whole world. If then the whole creation is supported by the Son of God ...' (Hermas Sim. ix. 14). Daniélou's comment is apt: 'It is hard to resist the temptation that what lies behind the present text is a train of thought in which not the "Name of the Son of God" but the "Name of God" sustained the creation and was equated with the Son of God.'[20] If this is so, then the tradition behind Hermas is that of the Gospel of Truth. 1 Clement is similar again: 'Your Name, which is the first source of all creation' (1 Clem. 59.2).

The Name is probably the most obscure and inaccessible of all the concepts used in the royal theology, and any attempt to synthesize such information as there is into a coherent system would probably distort more than it clarified. The Name was the nature, the power, the presence of Yahweh. The Name was the fundamental bond of the creation, such that Philo's contemporaries could understand it as the rational principle governing all natural phenomena. But the Name was also present in persons who mediated between the Most High and humankind, and those thus vested had the power of the Name. The high priest's duty of making atonement and offering life/blood to restore, renew and heal the people and their land is the clearest expression of the Name at work, renewing the covenant of peace which had been entrusted to the high priesthood (Num. 25.12–15). The Epistle to the Hebrews explains how Jesus, as high priest on earth and in heaven, renewed and restored this covenant with his own life/blood (Heb. 9.12).

Notes to chapter six

1 G. von Rad, *Studies in Deuteronomy*, ET D. Stalker SBT 9 London 1953, p.38.

2 J.E. Fossum, *The Name of God and the Angel of the Lord*, Tübingen 1985, p.87.

3 E.E. Urbach, *The Sages: their Concepts and Beliefs*, Jerusalem 1979, p.130, where he says that Avot de R Nathan Recension I xii is an explanation of Avot 1.13, 'Whoever uses the crown ...'

4 G.G. Scholem, *On the Kabbalah and its Symbolism*, ET R. Mannheim London 1965, p.130.

5 T.N.D. Mettinger, *The Dethronement of Sabaoth*, Lund 1982, p.124.

6 W. Horbury, 'The Messianic Associations of "the Son of Man"', JTS new series 36 (1985).

7 Mettinger, op.cit., p.123.

8 Scholem, op.cit., p.45.

9 Ibid., p.40.

10 Ibid., p.43.

11 Ibid., p.40.

12 W.H. Brownlee, 'The Ineffable Name of God', BASOR 226 (1977). Other suggestions are: it derived from the verb 'to fall' and referred to a sacred object which had fallen from heaven or the activity of one who caused rain and thunderbolts to fall; or it derived from the verb 'to blow' and referred to the God of storms and wind.

13 H.D. Betz, ed., *The Greek Magical Papyri in Translation*', Chicago 1986.

14 G.G. Scholem, *Jewish Gnosticism, Merkabah Mysticism and Talmudic Tradition*, New York (1960) 1965, p.71.

15 J. Naveh and S. Shaked, *Amulets and Magic Bowls*, Jerusalem/Leiden 1985, p.135.

16 Urbach, op.cit., p.134.

17 Scholem, *Jewish Gnosticism*, p.83.

18 Fossum, op.cit., p.81.

19   J.H. Bernard, *The Odes of Solomon*, Cambridge 1912, p.94.

20   J. Daniélou, *A History of Early Christian Doctrine before the Council of Nicaea, I: The Theology of Jewish Christianity*, ET London 1964, p.152.

Chapter seven The Evidence of Philo

Philo was a contemporary of the first Christians, a Jewish philosopher living in Alexandria where he was a leader of the community. His voluminous writings should provide the best possible background to any understanding of the New Testament but they are rarely used for this purpose because Philo's Judaism is very unlike the Judaism we have always assumed to be the 'orthodoxy' of Palestine. The nature of this supposed Palestinian Judaism is now being questioned as never before; many of the rabbinic writings on which it has been based are known to come from a later period, while many contemporary texts from Qumran point to something very different. The problem with Philo's writings is that he is not expounding the faith of his fathers in terms of his own culture but rather is transposing it into the world of contemporary Hellenism. He uses the language of the philosophers and yet time and again what he writes is not their philosophy.

The recovering of Philo's Judaism is more than an academic exercise. If it proves possible to determine what Philo transposed into the language of the philosophers, this will be a form of Judaism which was contemporary with Christian origins and *Philo's Judaism is chiefly remarkable for the fact that it has a second God, the Logos*. It has always been assumed that this second God, the Logos, was something unique to Philo, something which he adopted from contemporary philosophers and grafted into his Judaism, but this is unlikely. Could Philo have altered the fundamental monotheism of Judaism and still remained the leader and spokesman of his community? Or do we have in his writings evidence for a substantial Jewish community which was not monotheistic in the generally accepted sense of that word?

The key word, *logos*, is usually translated 'Word', but this is only one of several possible renderings. If our thoughts on Logos are limited to what could possibly be meant by the English 'Word' the results may well be far from anything that Philo would have recognized. Logos could mean a relation or correspondence, it could mean an analogy, an explanation, a rule or principle, the faculty of reason, a

114

speech, an oracle and much more. Since Philo describes the Logos as the Image of God (*On the Special Laws* I.81; *On Dreams* I.239) one would perhaps opt for 'correspondence' as an English equivalent, but since he also describes the Logos as the 'Covenant' (*On Dreams* I.237) and as the 'Seal of the Universe' (*On Flight* 12; *On Dreams* II.45) one could perhaps include 'rule or principle' as a part of what he meant by Logos.

Philo did not invent the term. The Jews of Alexandria already had the Wisdom of Solomon which shows how much of Israel's ancient religion had survived in the new environment of hellenized Egypt. Wisdom is there, the Spirit of God's power pervading creation. She it was who, in the role of Yahweh, delivered the Israelites from Egypt (Wisd. 10.15) and guided them all through their history. But the delivery from Egypt had also been accomplished by the all-powerful Logos:

> ... thy all-powerful *word* leaped from heaven, from the royal throne,
> into the midst of the land that was doomed,
> a stern warrior carrying a sharp sword of thy authentic command,
> and stood and filled all things with death,
> and touched heaven while standing on the earth. (Wisd. 18.15–16)

The old imagery is all there: the throne, the judgement and the warrior with a great sword. In the original story, however, the destroyer had been Yahweh (Exod. 12.12, 29). Even though the Wisdom of Solomon tells us nothing more about the Logos (except that the word is a healer, Wisd. 16.12), there can be no doubt that Philo's community of Jews remembered Wisdom as identical in her roles with those of Yahweh, and they described Yahweh as the Logos. Philo has many titles for the Logos: 'God's First Born, the Logos, who holds the eldership among the angels, their ruler as it were. And many names are his, for he is called, "the Beginning", and the Name of God and his Logos and the Man after his Image and "She who sees" that is Israel' (*On the Confusion of Tongues*, 146). The ruler of the angels and the Name had also been designations of Yahweh.

Several other writers link the Name and the Logos. Targum *Neofiti* to Exod. 6.7 suggests that both were aspects of Yahweh:

> And I will separate you to my Name as a people of holy ones,
> and my Word will be to you a Redeemer God,
> and you shall know that I am the Lord your God who redeemed and brought you out from beneath the yoke of the servitude of the Egyptians.

115

Christian writers said that Jesus was both Name and Logos; Clement of Alexandria, when writing on the prologue to the Fourth Gospel, equated Logos and Name, and in his *Excerpts from Theodotus* he shows that the gnostic Theodotus also called Jesus both Name and Logos (Excerpts 21; 26; 31).

Philo is quite clear what he meant by Logos; he was describing a second God: 'For nothing mortal can be made in the likeness of the Most High One and Father of the Universe but (only) in that of the Second God, who is his Logos' (*Questions on Genesis* II.62). This statement, though clear enough, has caused consternation, since it was thought impossible for a Jewish writer to speak of a second God. A.F. Segal wrote:

In doing this he has an entirely different emphasis than the rabbis. He is clearly following the Greek philosophers. Like them he is reluctant to conceive of a pure eternal God who participates directly in the affairs of the corruptible world. So he employs a system of mediation by which God is able to reach into the transient world, act in it, fill it, as well as transcend material existence without implying a change in his essence.[1]

He is certainly different from the rabbis, but this need not necessarily imply dependence on the Greek philosophers. What is said here about the Logos is very like what has been said by others of the Name in Deuteronomy. When we add to this the whole catalogue of significant titles which Philo gives to the Logos, of which King, Shepherd, High Priest, Covenant, Rider on the Divine Chariot, Archangel, and Firstborn Son can give a context for all the others, it seems more than likely that Philo drew his ideas of the mediator from his people's most ancient beliefs, and only *adapted* them to Greek ways of thinking. Any other evidence that he can give as to the role and function of the Logos/Name will be crucial for our understanding of how the Chief Angel of Israel was understood in the first century AD.

Philo was presenting the Judaism of his day in Greek terms, but what he was presenting was Judaism and not a vague syncretism. He used Greek terms for something which was essentially Jewish. Wolfson has this as a warning preface to his study of Philo:

With the example of Scripture before them (the Jews) were not afraid to make use in the description of their own religion of terms used in the description of other religions, but whatever common terms they used the difference was never blurred for them between truth and falsehood in religious belief and right and wrong in religious worship. For the understanding of the nature of Judaism throughout its history, and especially during the Hellenistic period, this twofold aspect of its attitude to other religions is of the utmost importance. Those who seem to see evidence of religious syncretization in every use of a pagan term by a Hellenistic Jew simply overlook this one important aspect in the attitude of Judaism toward other religions.[2]

Hellenization was largely a matter of language:

While with all other peoples in the Hellenistic world the adoption of the name of a Greek deity for one of their own gods meant a religious syncretism, in the case of the Jews it meant only a recourse to the convenience of language.[3]

Elyon, God Most High, was never Zeus; Shaddai, The Almighty, was never Hermes, even though for Greeks these were their special titles. When the Hebrew Bible was translated into Greek existing Greek words were used both for the descriptions of God and for the terms connected with worship.

Wolfson's view of Hellenistic Judaism may be over-rosy, but it still seems very unlikely that Philo could have *invented* a second deity and still have retained any credibility as a Jewish philosopher. A vast amount has been written about Philo and about the Logos, linking his work to Plato, to Aristotle and to the Stoics, but what Goodenough said of him is still largely true: 'No one seems to have tried to read Philo, if I may say so, with the grain instead of against it, to understand what Philo himself thought he was driving at in all his passionate labours.'[4] To discover the grain of Philo is no easy matter since he rambles in spirals around his themes, but one of the problems seems to be that we do not really know what 'his Judaism' was, and consequently it is not easy to see where he has made points of contact with other philosophical systems. Time and again he uses vivid imagery and then interprets it in philosophical terms, but modifies these terms as though he had some constraint. As a Jewish philosopher, this *must* have been his Judaism, which raises the question: What was there in his Judaism which put restraints on what could be said about 'the Logos'? Why if 'the Logos' resembles Aristotle's NOUS is it *not* Aristotle's NOUS? Why is it called the Logos? It has been suggested that Logos derives from the LXX's phrase *the Word of the Lord*, but there is a very large gap between this Word of the Lord and Aristotle's NOUS. Philo must have had a more proximate point of contact than that. Similarly it is suggested that Philo's philosophy started with Plato's theory of ideas, but again it would be more accurate to say that his Judaism found a point of contact with Platonism in the theory of ideas. The ancient Wisdom traditions of Israel already had a complex

117

system of heavenly counterparts. The temple itself was but a copy of the heavenly temple, the liturgy on earth a shadow of the worship of the angels.[5] The visions and the parables of the wise men all presupposed another heavenly realm which owed nothing to Plato.

If we set aside for a moment the contemporary Greek philosophical systems and the reconstruction of first-century Judaism based on much later ideas of orthodoxy which, as we shall see, went to great lengths to combat any notion of a second deity, and read Philo with the theology of the apocalyptists in mind, we find a natural setting for the Logos. The apocalyptists had kept much of the older royal theology, and it was their world of angelic hierarchies, visions of God, the heavenly temple and cosmic covenant binding all creation together which was the Judaism that Philo demythologized. Central to their theology was the Man. It cannot be 'a matter of indifference to us whether in Judaism before the time of Philo the personification of the term Logos meant that the Word of God was already considered as a real being created by God or whether its personification was merely a figure of speech.'[6]

When Philo mentions the second God he uses his words carefully. Nothing, he says, can be made in the likeness of the Most High but only in the likeness of the Logos. Note that the name for the greater deity is Most High, the ancient 'Elyon, and that this points to the remnants of the royal cult, as does his description of the Logos as the firstborn. This was not only a royal title; it shows that the Logos was begotten, a Son of God. He was 'neither uncreated as God, nor yet created as you' (i.e. human beings) (*Who is the Heir?* 206).

Philo knew of a process of creation in the divine realm which had preceded that of the material world. The Logos was 'antecedent to all that has come into existence' (*On the Migration of Abraham* 6). The primal existence is God and next to him is the Logos of God (*Allegorical Interpretation* II.86), 'the eldest and most all embracing of created things' (*Allegorical Interpretation* III.175), and the same had been said of Wisdom (Prov. 8.22–31). What Philo does with this ancient imagery suggests that it had survived intact and that it was probably the vehicle of a fairly sophisticated philosophical system even before he began to adapt it.

The question 'How many gods?' was known to Philo and not clearly answered. He touches on the issue when expounding the account of Jacob's dream at Bethel, a name which he takes to mean literally 'the place of God':

And do not fail to mark the language used, but carefully enquire whether there are two Gods; for we read 'I am the God that appeared to thee' not 'in my place' but 'in the place of God' as though it were another's. What then are we to say? He that is truly God is One, but those that are improperly so called are more than one. Accordingly the holy word in the present instance has indicated Him Who is truly God by means of the articles saying 'I am the God', while it omits the article when mentioning him who is improperly so called, saying 'Who appeared to thee in the place' not 'of the God' but simply 'of God'. Here it gives the title of 'God' to his chief Logos, not from any superstitious nicety in applying names, but with one aim before him, to use words to express facts (or 'to accommodate language to practical needs'). (*On Dreams* I 228)

'The God' means the true God (presumably the Most High, if Philo is consistent) and 'God' is a term applied to other heavenly beings such as the Logos. This important distinction must be borne in mind when reading the New Testament. The argument based on the meaning of Bethel is strange; does Philo *derive* the idea of the Logos as a separate divine being from this text (Segal p.162), or does he use the text to justify something which he already believes to be the case? The argument from the 'place of God' resembles one used by later rabbis,[7] suggesting that Philo already knew of a second deity who could be described as 'the place'. Elsewhere he describes those who serve the Existent, who 'in their thoughts ascend to the heavenly height', and he uses the account of Moses' ascent of Sinai in Exod. 24.10 (where the LXX differs from the MT and has 'they saw the place where the God of Israel stands'). Philo's interpretation is this: 'For then they shall behold *the place which is in fact the Logos*, where stands God the never changing ...' (*On the Confusion of Tongues* 96).

The mystic for whom Moses here is the pattern sees not God but the Logos. This must be Philo's way of describing the manifestation of God, either mystical, or in angelic and human form. Again, when he deals with Gen. 31.13, Philo shows that anthropomorphism is only for the unsophisticated:

Accordingly, when he says 'I am the God who was seen of thee in the place of God' understand that He occupied the place of an angel only so far as he appeared, without changing, with a view to the profit of him who was not yet capable of seeing the true God. (*On Dreams* I 238)

He continues his explanation of the two Gods thus:

For just as those who are unable to see the sun itself see the gleam of the parhelion and take it for the sun, and take the halo round the moon for that luminary itself, so some regard the Image of God, His angel the Logos, as His very Self. (*On Dreams* I 239)

What is he saying here? That the Logos is not divine, or that there are some who have identified the Logos with God, and that this is not correct? It seems to be that latter, in which case Philo could be criticizing *those who have identified the Logos with the Most High, i.e. Yahweh with Elyon*. This would mean that Philo, far from being a monotheist in our sense of the word, actually recognized several heavenly beings, one of whom, as we shall see, he calls Kyrios; *but he denies that he is to be identified with God.*

One of Philo's ways of interpreting Scripture was by allegory. The familiar stories of the patriarchs are all shown to have a hidden meaning which can relate to the philosophies of his contemporaries. What has not been recognized, however, is that Philo also used the mythology of Israel as an integral part of his exposition. Much of what has been thought to be his original contribution is in fact just Israel's old religion, but demythologized. The key to understanding him is to recognize that the Logos was the fulcrum of the system. He started from a Judaism which had a second God, one of whose titles was Logos. Among his pagan contemporaries, there was also a concept of Logos, but it meant Reason or the divine order manifested in the creation. Philo superimposed the one system on the other and by demythologizing the original Logos was able to relate it to the Logos of the philosophers.

The divine Logos was, for Philo, the Angel of Yahweh of Exod. 23.20, just as in his native Judaism. When he allegorized the journey into the promised land, the Angel who had led the travellers was given one of his other roles and was simultaneously the guiding angel of the apocalypses who led ascending souls into the presence of God. Both these became for Philo the journey of the man of Reason into the godlike state of true knowledge:

For as long as he falls short of perfection, he has the Divine Logos as his leader: since there is an oracle which says, 'Lo I send my messenger before thy face ...; for he will by no means withdraw from thee, for my Name is in him'. But when he has arrived at full knowledge, he will run with more vigorous effort and his pace will be as great as that of him who before led the way; for they will both become attendants on the all-leading God ... (*On the Migration of Abraham* 174–5)

Full knowledge of God in Philo is a synonym for the apocalyptists' knowledge or wisdom, that which transforms man into the angelic state. The wise who become like stars (Dan. 12.2) is an earlier expression of the same idea. Philo knew that all who lived 'in the knowledge of the One are rightly called 'sons of God' (*On the Confusion of Tongues* 145), and in the original mythology, the sons of God were the angels, those who had the heavenly knowledge. In the material which Philo uses, it looks as though the being whom he calls the Divine Logos, i.e. the Angel of Yahweh, guided the seeker after God into the presence of God where he too achieved divine status and became a son of God. In the parallel apocalyptic tradition the heavenly guide who brings the seeker into the presence of God is also a Yahweh figure: in the Apocalypse of Abraham (approximately contemporary with Philo) it was the angel *Yahoel*, and in the later 3 Enoch it was Metatron, the Lesser *Yahweh*.

In his *On the Confusion of Tongues* he has a similar treatment of Exod. 24.9-10, where the elders ascend Mount Sinai and see the God of Israel. Philo says that what they saw was the Logos, just as those who truly serve God ascend to the heights of Reason. What the seers described as the vision of God becomes for Philo intellectual enlightenment:

but it is the special mark of those who serve the Existent ... [that] in their thoughts they ascend to the heavenly height.
For then they shall behold the place which is in fact the Logos, where stands God the never changing ... for it well befits those who have entered into comradeship and knowledge to desire to see the Existent if they may, but, if they cannot, to see at any rate his image, the most holy Logos, and after the Logos, its most perfect work of all that our senses know, even this world. (*On the Confusion of Tongues* 95-7)

In all his philosophizing and allegorizing, Philo uses Logos in both its senses; it was the title of the Angel who appeared in human form but also the philosophers' Reason or the divine order apparent in the creation. Even when using the less momentous stories of the Old Testament he is consistent. Thus when Hagar ran away the Hebrew text says that she met the Angel of Yahweh (Gen. 16.9) but Philo says 'she met the angel or divine Logos' (*On the Cherubim* 3); she saw a more reasonable course of action. Balaam met with the angel of Yahweh (Num. 22.31) but Philo says 'the armed angel, the Logos of God', was standing in the way (*On the Cherubim* 35). The Logos was Yahweh.

One by one in the roles of the Logos we recognize the ancient Yahweh. He had been the high priest and the bringer of judgement; so too the Logos was 'appointed judge and mediator. Him he sets before the face' (*Questions on Exodus* II.13) again in an exposition of the Angel of Exod. 23.20 leading the seeker of God into the promised land of God's presence. The Logos was the High Priest (*On the Migration of Abraham* 102) and his temple was the whole universe: 'For there are, as is evident, two temples of God: one of them this universe in which there is also as High Priest His First-born, the Divine Logos, and the other the rational soul, whose priest is the real Man' (*On Dreams* I.215). The Logos was also royal 'at once high priest and king' (*On Flight* 118). He was the Man, presumably the 'likeness as it were of a human form ... the likeness of the Glory of Yahweh' (Ezek. 1.26, 28): 'God's Man, the Logos of the Eternal ... He is called the Beginning, and the Name of God, and his Logos, and the Man after his Image, and 'He that sees' that is Israel' (*On the Confusion of Tongues* 41, 146); 'The Image of God is the Logos through whom the whole universe was framed' (*On the Special Laws* I.81). He 'stood before the face' (*Questions on Exodus* II.13) and to him were given the roles of 'apostle and high priest' (Heb. 3.1), to stand between the material and spiritual worlds:

To his Logos, his Archangel, the Father of all has given the special prerogative to stand on the border and separate the creature from the creator. This same Logos both pleads with the immortal as suppliant for afflicted mortality, and acts as ambassador of the ruler to the subject. (*Who is the Heir?* 205)

He was the Branch of Zech. 6.12, a messianic text (*On the Confusion of Tongues* 62) and he was the viceroy appointed to sustain the universe: 'I sustained the universe to rest firm and sure upon the mighty Logos who is my viceroy' (*On Dreams* I 241; cf. *On Agriculture* 51). This status was symbolized by the high priest's diadem: 'This diadem is the symbol not of an absolute ruler but of a marvellous vicegerency' (*On Flight* 111). It bore a golden plate on which was engraved the sacred Name (*Life of Moses* II.114). Philo shows by this imagery that his Logos originated in the royal cult and it corroborates what we have deduced from other texts about the nature of that cult. Philo's detail fills out the picture of a cult which joined heaven and earth in its liturgy and in the person of its central figure. The *Songs of the Sabbath Sacrifice* which are approximately contemporary with Philo, also depict the heavenly liturgy but there is no pre-eminent angel figure who could have been the heavenly high priest even though other texts, as we have seen, do describe such a figure.

The Logos, in that his roles were cultic, affords an insight into aspects of the cult which, though implicit in other texts, are not clearly expressed. The high priests used to pass through the veil of the temple into the holy of holies, i.e. into the presence of God. Philo's description shows that the Logos also passed through the veil, but *from* the holy of holies and out into the material world. He was the manifested God. The high priests wore elaborate vestments which are described in detail in Exod. 28 and 39, but nothing is said of their significance. Philo's Judaism, however, knew that the high priest's robe 'depicted the whole world' (Wisd. 18.24). Ben Sira, which had been translated into Greek for the Jews of Egypt, also described the vestment as a 'robe of glory' (Sir. 50.11). Now 'robe of glory' was a phrase used to describe the dress of angels; the Peshitta of Dan. 10.5 and 12.7 says that the Angel who came to Daniel wore a 'robe of glory' and Yahoel in the Apocalypse of Abraham, as we have seen, wore the dress of the high priest. The Logos, as high priest, was the reality which the earthly priests represented in their rituals and the veil through which he passed was the material world in which he clothed himself to become visible. The temple veil divided the holy of holies, which represented the presence of God, from the *hekhal* which represented the world. Philo says that the veil of the temple represented the material world:

... he makes the curtains to be woven from such materials as are symbolical of the four elements; for they are wrought of fine linen, of dark red, of purple and of scarlet, as I have said. The linen is a symbol of earth, since it grows out of earth; the dark red of air, which is naturally black; the purple water, since the means by which the dye is produced, the shell fish which bears the same name, comes from the sea; and the scarlet of fire, since it closely resembles a flame. (*On the Unity of Study* 117; cf. *Questions on Exodus* II.85, 86; *Life of Moses* II.88)

He also says of it: 'The incorporeal world is set off and separated from the visible one by the mediating Logos as by a veil' (*Questions on Exodus* II.94). The garments of the high priest were of a similar fabric and, says Philo, they also represented the creation; the blue robe was the air, the flower and pomegranate patterns were the fruits and waters of the earth, the breastplate was heaven with its twelve precious stones the signs of the zodiac, the two emeralds on the shoulders represented the two hemispheres of the sky with their star signs, or the sun and moon (Philo knew that there were two traditions about this) (*On the Migration of Abraham* 102; *Life of Moses* II.117–26; *On the Special Laws* I.85–7).

Not only did the material world conceal the divine; it was also the means by which the second God became visible. The Logos as the real high priest passed through the veil from the presence of God and thus became robed in the four elements: 'Now the garments that the supreme Logos of him that IS puts on as raiment are the world, for he arrays himself in earth and air and water and fire and all that comes forth from these' (*On Flight* 110). The high priest as the outward and visible image:

offers the prayers and sacrifices handed down from our fathers to whom it has been committed to wear the aforesaid tunic which is a copy and replica of the whole heaven, the intention being that the universe may join with man in the holy rites and man with the universe. (*On Dreams* I.216)

In his role as the high priest the Logos was also the bond which bound all the creation together:

And the oldest Logos of God has put on the universe as a garment ... 'He does not tear his garments' for the Logos of God is the bond of all things, as has been said, and holds together all parts, and prevents them by its constriction from breaking apart and becoming separated. (*On Flight* 112)

He was called the Covenant (*On Dreams* II.237; cf. *On the Migration of Abraham* 181; *On the Confusion of Tongues* 137), a natural extension of his being the Bond, since the two words in Hebrew are related. He was also the Seal of the universe: 'The Logos of him who makes it is himself the Seal, by which each thing that exists has received its shape' (*On Flight* 12; cf. *On Dreams* II.45).

Philo must have known the tradition of Yahweh's name being the seal but he rejected the original magical associations such as are found in the tradition of sealing the abysses. Rather than the seal which secures it, for him the seal became the mould which forms the shape of the universe. The Logos also created by dividing, as did God in Genesis 1: '... the Severer of all things, that is his Logos' (*Who is the Heir?* 130), and he maintained order by keeping the conflicting powers apart: 'the earth shall not be dissolved by all the water ... nor fire be quenched by air; nor, on the other hand, air be ignited by fire. The Divine Logos stations himself to keep these elements apart ... he mediates between the opponents amid their threatenings, and reconciles them' (*On Planting* 10). Compare the role of the Angel Yahoel: 'I am the one who has been charged ... to restrain the threats of the living creatures of the cherubim against one another ... I am appointed to hold the Leviathans' (Ap. Abr. 10.9–10). The Logos was also the

124

Shadow, used as the means of creation; 'God's Shadow is his Logos, which he made use of like an instrument and so made the world' (*Allegorical Interpretation* III.96). This curious idea is significant because later gnostic writings presuppose a similar belief.[8]

The turban of the high priest was also important; on it was a golden plate 'with four incisions showing a name which only those whose ears and tongues are purified may hear or speak in the holy place and no other person nor in any other place at all. That Name has four letters ...' (*Life of Moses* II.114; *On the Migration of Abraham* 103). According to Exod. 28.36 the high priest's turban bears the words 'Holy to the Lord', a very significant difference. Why did Philo's high priest, who represented the Logos, bear the divine name while the Pentateuch implies only that the high priest was a consecrated person? Elsewhere Philo says that the golden plate bearing the name represented 'the original principle [idea] behind all principles, after which God shaped or formed the universe' (*On the Migration of Abraham* 103).

When the high priest entered the holy of holies on the Day of Atonement, he wore white linen garments (Lev. 16, m. *Yoma* 3.7). The Pentateuch does not say why he dressed thus, but it is possible that the high priest wore this in the holy of holies because this was the dress of the angels in the presence of God. Daniel had seen an angel described as a man clothed in linen (Dan. 10.5); throughout 1 Enoch the archangels were men in white (e.g. 87.2; 90.21, 31); and mortals who reached heaven were transformed and given similar robes, their garments of glory (e.g. 1 Enoch 62.16; 2 Enoch 22.8–10; Asc. Isa. 8.14; 9.3; Rev. 4.4). Philo does not in so many words associate the white of the high priest with the white of the angels, but he does say that linen was appropriate for the sanctuary because wool was 'the product of creatures subject to death' (*On the Special Laws* I.84). He also says that the high priest has a robe 'of linen made from the purest kind, a figure of strong fibre, imperishableness, most radiant light: for fine linen is hard to tear and is made from no mortal creature and moreover when carefully cleaned has a very brilliant and luminous colour (*On Dreams* I.216–17). Philo alludes to so much of his theology in this description; purity, the imperishable world of the angels, the strong bonds of the creation which cannot be torn, a robe not made from a mortal creature and radiant with light.

Philo's temple imagery is so closely and naturally a part of his exposition that it is hard to separate out the component parts. This is very clear when he deals with the *menorah*, the ancient sign of Yahweh's presence with his people in the temple, the seven eyes. But it was also the symbol of his plurality: the seven lamps were the seven spirits before the throne. Philo assumes all this, and uses it as the basis for a complex philosophical speculation. The Logos was the central stem of the *menorah*, dividing three lamps from three lamps (*Who is the Heir?* 215); Philo uses this to argue towards Heracleitus's theory of opposites, but he began with the fact that the Logos was represented by the *menorah*. He develops the plurality theme and describes the spirits or angels as the 'powers' which could operate in the material world: 'It is the powers only that can enter matter, for, though they are immaterial, their immateriality is presumably of a lower order than that of God, and they can therefore enter matter, even as the immaterial rational soul can enter a body.[9] By immaterial, Philo means holy, and it seems that the powers of which he so often speaks are the ancient angels who were manifested in the natural order. God is One, says Philo, but he has around him numberless powers which all assist and protect created being (*On the Confusion of Tongues* 171). Philo describes their function thus:

This aspect of Him which transcends his powers cannot be conceived at all in terms of place, but only as pure being; but that power of his by which he made and ordered all things, while it is called God in accordance with the derivation of that name*, holds the whole in its embrace and has interfused itself through the parts of the universe. (*On the Confusion of Tongues* 137)

These powers were not something derived from another system of philosophy, because Philo is careful to distinguish Moses' teaching about powers from that of 'Chaldeans'. Moses teaches that:

... the complete whole around us is held together by invisible powers which the creator has made to reach from the ends of the earth to heaven's furthest bounds, taking forethought that what was well bound should not be loosened; for the Powers of the universe are chains which cannot be broken. (*On the Migration of Abraham* 181)

This sounds very like the cosmic covenant, especially as Philo says that the powers are the angels, the host of heaven. They are the Glory of God. Moses says: 'By Thy Glory I understand the Powers that keep guard around Thee' (*On the Special Laws* I.45). Moses was told that he could not see the face of Yahweh but only what was behind him

(* The reference is to the similarity between *theos* and *tithemi*.)

126

(Exod. 33.23) and this was the powers in their visible manifestation in the universe. Philo says that this is like the 'forms', but again this is only a comparison; the original idea already existed in his own Judaism (*On Flight* 165; *On the Change of Names* 9). Similarly, his understanding of Exod. 33.23 is attested in the Targum: 'And I will make a troop of angels pass by who stand and minister before me and you will see the Word of the Glory of my Shekinah but it is not possible for you to see the face of the Glory of my Shekinah' (Targum *Neofiti* to Exod. 33.23). Thus Philo draws on a tradition of interpretation common to his community and that which produced the Targum.[10] He adapts it and says that the 'Powers around the Glory', what man can see of the presence of God, means their visible form in the universe.[11]

The powers express the same idea as did the robe of the high priest, the unbreakable bond of the creation:

The everlasting Logos of the eternal God is the very sure and staunch prop of the Whole. He it is who extending himself from the midst to its utmost bounds and from its extremities to the midst again keeps up through its length Nature's unvanquished course, combining and compacting its parts. For the Father who begat him constituted the Logos, such a Bond of the Universe as nothing can break. (*On Planting* 8–9)

The Logos as the Bond, the Logos as both the chief and the sum of the powers and as the sevenfold presence, lies behind several of Philo's illustrations. The six cities of refuge are the Powers, and these are colonies of the Word, who is 'the chiefest and surest and best mother city' (*On Flight* 94). The nature of the Powers is interesting; their leader is creative power, second is royal power, third is gracious power ... and at this point there is a lacuna in the text. Similarly the golden signet on the high priest's turban had represented the *single behind the plurality*: '... the original principle behind all principles, after which God shaped or formed the universe' (*On the Migration of Abraham* 103). Neither of these statements about the Logos can have derived from the passages in question; Philo demonstrates from them that this was the case, and each time the idea comes through that there were many powers and that their ruler was the creative power. The sacred name was also linked directly to the Powers: 'The third [commandment] is concerned with the knowledge of the name, not that name the knowledge of which has never even reached the world of mere becoming, but the name which is given to his Powers. We are commanded not to take this name in vain' (*Who is the Heir?* 170).

Discussing Deut. 4.39, 'God in heaven above and on the earth below', he says: 'Let no one suppose that he that IS is spoken of ... What is meant is that power of his by which he established and ordered and marshalled the whole realm of being' (*On the Migration of Abraham* 182). There were two chief powers called God (*'elohim*) and Lord (Yahweh), but these were but two aspects of the One. They were linked to and represented by the two cherubim of the throne:

> The two primary Powers of the Existing One, namely that through which He wrought the world, the beneficent, which is called God, and that by which he rules and commands that which he made, that is the punitive, which bears the name of Lord, are, as Moses tells us, separated by God himself standing above and in the midst of them. 'I will speak to thee', it says, 'above the mercy seat in the midst of the two Cherubim'. He means to show that the primal and highest Powers of the Existent, the beneficent and the punitive, are equal, having him to divide them. (*Who is the Heir?* 166; cf. *Questions on Genesis* I.57, *On the Unchangeableness of God* 109)

Philo uses the imagery of the cherubim in many ways; elsewhere it is Reason/Logos who stands between the two cherubim to unite them:

> While God is indeed One, his highest and chiefest Powers are two, even Goodness and Sovereignty ... And in the midst between the two, there is a third which unites them, Reason/Logos, for it is through Reason/Logos that God is both ruler and good. Of these two powers, Sovereignty and Goodness, the cherubim are the symbols, as the fiery sword is the symbol of Reason/Logos. (*On the Cherubim* 27–8)

Here Philo equates the cherubim of the Garden of Eden with those of the temple which represented Eden. Between the two cherubim in the Jerusalem temple was not the flaming sword (Gen. 3.24 does not say the sword was between them) but the throne. The cherubim and much of what they symbolized remain a mystery,[12] but what is clear is that Philo associates aspects of the Logos with the throne and the two Powers with the two cherubim. The gracious power is represented by the mercy seat between the cherubim. The passage in which Philo outlines this is not entirely clear, nor is it consistent with what he says elsewhere, a warning that he cannot be pressed too hard:

> ... the lid of the ark, which he calls the mercy seat, representing the gracious Power; while the creative and kingly Powers are represented by the winged cherubim that rest upon it. The divine Logos, which is high above all these, has not been visibly portrayed, being like to no one of the objects of sense ... nay he is himself the Image of God, chiefest of all beings intellectually

128

perceived, placed nearest with no intervening distance to the Alone truly Existent One. For we read 'I will talk to thee from above the mercy seat, between the two cherubim' (Exod. 25.22). (*On Flight* 100–1)

Had he said no more, we should have concluded that the Logos was the one who spoke to Moses, that is, that the Logos was Yahweh. But he then adds that the Logos is the charioteer to whom the occupant of the throne speaks! Both the highest powers, it should be noted, are equal and parallel, and both are subordinate to the High God.[13] Both the Powers were aspects of what Philo called the second God, and the double name Lord God (Yahweh Elohim) thus stands for the two aspects combined:

Why does scripture say that when Abraham was ninety nine years old, 'The Lord God appeared to him and said I am the Lord thy God'? It gives the appellations of the two highest Powers ... for by them the world came into being, and having come into being, it is governed by them ... (*Questions on Genesis* III.39)

Questions on Genesis IV.87 speaks of 'uttering a double invocation to the powers of the Father, the creative and the kingly'.

The Logos was also Wisdom; given how little evidence we have about Wisdom, it is impossible to say what distinguished it from Logos. We can see, however, that Wisdom's roles were very like those of the Spirit of Yahweh in the Old Testament, thus establishing another link between the Logos and Yahweh. A major source of evidence for the nature of Wisdom is the *Wisdom of Solomon*, which shows the remarkable similarity between Wisdom and Logos in the writings of Philo's own community. He himself gives the same titles to both. Moses, he says, 'has already made it manifest that the sublime and heavenly Wisdom is of many names: for he calls it 'Beginning' and 'Image' and 'Vision of God' (*Allegorical Interpretation* I.43), and the Firstborn, we recall, had the names 'Beginning, Name of God, *Logos* and Man after His Image' (*On the Confusion of Tongues* 146). The Logos was the Wisdom of God, 'highest and chiefest of his powers' (*Allegorical Interpretation* II.86). The initial objection, that the Logos is a male figure and Wisdom female is met by Philo himself, and the change of gender was not thought by him to be significant. Since Wisdom was second after God, he said, it was deemed feminine to express its subordinate place: 'Let us pay no heed to the discrepancy in the gender of the words, and say that the daughter of God, even Wisdom, is not only masculine but also father, sowing and begetting in souls aptness to learn' (*On Flight* 52). Philo's imagery is consistent with the tradition of the second God's double gender, but in other ways it is sometimes confused; Wisdom flows *from* the Logos (*On Flight* 137) while elsewhere she is *the mother* of the High Priest who represents the Logos (*On Flight* 110).

The simplest way to compare the Wisdom and Logos is to use the materials in chapter 5 above, and show how the Logos corresponds to them.

i   Both Wisdom and Logos are heavenly beings. To say that they are 'personified' begs several questions, and, since we know that anthropomorphism was actively suppressed by certain influential groups, personification as a late development is less likely than the other possibility, that these angelic beings survived from earlier times.

ii   Both Wisdom and Logos were associated with the *menorah*, the symbol of the presence of Yahweh.

iii   Wisdom was described as an image of God's goodness; the Logos was the Image of God.

iv   Wisdom was the first to be brought forth and the Logos was the firstborn.

v   Both Wisdom and Logos were the agents of creation. Wisdom was beside the creator, the master workman, or perhaps the favourite child; the Logos was the instrument by which the world was made (*On the Migration of Abraham* 6). Since Wisdom is depicted as the consort or counterpart of Yahweh, sharing his throne and sitting beside him, Wisdom may have been the feminine/creative aspect of Yahweh, and therefore also the feminine aspect of the Logos. The Wisdom described in Wisd. 7.25 is exactly Philo's Logos, 'a breath of the power of God, and a pure emanation of the glory of the Almighty'.

vi   Wisdom pervaded and penetrated all things (Wisd. 7.24); the Logos was the bond of the universe.

vii   Wisdom, like Yahweh, was given Israel for her inheritance (Sir. 24.8–10; cf. Deut. 32.9); the Logos is depicted as the Angel of Israel.

viii   Wisdom ministered before the creator in Zion; the Logos was the high priest in the temple.

ix   Wisdom entered holy souls and transformed them; the Logos guided the seeker after God until he was like one of the angels.

This list is not exhaustive, but is sufficient to show that those who would distinguish Wisdom and Logos, and separate them from their common root in the ancient temple cult, have a hard case to argue.

Finally, we must consider the 'stages' of the Logos in the light of my preliminary observations that there were 'stages' of divine sonship: there were the sons of Elyon who were heavenly beings, one of whom was Yahweh, and then there were the sons of Yahweh who were his human manifestations. Wolfson's conclusion on the nature of the Logos is most significant in that it says exactly the same: 'Our interpretation of Philo that his Logos, as well as his powers, has two stages of existence prior to the creation of the sensible world, one from eternity as a property of God and the other as something created by God, differs from interpretations hitherto advanced of Philo ..' These are the 'sons of Elyon'; Wolfson continues: 'We may also add here that besides the two stages in the existence of the antemundane Logos and the powers there is still a third stage, and that is their existence, after the creation of the world, as immanent in the world.'[14] These are the sons of Yahweh, those who have his Spirit, and the visible Glory in all its aspects.

Philo has none of the polemics of Palestinian literature; there is no deserted Wisdom, no sense that an ancient tradition has been betrayed. Our problem in reconstructing his Judaism is that we have only his transpositions into the language of another culture. He sets out to express in alien terms the essence of his own religion, with all its heavenly beings and elaborate temple symbolism. This makes the correspondence between his ideas and those of the extra-biblical books even more significant, for it corroborates my suggestion that post-deuteronomic monotheism, which we assume to have been characteristic of all Judaism, was in fact characteristic only of those in Palestine who had been influenced by the exile and who came subsequently to shape the way Judaism remembered itself after AD 70. The traditions in the apocalypses, which their authors claimed to be the true religion of the ancient cult, were also those of Philo.

Philo shows beyond any doubt that the Judaism of the first Christian century acknowledged a second God. The roles and functions of this God were exactly those of the ancient Yahweh, not only as recorded in the Old Testament but also as implied in the Wisdom and Angel texts of the inter-testamental period. It is now necessary to look at later texts, to see how these too remembered the second God. In the case of some Gnostic and early Christian texts it is often said that their consistency derived from a common dependence on Philo and his ideas, as though these ideas had originated with him. This is not so; the common elements in the Christian and Gnostic texts derive from their common roots in the Judaism which Philo knew, and the polemics apparent in Jewish texts from the early Christian centuries confirm that there was fierce debate about the second God, exacerbated by Christian claims that Jesus was the second God.

Notes to chapter seven

The quotations from Philo are taken from F.H. Colson, and G.H. Whittaker, *Philo*, 10 vols, Loeb Classical Library, London and Cambridge, Mass. 1929–1962, but I have in every passage left the Greek word Logos untranslated in order to emphasize the frequency of its occurence.

1 A.F. Segal, *Two Powers in Heaven*, Leiden 1978, p.165.

2 H. Wolfson, *Philo: Foundations of Religious Philosophy in Judaism, Christianity and Islam*, 2 vols, Cambridge, Mass. 1948, vol.I, p.10.

3 Ibid., vol.I, p.13.

4 E.R. Goodenough, *By Light, Light: The Mystic Gospel of Hellenistic Judaism*, New Haven 1935, p.5.

5 M.E. Stone, 'Lists of Revealed Things in Apocalyptic Literature', in F.M. Cross, W.E. Lemke, and P.D. Miller, Jr, eds, *Magnalia Dei: The Mighty Acts of God. Essays in Memory of G.E. Wright*. New York 1976, pp.414–52; C. Newsom, *Songs of the Sabbath Sacrifice*, Harvard Semitic Studies 27, 1985.

6 Wolfson, op.cit., vol.I, p.254.

7 Segal, op.cit., p.131.

8 See chapter 9, p.183.

9 Wolfson, op.cit., p.281.

10 Similarly, Targum *Neofiti* to Gen. 3.5 renders *'elohim* by 'angels'. Eating from the tree of knowledge made man an angel.

11 M.D. Hooker, in 'The Johannine Prologue and the Messianic

Secret', NTS 21 (1974), suggests that Exod. 33.12–23 also forms
the background to John 1.14–18, the revelation of the glory.

12 See R. Patai, *The Hebrew Goddess*, New York 1967, chapter 3,
noting especially his suggestion that the two cherubim
represented a male and a female.

13 The two powers being equal and subordinate to the High God is
not brought out in Segal, op.cit., n.1, which concentrates on the
ditheism implicit in the two powers texts rather than on the
plurality of the second power.

14 Wolfson, op.cit., p.239.

Chapter eight The Evidence of the Jewish Writers

Philo shows clearly that there was a belief in a second divine being among some first-century Jews. It is not possible to reconstruct exactly what this belief was since Philo was consciously expressing it in categories which his Greek contemporaries could grasp. Nevertheless, he is the nearest we have to a fixed point in this investigation, since his work can be dated and is known to reflect the thought of one man. Parts of the text may have been modified by later Christian writers, but there is no possibility that his writings were an accumulation of the belief of several centuries, expanded and revised to meet the changing needs of a religious community. The same cannot be said for the other Jewish writings we now have to consider. The Targums, for example, are virtually undateable. It simply is not known whether the material in them comes from one particular period, or that one text is definitely older than another. Informed guesses are possible in this area as in many others, but there are no fixed points beyond the actual existence of certain texts.

The Targums have several ways of referring to the divinity and these are usually regarded as circumlocutions of some sort. The Glory of Yahweh (*Kabod*), the Presence of Yahweh (*Shekinah*), the Name of Yahweh, and, commonest of all, the Word of Yahweh (*Memra*) appear frequently where the translator had only 'God' or 'Yahweh' in his Hebrew original. All except 'the Word' have counterparts in the Old Testament. The Glory of Yahweh occurs often in the Pentateuch, e.g. Lev 9.6, and in the prophets, e.g. Isa. 60.1; Ezek. 1.28; the Name of Yahweh, as we have seen, was a common term, although its meaning changed dramatically in the hands of the reformers, and the Presence of Yahweh, the Shekinah, derived from the Tabernacle (*mishkan*) in which he was said to be present with his people (e.g. Ps. 46.4 and throughout Exodus and Chronicles). There are, however, considerable problems as the origin of 'the Word' (*Memra*), since it does not translate 'the word of the Lord' in the Old Testament. This phrase was rendered in the Targums by other Aramaic words, thus emphasizing that Memra was not 'word' in our

134

sense. G.F. Moore studied the problem and concluded: 'Wherever "the word of the Lord" is the medium or instrumentality of revelation, or of communication to men ... the term employed for this medium in the Targums is not memra, but pitgama, or (seldom) as in ... Ps 33.6, milla.'[1] It is curious and probably significant that of all Philo's names for the second God it is again only 'the Word' which has no obvious basis in the Old Testament, suggesting that the Memra of the Targums and the Logos of Philo both represent something now lost in our reading of the Old Testament. Since the Logos was Yahweh, it cannot be coincidence that the Memra in the Targums was also the commonest way of referring to Yahweh. Problems have arisen because Yahweh is always assumed to have been the name for the supreme God in the Old Testament, but this, as we have seen, was true only for one particular group among the heirs to Israel's cult. It has often been observed that Memra in the Targums refers to the *presence* of Yahweh with his people; this would have been an accurate recollection of the older Yahweh who passed between earth and heaven as the mediator figure. I suspect that Philo used Logos as the Greek equivalent for a Hebrew designation already known to him, and it was this designation which also gave rise to the Aramaic Memra. The vital evidence must lie in the Hebrew original which has either been lost, or else has survived but not been recognized for what it is.

Logos is the earliest evidence for this title; but Logos does not only mean Word. If, as I have suggested, a more likely meaning *in view of the way that Philo actually used the term* is 'relation', 'correspondence', this would suggest that the term underlying Logos was not originally *Memra*, an Aramaic word for which there is no Hebrew counterpart used of the Lord, but rather a Hebrew term which occurs so frequently in accounts of visions of the Lord in human form, *mar'ah* or *mar'eh*, meaning vision or appearance. The most detailed accounts of theophany in the Old Testament are those of Ezekiel which distinguish between the appearance (*mar'eh*) and the likeness (*d'mut*) of the Glory of Yahweh (Ezek. 1.26, 28). The appearance, the manifestation of the Lord, was especially emphasized but this is such a common theme in the Old Testament writings that it passes without comment. The expression was not confined to any particular tradition, although it does not appear in Deuteronomy. Given this tradition's aversion to anthropomorphism, this is hardly surprising.

Apart from the account of the appearance in Ezekiel, there is the detailed description of Judg. 13, where the angel of Yahweh and

135

Yahweh are not distinguished; the figure had the countenance of an angel (RSV has 'countenance' for Hebrew *mar'eh*, Judg. 13.6). The angel figure in Daniel is similarly described; he saw the *appearance* of a man (Dan. 8.15; 10.18), and the angelic face with the *appearance* of lightning (Dan. 10.6). The people of Israel saw the *appearance* of the Glory of Yahweh (Exod. 24.17) and the *appearance* of fire covered the tabernacle at night (Num. 9.15–16). In the verbal form, the word occurs even more often. Yahweh *appeared* to the patriarchs (Gen. 12.7; 17.1; 18.1; 35.1; 48.3). Yahweh, often as the Glory of Yahweh, *appeared* to the people throughout the desert wanderings (Exod. 16.10; Lev. 9.4, 6, 23; 16.2; Num. 14.10, 14; 16.19, 42; 20.6). Yahweh *appeared* to Samuel (1 Sam. 3.21), to David (2 Chron. 3.1) and to Solomon (1 Kings 3.5; 9.12) to Israel (Jer. 31.3). The Glory of Yahweh *appeared* to his people (Isa. 60.1–2), coming like a rushing stream driven by the wind of Yahweh (Isa. 59.19) just as Yahweh had earlier *appeared* on the wings of the wind, upon the cherubim (2 Sam. 22.11). The *appearance* of Yahweh does seem to have been associated especially with the temple or the desert tent which was the earlier counterpart. It was also frequently an appearance in human form.

Bearing in mind that the terms Memra in the later Targums and Logos in the writings of Philo have no obvious antecedent in the Old Testament even though what they represent is well attested, and that the *appearance* which is so important in the earlier traditions has no obvious equivalent in any of these later writings, let us now look at some of the debates which have centred on this Memra.

Jewish discussion of Memra has linked it to the problem of anthropomorphism in Scripture, and this is significant. Maimonides said that Targum *Onkelos* (hereafter T.O.) paraphrased passages in which God was said to perform human activities such as coming and going; the Targums described more accurately the presence of God by referring to the light which manifested his presence as his Glory and the voice as his Word. R. Moses ben Naḥman taught that the Memra was God in certain modes of self-manifestation.[2] More recent scholarship has trodden the narrow line between saying that the Memra was a personification and that the Memra was a person. All recognize that there was more to Memra than simply a word. Kohler defined Memra thus:

Just as the references to God's appearing to man suggested luminous powers mediating the vision of God, so the passages which represent God as speaking suggest powers mediating the voice. Hence arose the conception of the Divine Word (capital W), invested with divine powers both physical and spiritual.[3]

Strack-Billerbeck, which has had such an influence on Christian scholars, concluded that Memra was a paraphrase, a reverent substitute for the divine name, which arose on account of the commandment not to take the name of the Lord in vain. Word of God was one of the substitutes offered.[4]

Christian scholars, on the other hand, saw in the Memra the antecedent of the Logos of the Fourth Gospel. J.W. Etheridge, in the preface to the first volume of his translation of the Targums to the Pentateuch (1862), wrote:

In reading only the Targum of Onkelos on the Pentateuch I have made a memorandum of more than a hundred and fifty places where the Memra de Yeya is spoken of in one way or another. And with the facts before us which I have stated above, it seems, I repeat, impossible to restrict the signification of the epithet in question to a mere figurative personification, and not perceive that St John, when he wrote the first verses of his Gospel, communicated to the gentile churches a mystery of the truth *which had long been held sacred by the ancient people of God*.[5]

Others of his generation were equally certain; B.F. Westcott thought that Memra had influenced the writing of the Fourth Gospel, and that *it tended towards the idea of a divine person subordinate to God*.[6] A. Edersheim wrote 'if words have any meaning, the Memra is a hypostasis'.[7]

The next generation decisively rejected this point of view and the turning point was an article written in 1922 by G.F. Moore, 'Intermediaries in Jewish Theology'. It begins thus:

The Christian interpretation of the Old Testament was early set upon finding in it a figure corresponding to the Son, or the Word (Logos), in the New Testament, a divine being, intermediary between God the Father and the world in creation, revelation and redemption. For Christian theology with its philosophical presumptions, a God who visibly and audibly manifested himself to men in human form and action was necessarily such a being; the Supreme God, in his supramundane exaltation or his metaphysical transcendence, could not be imagined thus immediately to intervene in mundane affairs. In this assumption and to a considerable extent in their particular interpretations the Fathers had a precursor in the Jewish theologian Philo.[8]

The implication of the pages which follow is that both Philo and the Christian Fathers had been wrong in what they said about the Logos, the second God. The fact that the Targums frequently referred to the Memra of the Lord, along with other terms such as the *Shekinah* (Presence) and the *Kabod* (Glory) was not thought to be in any way connected: 'Christian investigation and discussion of the terms Memra and Shekinah have thus in all stages been inspired and directed by a theological motive, and the results come around in a circle to the theological prepossessions from which they set out.'[9] This may be so, but Christian motives do not explain the Logos in Philo, nor why the first Christians who set out to demonstrate certain things from the Old Testament should have used the same ideas as Philo. Did they 'copy' him or did they have a similar way of understanding the Old Testament in the first place? In other words, was Philo's Judaism the norm for this time, and is the difference which we can see between that Judaism and the later 'orthodoxy' of the rabbis an indication of how far later Judaism had altered? Moore then implied that the *Jewish* understanding of Memra was not directed by a theological motive: 'Jewish discussion of the subject has generally approached it as a phase of the *problem of the anthropomorphisms of scripture*.'[10] Anthropomorphism again! This article has become a classic, said to mark a watershed in New Testament scholarship. Its hidden agenda, alas, was that Jewish interpreters had no reason to modify any understanding of Scripture whereas Christians did and they distorted the true meaning of Scripture in the process. Moore demonstrated that the Memra of Yahweh did not represent the Old Testament expression 'the Word of Yahweh' (where 'word' is *dabar*) which is undoubtedly true. Nor, he said, did it mean a mode of divine manifestation, and such semblance of personality as attached to it was because it was used to avoid the sacred name.

After the publication of Moore's article the fashion in New Testament scholarship changed and Memra was not considered relevant to the Logos problem. C.K. Barrett spoke for the current orthodoxy of Johannine scholarship when he wrote in 1965, 'Memra is a blind alley in the study of the biblical background of John's Logos doctrine.'[11] Bultmann similarly opted for the view that the Logos had no relationship to the Memra.[12] R. Schnackenburg was just as confident:

We may exclude completely, as is now sufficiently obvious, the appeal to the Memra d' Adonai (the word of the Lord) in the Aramaic translations of the Bible. This has nothing to do with speculation on hypostatisation, but is merely a periphrasis for God, to avoid irreverence ... Wisdom literature has still no inkling of the personal character of the Logos.[13]

(One assumes that he had not read Wisd. 8.15: 'Thy all powerful Logos leapt from heaven ... a stern warrior'!)

This change in scholarly opinion was not caused by any great influx of new evidence such as was afforded by the discovery of the Qumran texts. It was simply a change of fashion; whereas it had formerly been the fashion to follow the early Christian fathers in their treatment of the subject, it became instead the fashion to follow modern Jewish scholars:

This current scholarly attitude towards the Memra is due almost entirely to careful and painstaking work of students of Rabbinic Judaism, who were fully conscious that Memra *could not* be a hypostasis. The fundamental monotheism of mainstream Judaism reflected in the Targums rules out the existence of any such independent or semi-independent entity between God and creation ... The work of these experts must stand as an assured result of Jewish scholarship ...[14]

This assured result is, however, based on the assumption that the monotheism of Rabbinic Judaism was the unchanged tradition from pre-Christian times and that this fundamental monotheism as expressed in the Targums was a valid tool for reconstructing the Judaism of the first century AD.

Two serious questions arise:

i   If there is no real evidence for the dating of the Targums to the Pentateuch, should they be used with such confidence as early evidence for monotheism?

ii How well do we understand the Targums if Memra was introduced as a way of explaining and clarifying the meaning of the Hebrew and we find that word incomprehensible? There must have been something in the Targumists' understanding of the Hebrew text which we no longer know. The missing evidence concerned their understanding of Yahweh.

The crux is: Was the Memra personal or impersonal? The debate is conducted in terms of 'buffer words' but there is no agreement as to whether this buffer word denoted a person or was simply a flowery circumlocution. Several scholars have concluded that Memra served as a way of making God less personal rather than more so:

In many instances it [Memra] is clearly introduced as a verbal buffer ... one of many such in the Targums ... to keep God from seeming to come to too close quarters with men and things; but it is always a buffer word and not a buffer idea; still less a buffer person.[15]

[handwritten: presence — touch of healing — miracle]

The examples given to justify this conclusion are often ambiguous.

i   T.O. to Num. 11.20 has: ... you have felt dislike to *the Word of Yahweh, whose Shekinah dwelleth among you.* The Hebrew has *you have rejected Yahweh who is among you.*

[handwritten: power of miracles]

ii   T.O. renders Num. 14.41: Wherefore do you transgress against *the decree of the Word of Yahweh?* The Hebrew has *the command of Yahweh.*

iii   T.O. says Adam and Eve heard *the voice of the Word of Yahweh Elohim* whereas the Hebrew has *the sound of the Yahweh Elohim.* It was also the Word which met the people in the tabernacle.

[handwritten: sound utterance]
[handwritten: re-configurated]

iv   T.O. to Exod. 25.22 reads: *And I will appoint my Word with thee there and I will speak with thee* ... where the Hebrew has *there I will meet with you.*

v   T.O. to Exod. 29.42–3 is most detailed of all: *the door of the tabernacle of ordinance before Yahweh where I have appointed my Word with you to speak with you there. And I will appoint my Word there unto the sons of Israel and with my glory I will sanctify it.* In the Hebrew is *at the door of the tent of meeting before Yahweh where I will meet with you and speak there with you. There I will meet with the people of Israel and it shall be sanctified by my Glory.*

vi   It was the Word which fought for Israel; T.O. to Deut. 3.22 says *the Word of Yahweh your God will fight for you,* whereas the Hebrew has *it is Yahweh your God who fights for you.*

vii   The covenant was made with the Word; T.O. to Gen. 9.13 has *I have set my Bow in the cloud and it shall be for a sign of the covenant between My Word and between the earth,* while the Hebrew has *... a sign of the covenant between me and the earth.*

Now it is true that these examples could be showing nothing more than an impersonal buffer word, something to avoid bringing the Lord into too close a contact with the earth, but the very fact that such an expression is used time and again in a Targum which does not avoid anthropomorphism suggests that there is another explanation. T.O's account of Adam and Eve describes how the Lord made clothes for them and when the three visitors came to Abraham, the Lord accepted hospitality: 'Accept now a little water and wash your feet, and recline under the tree and take a mouthful of bread ...' (T.O to Gen. 18.4). Anthropomorphism cannot have been a problem for a targumist who could describe the Lord eating and drinking. Perhaps this Targum was retaining a traditional form of expression which had been used far more frequently in the other Targums.

All the examples offered by Moore to prove that Memra was simply a buffer idea, come from the Targum of Onkelos which is thought to represent the Babylonian tradition. The other tradition, the Palestinian, is found in several Targums, all of which use Memra far more often and they make it clear that Memra was more than a mere buffer word or a stylistic device. When man was created he was made in the image of the Memra of Yahweh (Targum *Neofiti*, hereafter T.N., to Gen. 1.27) whereas T.O has him created in the image of Yahweh. The Memra of Yahweh shut the door of the Ark (Targum *Pseudo-Jonathan*, hereafter T. Ps-J., to Gen. 7.16). The Memra of Yahweh killed the firstborn of Egypt (T.Ps-J. to Exod. 12.29). The Memra opposed the works of Balaam (T.Ps-J. to Num. 23.8). The Memra was the offered worship and prayer and was the warrior leader of Israel:

The Memra of Yahweh sitteth upon his throne high and lifted up and heareth our prayer what time we pray before him and make our petitions. (T.Ps-J. to Deut. 4.7)
Hear, O Memra, the voice of the prayer of Judah and bring him back safely from the battle lines to his people in peace. (T.N. to Deut. 33.7)
Arise now, O Memra of Yahweh, in the power of thy might ... (*Fragment Targum*, hereafter F.T., to Num. 10.35)
Let the Memra of Yahweh now be revealed ... Return now, thou Memra of Yahweh, in the goodness of thy mercy and lead thy people Israel ... (T.Ps-J. to Num. 10.35–6).

If the various Targums differ in their use of Memra, the question then arises: What is the nature of this difference and how did it come about? The most obvious difference is that the Babylonian tradition in T.O. uses Memra far less often that does the Palestinian tradition in T.Ps-J., T.N. and F.T.

i In Gen. 1, T.N. uses the Memra of Yahweh seventeen times, the marginal readings of T.N. (hereafter Ngl) add two further instances, and the F.T. uses Memra once and T.O. not at all.

ii In Gen. 2–3 T.N. uses Memra three times, Ngl has fourteen further instances, T.Ps-J., F.T. and T.O. each have two instances.

iii In Gen. 22, T.N. has three instances, Ngl a further three, T.Ps-J. has three, and T.O. and F.T. both two.

iv In Exod. 12 T.N. and T.Ps-J. say that it was the Memra which destroyed the Egyptians, T.O. that it was the Lord.

In the three prayers quoted above (Deut. 4.7; 33.7; Num. 10.35–6), T.O. always refers to Yahweh and never to the Memra of Yahweh. The general picture which emerges is that T.O. stays closer to the original Hebrew than do the Palestinian versions which are more inclined to use Memra.

In addition, these Palestinian Targums incorporate far more non-biblical material into their translations. When Adam and Eve were driven from the garden, for example, T.O. says that the cherubim were placed to guard the way to the Tree of Life exactly as in the Hebrew text. The Palestinian versions, however, elaborated the account with old temple lore in which the temple was the Garden of Eden; the glory of the Shekinah above the cherubim of Eden is the glory in the temple above the cherub throne: 'And he cast out Adam and made the glory of his Shekinah to dwell at the front of the east of the garden of Eden, above the two cherubim' (F.T. and T.N.). In T.Ps-J. the fallen ones of Gen. 6 are named Semiḥaza and Uzziel, just as they are in 1 Enoch; in T.N. they are *the sons of the judges*, but in Ngl *the sons of the kings/angels*. In T.O. they are the *sons of the mighty*. Now the earliest known understanding of this verse is that of 1 Enoch which actually names the leaders of the fallen ones as Semiḥazah and Asael. Given that this text in its Qumran form may be from the third century BC and could represent something a great deal older, it seems as though Ngl and T.Ps-J. represent this older tradition about fallen angels, which later exegetes tried to sanitize. The first dateable evidence for this is from the middle of the second century AD when the interpretation of Gen. 6 was clearly being altered: 'R. Simeon ben Yoḥai called them *the sons of the nobles*; R. Simeon ben Yoḥai cursed all who called them *the sons of God*' (Gen. Rab. 26.5, 20).[16] We could then tentatively suggest that the Targums which translate using Memra represent the older tradition and that this was replaced by one hostile to the angel figures, the sons of God, and wary of using Memra. There is also a telling piece attributed to R. Eliezer:

R. Eliezer said: 'He who translates a verse literally is a liar. He who adds to it commits blasphemy. For instance, if he translated [Exod. 24.10] *And they saw* the God of Israel, he spoke an untruth; for the Holy One ... sees, but is not seen. But if he translated, *And they saw the Glory of the Shekinah of the God of Israel* he commits blasphemy; for he makes three (a trinity) viz. Glory, Shekinah and God.'[17]

The version condemned as blasphemy is that of the Palestinian tradition. Both T.N. and T.Ps-J. read for Exod. 24.10: 'And they saw the glory of the Shekinah of Yahweh ...' Notice that it is 'seeing' God which is condemned.

Memra is not only used in the Targums to the Pentateuch. It is the commonest 'paraphrase' for God in the Targums to the prophets. Chilton listed several examples for each of the distinctive motifs associated with this usage in the Targum to Isaiah (hereafter T.Isa.)[18]:

Israel rebelled against the Memra:
    ... if you refuse and do not obey my Memra ... (T.Isa. 1.20)
Israel would be punished by the Memra:
    ... his Memra will be among you for punishment ... (T.Isa. 8.14)
    ... my Memra, as whirlwind the chaff, will destroy you ... (T.Isa. 33.11)
    Cf. T. Hosea 13.14 ... now my Memra will be among them for death.
Israel was to obey the Memra:
    If you are willing and obey my Memra (T.Isa. 1.19)
Memra represented the edict of Yahweh:
    ... by the Memra of Yahweh of Hosts will this be done (T.Isa. 9.6)
    Have I come up without the Memra of Yahweh against this land to destroy it? (T.Isa. 36.10)
Memra has a voice:
    And I heard the voice of the Memra of Yahweh (T.Isa. 6.8)
    And Yahweh shall cause the glorious voice of his Memra to be heard (T.Isa. 30.30)
    ... a voice from the temple, the voice of the Memra of Yahweh who rendereth recompense to his enemies. (T.Isa. 66.6)
    Draw near unto my Memra, hear ye this ... And now Yahweh Elohim has sent me and his Memra (T.Isa. 48.16)
Memra was a guardian:
    ... when ye passed through the Red Sea my Memra was your support. (T.Isa. 43.2)
    ... and his Memra was their saviour ... (T.Isa. 63.8)
    ... the Memra of Yahweh led them ... (T.Isa. 63.14)
    My Memra shall go before thee and I shall trample down walls ... (T.Isa. 43.2)
Memra is an assurance:
    By my Memra have I sworn ... (T.Isa. 45.23)

For my Name's sake, for my Memra's sake, will I do it ... (T.Isa. 48.11)
Memra was an intermediary:

I let myself be entreated through my Memra ... (T.Isa. 65.1)

Then there is the evidence of the Job Targums. The Second
Targum, a fourth- or fifth-century Palestinian text, avoids all anthropomorphism and uses Memra frequently, whereas the fragments of
the Qumran Targum of Job (11QtgJob), a pre-Christian text, does
not avoid anthropomorphism and offers two examples of Memra.
One is particularly interesting. The Targum renders Job 39.26–7
thus:

Is it by your Wisdom that the falcon is stirred ...
It is by your Memra that the eagle lifts itself aloft ...

The Hebrew has respectively 'your discernment' and 'your command'
(lit. 'mouth'). Why this particular change in parallel lines? Presumably
because Memra and Wisdom were equivalents.[19]

The relevance of the Memra to any enquiry into the nature of
second God, as this was understood in the first century AD, must
depend largely on the age of the Targums in question. The first point
to establish is the relative age of the two major traditions. T.O. has
fewer instances of Memra than the Palestinian Targums and, since it
is usually assumed that monotheism is the most desirable reading of
the Old Testament and it would be hard to maintain that none of the
references in the Palestinian Targums is personal, we have to ask if the
Memra was something added to the tradition as it degenerated, or
removed from the tradition as it was sanitized. Memra does not occur
in any later rabbinic writings and so the first indication would be that
Memra fell out of the tradition and that the Palestinian Targums
represent something older than T.O. or the Mishnah. In the light of
second-century hostility to other interpretations of the Pentateuch
known to have been pre-Christian, interpretations which included
heavenly beings, and in view of the fact that Christian writers used the
Memra as a designation for Jesus, it is more likely that Memra
dropped *from* the tradition at this time than that it was added to it at a
later date.

Much modern dating of Targums derives from the work of Paul
Kahle who argued that T.O. was compiled wholly in Babylon and was
unknown in Palestine until as late as AD 1000. Of the other Targums,
he said, T.N. and the F.T. represented an ancient tradition, far older
than T.O., current in Palestine before the compilation of the Mishnah

because it included traditions contrary to those of the Mishnah. It could even have been pre-Christian. T.Ps-J. represented a different Palestinian tradition. Unfortunately, the earliest actual evidence for these Targums is fragments from the Cairo Geniza dated between AD 700 and 900 and it is not easy to argue convincingly for a first-century date from eight-century evidence.[20] Earlier generations of Targum scholars had argued that Onkelos was produced in Palestine, and that it was the earliest of the Targums to the Pentateuch. G.F. Moore thought that the Palestinian Targums were of little value, even though he acknowledged that they contained some old material,[21] and it was on the basis of material drawn only from T.O. that he argued for the Memra's having been nothing more than a figure of speech. When G.H. Box wrote in strong disagreement with Moore, 'that Memra and allied terms are not merely verbal counters but have a more positive theological significance'[22] it is interesting that the material used to argue *for* a personal Memra was drawn from the Palestinian Targums. Nowhere, however, is there any concrete evidence that the Targums as we now know them existed at an early date.

Tradition records that T.O. was composed during the second century AD and the Targum to the Prophets was composed in the first century by a student of Hillel:

R. Jeremiah ... or some say R. Hiyya b. Abba ... also said: The Targum of the Pentateuch was composed by Onkelos the proselyte under the guidance of R. Eleazar and R. Joshua. The Targum of the Prophets was composed by Jonathan ben Uzziel under the guidance of Haggai, Zechariah and Malachi. (b. *Megillah* 3a)

There are references to written Targums in the Mishnah (*Megillah* 4.10; *Yadaim* 4.5), and several references to a Targum to Job in other rabbinic writings (b. *Shabbath* 115a; j. *Shabbath* 15c; Tosefta *Shabbath* 14) and fragments of a Job Targum at Qumran (11Qtg Job). Modern scholarship has also concluded that the basis of the Targum of Isaiah comes from the first century.

Written Targums, however, are a very different matter from the translations offered at public worship, and it is not known how the need to render the Bible into the Aramaic of everyday speech eventually resulted in the official written Targums, how the traditions of hundreds of translators in hundreds of synagogues became what we read today. The earliest description of their activity is when Ezra read the Law in Jerusalem (Neh. 8.1–8) and the Levites explained it to the people. Amongst all this uncertainty, which gives a margin of several centuries for evidence of the use of Memra, one fact is beyond dispute. *The Targums were made to help uneducated people understand the Scriptures and therefore any term which is found in them must have been one in common use, one which would have been immediately helpful to the hearers.* Memra was such a term, and the fact that we have such difficulty in placing it in our reconstruction of Judaism at this time *is a sure indication that we know less about that Judaism than we commonly suppose.*

A comparison of the Logos of Philo and the Memra of the Targums, especially the Palestinian Targums, shows that, whatever the date of the latter, they reproduce faithfully what Philo knew. The translators of the Targums could assume that the ordinary Jews of the synagogues had more or less the same beliefs as Philo and used the same imagery to express them. This can be shown by comparing some of the descriptions of Philo's Logos with Memra passages in the Targums.

i   The Logos was the Name (*On the Confusion of Tongues* 146):

> And I will separate you to my Name as a people of holy ones and my Word will be to you a redeemer God (T.N. to Exod. 6.7).

ii   Man was made in the image of the Logos (*Questions on Genesis* II.62):

> And the Memra of Yahweh created man in his likeness (F.T. to Gen. 1.27).

iii   The Logos was the viceroy of a great King (*On Dreams* I.241; *On Agriculture* 51):

> ... the Memra of Yahweh hath sworn by the throne of his Glory (T.Ps-J. to Exod. 17.15);
> ... the Memra of Yahweh sitteth upon his throne high and lifted up and heareth our prayer what time we pray before him and make our petitions (T.Ps-J. to Deut. 4.7).

iv   The Logos was the angel of Yahweh who guided Israel in the desert (*On the Migration of Abraham* 174):

> And the Shekinah of the Memra of Yahweh will go before thee (T.Ps-J. to Deut. 31.6).

v The Logos was the heavenly judge (*Questions on Exodus* II.13):

> Woe to them that are alive at the time when the Memra of Yahweh shall be revealed to give the good reward to the righteous and to take vengeance on the wicked ... (T.Ps-J. to Num. 24.23);
>
> His Memra will be among you for vengeance (T.Isa. 8.14).

vi The Logos was the mediator (*Questions on Exodus* II.13):

> I let myself be entreated through my Memra by them that enquired not from before me (T.Isa. 65.1).

vii The Logos was the high priest (*On Dreams* I.215):

> By his Memra he will make atonement for his land and for his people (T.Ps-J. to Deut. 32.43).

viii The Logos was the agent of the creation (*On the Special Laws* I.81):

> The Memra of Yahweh said: Let there be light (T.N. to Gen. 1.3 and *passim*);
>
> They forgot the Memra of Yahweh who had created them (T.N. to Deut. 32.15);
>
> I have made the earth by my Memra (T.Isa. 45.12);
>
> The world was made by his Memra (T.O. to Deut. 33.27).

ix The Logos was the Covenant (*On Dreams* II.237):

> The covenant between my Memra and the earth (T.Ps-J. to Gen. 9.12);
>
> I will set my Covenant between my Memra and thee (T.Ps-J. to Gen. 17.2);
>
> [cf the angel of the Covenant is the Memra, T. Malachi 3]

x The Logos spoke from above the cherubim (*On Flight* 101; *Who is the Heir?* 166):

> And I will appoint my Memra with thee there, and will speak with thee from above the mercy seat, between the two cherubim (T.N. to Exod. 25.22).

And perhaps the Memra was also Wisdom (11QtgJob); cf. Logos was Wisdom, the chief power (*Allegorical Interpretation* II.86).

The correspondence is striking, and, since Philo's Logos was the 'second God', the original significance of Memra becomes a very interesting question. It is not possible to say that Philo's Logos was a second divine being, therefore it cannot have been true to the Old Testament tradition, and it cannot represent anything within what may reasonably be called Judaism. The 'assured result' of modern rabbinic scholarship is that Memra could not be a hypostasis only because this is the concealed premise of the investigation. The monotheism of mainstream rabbinic Judaism which is now reflected in the Targums may not have been the Judaism of the people to whom they were originally addressed. The fact that Memra is opaque to us, even though originally intended as a translation and clarification, must stand as a warning.

The self-revelation of Memra has been the subject of considerable debate, since what is revealed is not the name by which he is addressed, *Yahweh*, i.e. 'He who is/ He who causes to be', but rather the personal form by which he reveals himself, i.e. *'Ehyeh*, 'I who am/I who cause to exist'. The Palestinian Targums hint at the significance of this self revelation in their translations of the *'Ehyeh 'asher 'Ehyeh*. The RSV of Exod. 3.14 renders this 'I am who I am' and T.O. leaves the name untranslated, whereas the Palestinian Targums show that the *'Ehyeh 'asher 'Ehyeh* was associated with creation both past and present. The first *'Ehyeh* refers to the past and the second to the future, showing the continuous creative power:

> I AM HE WHO IS AND WHO WILL BE, hath sent me unto you. (T.Ps-J. Exod. 3.14);
> He who spake to the world, Be, and it was; and who will speak to it, be, and it will be. (F.T. to Exod. 3.14);
> He who said and the world was from the beginning and is to say again to it: Be! and it will be. (T.N. to Exod. 3.14).

The name by which his people addressed him was Yahweh, whereas the name by which he revealed his own presence was *'Ehyeh*:

> And I was revealed in my Memra to Abraham, to Isaac and to Jacob as the God of the heavens, but *my mighty name the Lord** I did not make known to them. (T.N. to Exod. 6.3; F.T. is almost the same)

T. Ps-J. is significantly different in that it is a straight translation of the Hebrew: 'I appeared unto Abraham and to Isaac and to Jacob by

*margin reading is *the name of the Word of Yahweh.*

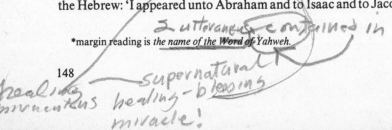

(the name) El Shaddai, but by my name Yahweh I was not known to them.' T.N. preserves another curiosity at Lev. 16.8–9 where Aaron chooses by lot a goat *for Yahweh* on the Day of Atonement. Both T.O. and T.Ps-J. render this *a goat for the name of Yahweh* but T.N. has *a goat for the name of the Memra of Yahweh*.

This distinction between *'Ehyeh* and Yahweh involves some complex arguments, not all of which are entirely convincing; but in an area as fraught with problems as this, the distinction does seem to provide a valuable working tool and it will be hard to come by solid proof given the nature of the materials.[23] It is not unreasonable to suggest that Memra indicated the manifested (i.e. the present) power of the Lord in creation, when creation is understood in the broadest sense of the ongoing ordering of all aspects of the created world. This is implied in the hymns of Revelation:

Holy, holy, holy, is the Lord God Almighty
who was and is and is to come ...
for thou didst create all things,
and by thy will they existed and were created. (Rev. 4.8, 11)
We give thanks to thee Lord God Almighty, *who art and who wast*,
... for destroying the destroyers of the earth. (Rev. 11.17, 18)

The destruction was part of the creation, or rather the preliminary to the recreation. This was the most ancient pattern of the autumn festivals, where the judgement enacted by Yahweh/the King preceded the renewal of the earth with the autumn rains. Thus the Memra, the creating presence of Yahweh, was revealed in destruction wrought by the avenging angel, as well as in creation.

Memra was not used in an arbitrary way but, although patterns of usage are apparent, it is not always possible to account for the changes. T.O.'s less frequent use of the term may suggest that it was falling from favour or was no longer understood. Within the Palestinian tradition also there is discrepancy; the marginal readings of T.N. have far more instances of Memra than does the main text. Not only does the margin have more instances of Memra, but it uses it as the subject of a whole range of verbs whereas the main text is much less free. The main text has 133 examples of verbs other than 'to be' used with Memra as the subject; these verbs represent 39% of the total, and their range is restricted. The margin has 549 examples of a wide range of other verbs, forming 87% of the total usage.[24] There are two possible explanations of this: either the margin represents the earlier tradition, when Memra was used widely to describe the divine mode of communicating with the world and thus could be the subject of a large range of verbs, or the main text represents the earlier tradition, when descriptions of the divine mode of communication were more carefully restricted to verbs of speaking, revealing and visiting. There is no certain way of choosing between these two, except to note that in general the trend seemed to be away from Memra, and that one would therefore expect the usage to diminish rather than to increase. The battle fought by the rabbis against an over-literal understanding of anthropomorphism in the Old Testament may also have been a factor in the fate of Memra, since the manifestation of Yahweh was associated with the human form. This opposition to anthropomorphism, fuelled by controversies in the early Christian centuries, could well have been a factor in the reduction of the activities of the Memra; the main text of T.N. would then represent a less primitive description of the Memra and the margin the older readings, when the Memra intervened in the world with a full range of activities.

The New Testament, especially the Johannine writings, used Memra extensively, not in the sense that there was a direct literary dependence on Philo or a primitive edition of any known Targum, but in the sense that this was a major part of the Judaism from which Christianity grew. The Memra could and did manifest itself in human form and man was created in the likeness of the Memra: 'And the Memra of Yahweh created man in his likeness, in the likeness of the presence of Yahweh He created him' (F.T. to Gen. 1.27). Philo had been embarrassed by this and argued that the likeness was not to the human figure but was a similarity of minds (*Questions on Genesis* II.62). Ezekiel, the priest of the older cult, had had no such problems. For him, the *appearance* of the likeness of the Glory of Yahweh was a human form originally on the cherub throne in the temple, but later removed to Babylon. The Prologue to the Fourth Gospel retains all this and more. The Glory of the Son is manifested in human form (John 1.14). There is Philo's distinction between *God* and *the God*; the former indicated the Logos, the second God, whereas the latter, *the God* indicated God Most High: 'In the beginning was the Word and the Word was with *the God* and the Word was God' (John 1.1).

The Word was the agent of the creation (John 1.10), and *tabernacled* on earth (John 1.14), just as the Memra/Logos had been associated with the tabernacle in the desert and its successor, the temple, and the visions of the Lord in the prophets and the apocalyptic writings had been set there. There were many traditions of the Angel who lived in the sanctuary and appeared in times of crisis. These, too, were a part of the same belief in the presence and manifestation of the presence of the Lord with his people. 1 John begins with an emphasis upon the *manifestation* of the Word of life (1 John 1.1–2). The Word appeared at the beginning of John's vision of the judgement: 'I am the Alpha and the Omega, says the Lord God, who is and who was and who is to come, the Almighty' (Rev. 1.8), and the Targum is similar:

When the Memra of Yahweh shall reveal himself to redeem his people, he will say to all nations: behold now, that I am He who Am and Was and Will be and there is no other God beside me; I in my Memra kill and make alive ... (T.Ps-J. to Deut. 32.39)

He was the heavenly warrior with the secret Name, the Word of God (Rev. 19.11–16), just as in Wisd. 18.15–16 where the Logos killed the firstborn of Egypt. T.Ps-J. to Exod. 12.29 says that it was the Memra who killed them.

Elsewhere the Word is described as the one who severs: 'sharper than any two edged sword, piercing to the division of soul and spirit' (Heb. 4.12). Compare Philo, *Who is the Heir?* 130: 'the Severer of all things, that is the Word'. The Word of God is the creator and judge of the earth: '... by the Word of God heavens existed long ago ... by the same Word the heavens and earth that now exist have been stored up for fire, being kept until the day of judgement and destruction of ungodly men' (2 Pet. 3.5, 7). In addition there are places in the New Testament where Jesus is described in terms strongly reminiscent of the Word, even though the title is not actually mentioned. The most detailed of these are in Colossians and Hebrews. In Col. 1.15–20 the beloved Son is:

i   The image of the invisible God (cf. 'The image of God is the Word', *On the Special Laws* I.81).

ii The firstborn of all creation (cf. 'God's firstborn, the Word', *On the Confusion of Tongues*, 146).

iii In him all things were created (cf. 'the Word through whom the whole universe was framed, *On the Special Laws* I.81).

iv In him all things hold together (cf. 'the complete whole is held together by invisible powers', *On the Migration of Abraham* 181. The Word was the chief of the powers).

v He is the beginning (cf. 'And many names are his, for he is called the Beginning ...' *On the Confusion of Tongues*, 146).

The beloved Son made peace by means of blood (Col. 1.20); one thinks of the Word as the heavenly high priest. Later in the chapter Paul speaks of the Word of God as 'The mystery hidden for ages and generations but now made *manifest* to his saints ... (Col. 1.26).

Hebrews describes a Son:

i Through whom the world was created (Heb. 1.2).

ii Reflecting the glory of God (Heb. 1.3; cf. *On Dreams* I.239: the Word is light around the sun, not the sun itself).

iii Upholding the universe (Heb. 1.3, cf. *On the Migration of Abraham*, 181).

iv Making purification for sins (Heb. 1.3).

v Acting as the heavenly high priest (Heb. 8.1, cf. *On Dreams* I.215, as high priest his First Born the Divine Word).

vi Mediator of the new covenant (Heb. 8.6, cf. 1 Tim. 2.5, there is one mediator between God and men, and *Questions on Exodus* II.13, the Word was appointed as Judge and Mediator).

Jesus was *manifested in the flesh* (1 Tim. 3.16), the Shepherd and Guardian (1 Pet. 2.25) and the heavenly king who ruled under Another (1 Cor. 15.28), cf. 'setting over it [the creation] His true Word and Firstborn Son who shall take upon him its government like some viceroy of a great king ...' (*On Agriculture* 51).

There can be little doubt, in the light of passages such as these, that Jesus had been identified with the second God, whom Philo called the Logos, and whom the Targumists remembered as the Memra, the manifestation of Yahweh with his people. Problems have arisen in the understanding of the Targums because proper account has not been taken of this second God, the great Angel. The final transmitters of the Targums were those who had inherited the tradition of the Second Isaiah and the Deuteronomists: for them, Yahweh and Elyon had become one and the same, and there was no form of Yahweh manifested. Thus they made for themselves the twin problems of anthropomorphism and the 'second power in heaven'. It is to these controversies that we now turn.

The rabbinic writings from the first Christian centuries show that they were engaged in a controversy with heretical groups, who taught that there were two powers in heaven.[25] It is not possible to identify these groups with certainty because they are never named, but investigations have shown that the controversy was 'almost entirely confined to Palestine ... The defence against the heresy is attributed only to Palestinian sages or to Babylonian sages who emigrated to Palestine.'[26] In addition, the earliest evidence for this dispute centred on the understanding of particular passages of Scripture which the heretics had been using to demonstrate that there were two powers in heaven. These heretics did not see the two powers as opposing one another, i.e. they were not early gnostics, but rather they saw them as a far God and a near God. This suggests that the heretics were the Christians; they originated in Palestine, they believed in a second divine person and they took as one of their key scriptural passages the son of man vision in Dan. 7, the very text which formed the starting point of the rabbis' polemic. It is possible to reconstruct only the outlines of what must have been a bitter dispute, but the strength and ferocity of the debates, added to the enormous length of time over which the arguments were refined, shows that this was a cause of great concern.

The earliest account is in a midrash on Exodus, the *Mekhilta* of R. Ishmael. The text of Exodus apparently gives two different accounts of the appearance of Yahweh; as a young warrior in Exod. 15.3, 'Yahweh is a man of war' and as an old man in Exod. 24.10, 'they saw the God of Israel'. There is nothing in the latter to say that the manifestation at Sinai was of an old man, but later tradition shows that this was assumed since Law is best when given by the old. Thus there was a young man figure named Yahweh who brought justice for his people and there was an old one named God who showed mercy to them (Exod. 24.11). In order to ensure that the readers of Exodus did not draw these dangerous conclusions, the two manifestations were related to the vision of Dan. 7 in order to show that the Lord could be manifested in two ways yet be the same God. Now the vision of Dan. 7 is not perfectly clear, but it would not seem to be the most obvious choice of texts to make the point that there was only one God, since the one thing the passage does make clear is that there were two: there was the Ancient of Days, seated on a throne of fiery flames, and there was a man-like figure who went up to him to be given dominion and glory and kingdom (Dan. 7.14). Since the man-like figure seems to have triumphed over the beasts, he must have been the young

153

warrior, and the seated figure must have been the one seen at Sinai. Thrones, plural, had been placed in heaven, one for the Ancient of Days and one for the man figure. The rabbis maintained, nevertheless, that the vision was of two differing manifestations of the same God.

I am YHWH your God: why is this said? Because when He was revealed at the sea he appeared to them as a mighty hero making war. As it is said, *YHWH is a man of war*. He appeared at Sinai like an old man, full of mercy as it is said: *And they saw the God of Israel*. And of the time after they had been redeemed what does it say? *And the like of the very heaven for clearness*. Again, it says *I beheld till thrones were set down*. And also it says *A fiery stream issued and came forth from him*. Scripture would not give an opportunity to the nations of the world to say 'There are "two powers"', but declares *I am YHWH your God*.' I was in Egypt. I was at the Sea. I was in the past, I will be in the future to come. I am in this world, I am in the world to come.

They did this by adducing texts from Deuteronomy and the Second Isaiah, significant sources since it was the innovative monotheism of the Second Isaiah which had first identified El Elyon with Yahweh and it was the reforming zeal of the Deuteronomists which had first made this monotheism central to the presentation of Israel's tradition:

As it is said: *Behold now, that I, even I, am He* etc (Dt 32.39). *Even unto old age I am the same* (Is 46.4). *Thus says YHWH the king of Israel and his Redeemer the Lord of Hosts. I am the first and the last* (Is 44.6) And it says *Who has wrought and done it? He that called the generations from the beginning. I the Lord who am the first, and to the end I am He* (Is 41.4).

R. Nathan, who taught in the mid-second century, added to the argument the fact that no other God is reported to have questioned the claims of the Lord to be the only God: 'Rabbi Nathan says: from this one can cite as refutation of the heretics who say: "There are two powers". For when the Holy One, Blessed be he, stood up and exclaimed: "I am Yahweh thy God" was there anyone who stood up to protest against him?' There could have been no second power.

Later elaborations of the argument introduced the themes of the justice and mercy of God; the former was the characteristic of the warrior, Yahweh, and the latter of the old man, *'elohim*. The various manifestations emphasized these different aspects, but they could be seen to be one God because, it was argued, passages such as Exod. 20.2 used both names: I am *Yahweh thy God*. These 'two attributes' of God were to become an important part of later rabbinic teaching, although, curiously, the associations were reversed and *Yahweh* came to represent the merciful aspect and *God* the just. Philo, it will be recalled, also knew of the two aspects of God which were represented in the Old Testament by *the Lord* and *God* but he related them as did the earlier rabbis: *the Lord, kyrios* signifying justice and *God* mercy (*Who is the Heir?* 166). For Philo these were not the attributes of the far God and the near God, the Ancient of Days and the warrior, but rather they were both aspects of the *second* God, the Logos; the far God was known as the 'pre-Logos God' (*Questions on Genesis* II.62), the Highest of Causes (*On Dreams* I.190). 'In the first place he who is elder than the one and the monad and the beginning, and then second comes the Logos of the Existent One' (*Questions on Exodus* II.68). This was God Most High. It is not hard to see how those coping with the problem of demonstrating monotheism from the Old Testament texts adapted this older belief and used the tradition of the two names of the one Logos to demonstrate the two names of the one God. The fact that this tradition exists in two exactly contradictory forms, with *the Lord* signifying first justice and later mercy, shows that it was being used for a purpose rather than faithfully handed on intact!

Tradition attributes the earliest discussion of these two attributes of God to R. Akiba and his successors in the mid-second century; this would suggest that the underlying form of the debate, the one involving only the two figures of the warrior and the Ancient of Days based on Dan. 7, came from an earlier period, say the first century, exactly when the Christians were using this 'son of man' text to give shape to their own expectations. The crux of the problem was the *two* thrones of the vision. Later tradition says that R. Akiba had originally taught that the second throne was for the Messiah, but that this was opposed by R. Yosi:

One passage says: *His throne was fiery flames* (Dan. 7.9) and another passage says: *Until thrones were placed; and One that was Ancient of Days did sit ... there is no contradiction;* one (throne) for him and one for David: this is the view of R. Akiba. Said R. Yosi the Galilean to him: Akiba, how long will you treat the divine presence as profane! Rather, one for justice and one for grace. Did he accept this explanation from him or did he not accept it? ... come and hear. One for justice and one for grace; this is the view of R. Akiba. (b. *Hagigah* 14a)

As with all the sayings attributed to the rabbis, this one is not easy to extract from its highly stylized setting. R. Akiba's interpretation was opposed by his colleague who insisted that the two thrones were for the two aspects of the one God. There is nothing to suggest that R. Akiba saw the Davidic messiah figure, for whom the second throne was set, as merely human; he could have viewed the Messiah as a manifestation of the second *divine* figure. He saw in Bar Kochba a political messiah, but this does not exclude the possibility that that Messiah figure was thought to have had a heavenly aspect. Eschatology and politics were closely linked at the time, which may account for later generations recording that R. Akiba was converted to a less dangerous view of the verse! The Bar Kochbar revolt, fuelled by messianic fervour, had ended in disaster just when the Christians were demonstrating that the second divine figure in heaven had been Jesus. It is interesting that when Justin debated the matter with the Jew Trypho at exactly this time (*Dialogue with Trypho* 32), the problem was not over the whether the second figure in Daniel's vision was the glorious and exalted Messiah, but whether or not this figure could have been Jesus. In the early second century, then, this son of man figure which was later to be explained as the second attribute of God *was* understood by Jews as the Messiah, and presumably therefore as the second power in heaven.

The most anthropomorphic descriptions of God in this period are those of the *Shi'ur Komah* which speculates as to the dimensions of the divine figure who is identified as the Beloved of Song of Songs 5.11–16. Although traditionally attributed to R. Akiba and R. Ishmael it has proved almost impossible to date the text. Nevertheless, the traditional attribution may point to speculation about the divine form having antedated the second-century rabbis. Stroumsa's study concluded: 'There is strong reason to presume that the original Jewish speculation on the macrocosmic divine body is pre-Christian.' He then raised the important question; Who was the divine figure whose dimensions were given? He quoted from Scholem:

We may ask whether there did not exist ... a belief in a fundamental distinction between the appearance of God the Creator, the Demiurge, i.e. one of his aspects, and his indefinable Essence? There is no denying the fact that it is precisely the 'primordial man' on the throne of the Merkabah whom the Shi'ur Komah calls 'Yotser Bereshith' ... The Shi'ur Komah referred not to the 'dimensions' of the divinity but to those of its corporeal appearance.[27]

Other traditions from the second century show that this second power, in its heavenly aspect, was the great angel who bore the secret name. The ill-fated Elisha ben Abuya, known as Aher (*the other one*, to avoid saying his name!), was a mystic who had a vision of the heavenly throne. There are various versions of the story, but they all show that Aher was in touch with the most ancient temple traditions since he saw the divine throne when he entered the heavenly garden, the ancient Eden. He saw a second *seated* figure in heaven:

> What does it refer to? ... he saw that permission was granted to Metatron to sit and write down the merits of Israel. Said he: 'It is taught as a tradition that on high there is no sitting and no emulation, no back and no weariness.' Perhaps, God forfend ... there are two divinities (two powers). Thereupon they led Metatron forth and punished him with sixty fiery lashes, saying to him: 'Why didst thou not rise before him when thou didst see him?' Permission was then given to him to strike out the merits of Aḥer ... (b. *Hagigah*, 15a)

Another version of the story is told in 3 Enoch. R. Ishmael ascended to the divine presence, guided by Metatron, who told him how Aḥer had mistaken his role in the heavenly court:

> When Aḥer came to gaze upon the vision of the merkabah, he looked at me and he was afraid and trembled before me. His soul was so agitated even to leaving him because of fear, horror and dread of me, when he saw me sitting on a throne like a king and ministering angels sitting before me like servants and all the princes of the kingdoms around me adorned with crowns. At that moment Aḥer opened his mouth and said 'It is true, there are two powers in heaven.' (3 Enoch 16)

At this point the great angel Aniyal came to punish Metatron and made him *stand* before the throne. Since 3 Enoch records that one of the names of Metatron was 'the Little Yahweh', it was the *second power* who had the sacred name. Further, the angel Metatron whom R. Ishmael met on his ascent explained that he had been Enoch the seer before his exaltation. The second power not only had the sacred name but also had human manifestations on earth.

There is also the tradition recorded of R. Idi, a teacher who probably lived in the middle of the third century, which indicates another of the heretics' uses of Exod. 24.1: 'And He said to Moses, "Come up to Yahweh"'. This implies that 'He' i.e. God, and 'Yahweh' are not identical, otherwise the text would have read 'And He said to Moses "Come up to me"'.

> Once a *Min* said to R. Idi: 'It is written, *And unto Moses he said: Come up to Yahweh (Ex. 24.1). But surely it should have stated, Come up to me!*' 'It was Metatron,' he replied, 'whose name is similar to that of his master, for it is written, *For My name is in Him*' (Ex 23.21). 'But if it is so, we should worship him!' 'The same passage, however,' replied R. Idi, 'says: *Be not rebellious against Him* [i.e. exchange Me not for him]. But if it is so, why is it stated: *He will not pardon your transgression?*' (Ex 23.21). He answered: 'By our troth [lit. "we

157

hold the belief"] we would not accept him even as a messenger, for it is written. And he said unto him, *If thy presence go not ...*' (Ex 33.15) (b. Sanh 38b)

Two things can be deduced from this tightly written piece. First, we learn that the Min (heretic) considers the second power in heaven to be a second God named *Yahweh*, whereas the rabbi will concede only that this was an angel who bore the sacred name. We do not, however, know what was meant by this. Second, the heretic asks why at this point the 'angel' did not forgive Israel's sins; presumably the 'angel' would normally have done this, or else the remark is pointless. This must have been the mediator angel, and the heretics knew him as *Yahweh*.

The battle against the 'two powers' heretics began with the exegesis of Scripture, especially with vision of Dan. 7; the earliest debates were probably in the first century; they became increasingly complex and their arguments more refined and the debates were always associated with Palestine. *All this points to a crisis precipitated by the rise of Christianity*. The people involved in this controversy will have been the same as those who formed the Palestinian Targums, those who used the term Memra to explain certain manifestations of Yahweh. Memra must have been the term used by the Palestinian Christians, before John expressed it in Greek as the Logos just as Philo had done, and yet all three, the Memra, the Logos of Philo and the Logos of John have caused endless debate. The problem of the Memra, the problem of the Logos and the problem of the two powers are all one problem, caused by our losing sight of the Great Angel, and by the curiously perverted refusal on the part of Christian scholars to believe the claims of the first Christians. The monotheism of rabbinic orthodoxy is not a valid basis from which to reconstruct the earliest Christian beliefs, and to accept that the Memra 'cannot' have represented anything other than a figure of speech because this is the assured result of Jewish scholarship, is as dubious as accepting that 'son of man' was no more than a figure of speech, just because this, too, was the result of Jewish scholarship.

The problem of anthropomorphism has continued to exercise Jewish scholars. J. Neusner, for example, in his fascinating study *The Incarnation of God*,[28] was bold enough to tackle the problem even though he could not bring himself to address the central issue. He analysed the Jewish texts of the first seven Christian centuries to see how they depicted God and recognized that 'the incarnation of God' was profoundly characteristic of Judaism (p. 6), even though his definition of incarnation is not one which everyone could accept: 'It is *the representation of God as a human being* who walks and talks, cares and acts, a God who not only makes general rules but also by personal choice transcends them and who therefore exhibits a particular personality' (p.21, *my emphases*).

This way of 'framing the direct encounter with the living God' did not find a real place in Judaism of the early Christian centuries, he said, until the period of the Babylonian Talmud, the sixth or seventh century AD, and only then in a community not threatened by Christianity. Neusner recognized that this direct encounter had been a part of the original expression of the Scriptures and argued with a great deal of evidence that when the writers of this period 'began to represent God as personality ... they *reentered* the realm of discourse about God that Scripture had originally laid out' (p.28, *my emphases*). He hints at the reason for abandoning the older ways. When the earlier Talmud, the Jerusalem Talmud, had been formed within the Palestinian community it had addressed the threat posed by the newly influential Christianity in the fourth century AD, and, since Christianity had its own way of reading the Old Testament, a '*Judaic response took the form of a counterpart exegesis*' (p.107, *my emphases*). The Jewish sages adapted Scripture to their new needs. 'When the sages ... read and expounded Scripture it was to spell out *how one thing stood for something else* ... The as-if frame of mind brought to Scripture *renews* Scripture, with the sage seeing everything with fresh eyes' (p.125, *my emphases*). As the Christians were explaining how Jesus was both God and Man and finding him in the Old Testament as the manifested God, Jewish scholars writing in Roman Christian Palestine 'clearly treated with reticence and mainly through allusion the perfectly available conception of God as incarnate' (p.196). Scholars in Babylon, however, were under no such pressures: 'Consequently, it was in the Bavli (the Babylonian Talmud) in particular that God became Man' (p.166), even though, as we have seen, it is the 'Babylonian' Targum which has the fewest instances of Memra.

It is studies such as this which highlight the need for a very careful use of ancient texts. Jewish sources, though still something of a novelty for many Christian scholars, are not necessarily a more authentic way of understanding Christian origins. Their novelty must not allow us to give them a weight they cannot bear. Terrible traumas are buried in the earliest years of the Jewish-Christian separation and all our present discussion of ancient texts must not lose sight of this.

Notes to chapter eight

1 G.F. Moore, 'Intermediaries in Jewish Theology', HTR xv (1922) p.46.

2 Ibid., p.43 for a survey of various interpretations offered by Jewish scholars.

3 K. Kohler, *Jewish Theology Systematically and Historically Considered*, New York 1918, p.198.

4 H.L. Strack and P. Billerbeck, *Kommentar zum neuen Testament aus Talmud und Midrasch*, Munich 1924, vol.II, p.302.

5 J.W. Etheridge, *Targums to the Pentateuch*, London 1862, p.19.

6 B.F. Westcott, *An Introduction to the Study of the Gospels* (4th edn), London 1872, p.147; *The Gospel according to St John*, London 1908, vol.I, p.5ff.

7 A. Edersheim, *The Life and Times of Jesus the Messiah*, London 1890, vol.I, p.47.

8 Moore, op.cit., p.41.

9 Ibid., p.42.

10 Ibid., although Kohler, op.cit., p.199, n.3, suggested that the rabbis abandoned the personified Memra because of the Christians.

11 C.K. Barrett, *The Gospel According to John*, London 1965, p.128.

12 R. Bultmann, *The Gospel of John*, Oxford 1971, p.22.

13 R. Schnackenburg, *The Gospel of John*, London 1968, p.485.

14 C.T.R. Hayward, 'The Holy Name of the God of Moses and the Prologue of St John's Gospel', NTS 25 (1978), p.19 (my emphases).

15 Moore, op.cit., p.53.

16 P.S. Alexander, 'The Targumim and Early Exegesis of the Sons of God in Gen 6', JJS 23 (1972).

17 Midrash ha-gadol quoted by G.H. Box in 'The Idea of Intermediation in Jewish Theology', JQR xxiii (1932), p.112 and by R. Patai in *The Hebrew Goddess*, New York 1947, p.150.

18 B.D. Chilton, *The Glory of Israel. The Theology and Provenience of the Isaiah Targum*, Sheffield 1982.

19 J.A. Fitzmyer, 'The Contribution of Qumran Aramaic to the Study of the New Testament', reprinted in Fitzmyer, *A Wandering Aramaean: Collected Aramaic Essays*, Missoula 1979, p.95.

20 A.D. York, 'The Dating of Targumic Literature', JSJ V.i (1974).

21 G.F. Moore, *Judaism in the First Centuries of the Christian Era: The Age of the Tannaim*, 3 vols, Cambridge, Mass. 1927–30, vol.I, p.175.

22 Op.cit., p.110, n.17.

23 Op.cit., n.14.

24 C.T.R. Hayward, 'The Memra of Yahweh and the Development of its Use in Targum Neofiti I', JJS xxv (1974).

25 A.F. Segal, *Two Powers in Heaven*, Leiden 1978, is the major treatment of this theme and my examples are drawn from it.

26 Ibid., p.174.

27 G.G. Stroumsa, 'Form(s) of God: Some Notes on Metatron and Christ', HTR 76.3 (1983), p.277; quoting from G.G. Scholem, *Major Trends in Jewish Mysticism* (3rd edn) New York 1961, p.65.

28 J. Neusner, *The Incarnation of God. The Character of Divinity in Formative Judaism*, Philadelphia 1988.

Israel's oldest religion was not monotheistic. It is not possible to say how it survived, but the fact that it can be seen in both Daniel and Philo, which are dateable texts, shows that it did not disappear. Philo spoke of the seven aspects as the powers who were the visible manifestation of the Glory in the creation; the second God, the Logos, was their chief. Each power had a name and the two chief powers were named Yahweh and Elohim. At the point where Philo enumerates all the powers there is a break in the text after the first three, viz. creative power, royal power, gracious power ... (*On Flight* 94). Were the rest of this piece extant we might have been able to discover a great deal about the compound nature of the second God. As it is we have to reconstruct what we can from the two recurring patterns used by Philo to describe the powers; one has six-plus-one, derived doubtless from the *menorah*, and the other has two equal powers represented by the two cherubim of the throne. Whilst the second God is above the throne, he is still thought in some way to *be* those two powers which are beneath him, a fact which must be borne in mind when we read of the gnostic archons (rulers) emanating from a higher source. Yahweh was known as Yahweh of Hosts, the chief of the heavenly hosts. He was also Yahweh Elohim, which may once have indicated something very similar, viz. Yahweh of the Elohim. In addition there had been a female deity or rather, a female aspect of Yahweh.

The original setting for these beliefs had been the temple cult in Jerusalem. Their framework was the myth of the fallen angels and the great Day of Yahweh when they and their evil would be judged by Yahweh the heavenly judge, before his enthronement as the heavenly king, the chosen one of El Elyon. This enthronement would be the beginning of the new creation. Temple traditions survived in the apocalypses where there were evil angels in abundance and the memory that Wisdom had been lost or displaced at the end of the first temple period. There is not one myth of the fallen angels, but, in the texts we have, a considerable diversity, suggesting that something

162

very ancient was involved, something, furthermore, which had had time to develop without any centralized control or imposed interpretation. There was a version which attributed evil to the pride of the angel figure who wanted to set his throne above Elyon's; another taught that evil had been caused by the corruption of heavenly knowledge brought to earth by the lustful angels; yet another said that the angels had come to earth to bring civilizing knowledge but had been corrupted by the daughters of men. There were several traditions about the archangels; one knew of seven and another of four. There were also different traditions about their names and the number of heavens they inhabited. Such diversity is an important factor to be borne in mind when attempting to locate their date and place of origin. It is pointless to try to find the authentic original myth from which all the others degenerated. This myth was a basic working tool by means of which several different points of view were expressed; what is important is that the myth was sufficiently central to the world-view of many people that it remained the means by which they expressed beliefs, even when they differed. One might perhaps compare here the widely differing beliefs that Christian denominations have built on the story of the last supper. Were we to start from the present day and try to retroject to what the story might have been, it would be extremely difficult to make anything like a reconstruction of what is actually in the Gospels. And then there is the problem of what lay behind them, and so on. We have to take the whole set of the angel myths and resist the temptation to tidy it up.

This diversity in the angel mythology accounts for the diversity in the later gnostic systems. Stroumsa has shown that 'a radical transformation of this myth (the fallen angels) forms the basis of the Gnostic mythological consciousness of evil',[1] but the problem for the gnostics, he said, was not 'How can there be evil if God is good?' but rather 'How can good mix with evil, the spiritual with the material?' The former is supposed to have been the traditional view point of the Old Testament, with God all good and the material world good also. A careful reading, however, leaves one with the unmistakable feeling that the roots of the gnostic viewpoint *could have been in the earliest strata of the Old Testament*. The Old Testament does not depict a God who is wholly good; he has evil spirits at his command (1 Kings 22.22) and wreaks terrible vengeance on his enemies. The material world is not wholly good either; it is a place of thorns and thistles, pain and death, by the express command of Yahweh Elohim (Gen. 3.14–19).

163

Job said everything there was to say about the world as a place of evil. The later gnostic motif of separating sacred from profane also runs right through the ancient texts. The angels in 1 Enoch were condemned for mixing the spiritual with the earthly: 'though ye were holy, spiritual, living the eternal life, you have defiled yourselves with the blood of women ...' (1 Enoch 15.4).

Further, the possession of knowledge made one wise like the angels, and this too is not far from the gnostic position. In 2 Sam. 14.20 the phrase seems to be proverbial, but in Gen. 3.5 and 22 it is the key to the whole story. Mankind was forbidden the knowledge which could make him like the *'elohim*, like the angels. It would be easy to read this chapter as a polemic against someone who was teaching that knowledge could make a human being divine. It was the desire for this knowledge, says the writer, which had caused the corruption of the earth and man's sorry state. Now there is no doubt that Genesis begins by setting out various possible accounts of the origin of evil; why should there have been such a distinctly polemical tone about the explanation offered in Gen. 3 unless the opposite position was the one being denounced? Was there a knowledge which transformed the human into the divine even in the cult of the first temple? And why does the first story of the creation in Gen. 1 emphasize that what was made by God was good? It has long been suspected that other, older views were being replaced by this account: the sea monsters of Gen.1, for example, were not hostile powers opposed to God but were only his creatures; the sun, moon, and stars were only to separate light from darkness. There were accounts of the creation in which the sea monsters and the stars had played a very different role: the sea monsters and the savage waters of chaos had been conquered by the arm of Yahweh (Isa. 51.9; Letter of Manasseh, 3) and the stars and the sons of God had shouted for joy when the foundations of the earth were put in place (Job. 38.7). These monstrous angelic beings and the waters of chaos all appear in the gnostic mythologies, but the texts are several centuries later. The unanswerable question is: Was there an unbroken tradition of another creation story which went back to the oldest strata of the Old Testament, or did the gnostic teachers simply cobble together all the pieces they could find which would contradict what was in the 'official' account? We cannot *assume* the latter, although this is usually done. It is possible that the Old Testament editors, who are increasingly being recognized as creative theologians in their own right, were opposing a view of creation which had a place for the hostile sea, monsters, star angels, knowledge which made human beings like the heavenly beings, and a belief that the material world was evil. A good case can be made for seeing the preface to Deuteronomy as a manifesto excluding the position of the apocalyptists, namely Wisdom, the visible form of God and the veneration of the heavenly host (Deut. 4.6, 12, 19). Was the older view of creation also excluded as part of the same process? This cannot be answered with certainty, but that does not prevent our asking the question. The older strata of the Old Testament *do* look very like the roots of the later gnostic systems and it is significant that the gnostics had links to the older, i.e. superseded, strata. Were the gnostic teachers such expert textual critics that they chose only the older material, or did they know another tradition behind what we read in the Old Testament? They certainly knew of a great variety of beliefs within Judaism, and again this is something which we tend not to take as a serious possibility in our reconstructions.

The *Tripartite Tractate* said that the prophets had spoken of a coming Saviour, a common enough sentiment among Christian writers: 'Sometimes they speak as if it will be and sometimes it is as if the Saviour speaks from their mouths' (*Tripartite Tractate* CG I.5.113), indicating that the Saviour had existed during the time of the Old Covenant. It also said that those who heard the prophets,

have accepted the scriptures in an altered way. By interpreting them they established many heresies which have existed to the present among the Jews. Some say that God is one, who made a proclamation in the ancient scriptures. Others say he is many. Some say that God is simple and was a simple mind in nature. Others say that his activity is linked with the origin of good and evil. Still others say that he is the creator of that which has come into being. Still others say that it was by the angels that he created. The multitude of ideas of this sort, the multitude of forms and the abundance of types of scripture is what produced their teachers of the law. (*Tripartite Tractate*, CG I.5.112–13)

This passage probably represents the teachings of Heracleon, a disciple of Valentinus. What is interesting is the implication that our 'normal' reading of the Old Testament, that God is one and spoke through the ancient Scriptures, is thought to be a heresy established by misreading.

Let us take some aspects of this older system and trace their gnostic counterparts: (i) the Great God; (ii) the Great Angel who was the patron of Israel, the chief of the angels and the creator; (iii) the plural nature of the Great Angel; (iv) the fallen angels as the source of evil through pride or rape; and (v) the female aspect of the Great Angel. In addition we need to note throughout their setting in the ancient temple cult, and try to imagine what might have happened to the ancient ways after the reforms of the Deuteronomists and the ardent monotheism of the Second Isaiah. The prophet had declared that El and Yahweh were one and the same (Isa. 40.28); the Deuteronomists had declared that the Law was to be the wisdom of Israel (Deut. 4.6), that there was no visible form of God (Deut. 4.12) and that 'Yahweh our Elohim is one Yahweh' (Deut. 6.4). This latter is so familiar that its strangeness can be overlooked; it was emphasizing that the plurality of the Elohim was One, and that that One was the Yahweh of the Deuteronomists. Someone also seems to have rewritten the myth of the Garden of Eden so as to teach that human disobedience and the craving for knowledge were the source of all evil, rather than the corruption of heavenly knowledge by the fallen angels and the sin of pride in heavenly places such as we find in the earlier Eden of Ezekiel, the priest of the first temple. Not everyone accepted the new ways of the reformed and reforming exiles when they returned to Jerusalem; how might these other people have perpetuated and adapted their ancient beliefs?

In the first place, many will have left their homeland and gone to live in the Diaspora. There they will have found themselves, as did Philo some centuries later, in the midst of another culture, and their own beliefs will not have been kept free of other influences. Anything we detect in later texts will not reflect the original beliefs of the dispossessed, but rather the way in which the basic materials were used to cope with their new situation. We should expect to find some expression of the anger felt by the worshippers of Yahweh who had been excluded by the purists of the restored community, those who were declaring that Yahweh and El were one. We should expect to find hostility to the Jews, since this was the name by which the returned exiles were known. We should expect to find a role for the Lady Wisdom since we know even from Jeremiah that it was those who fled to Egypt who believed that the neglect of her cult had caused the disaster (Jer. 44.18). We should expect to find a belief in the plural nature of Yahweh. We should expect to find a cult of angels and heavenly powers with vestiges of the original temple setting. We should expect to find a view of the origin of evil akin to that of the myth of the fallen angels, and we should expect hostility towards the

166

Mosaic Law which characterized the religion of those who both replaced and displaced the ancient cult.

I believe that all these can be found in the gnostic texts, and shall devote this chapter to showing that the ancient temple cult was transformed into the gnostic systems both by alien influences and bitterness. What comes through most clearly, and this is what I wish to demonstrate, is the universal belief that the *second* God was the creator and the revealer, that *he* was the God of the Jews, and that beside him or above him was a female figure, Wisdom. This, I suggest, is yet further evidence that the older beliefs of Israel have survived as the basis of the later system. The gnostic texts themselves are undateable. The earliest full account of their teachings was written towards the end of the second century AD by Irenaeus who described several varieties of gnostic teaching, but although he wrote in considerable detail, he also wrote to discredit them and cannot therefore be used as an unbiased source. Christian commentaries have often taken their tone from Irenaeus:

It may be a matter of regret that so large a portion of the work of Irenaeus is given to an exposition of the manifold Gnostic speculations. Nothing more absurd than these has probably ever been imagined by rational beings ... by deserting the guidance of Scripture, they were betrayed into the most pernicious and extravagent systems. (ANCL V p.xv)

Irenaeus himself says that much of what was taught was the result of rival teachers setting up on their own; and 'a multitude of Gnostics have sprung up, and have been manifested like mushrooms growing out of the ground' (*Against Heresies* I 29). Mushrooms they may have been, but the decaying memories on which those mushrooms grew are of considerable interest! The followers of Basilides described themselves as 'no longer Jews' (*Against Heresies* I 24.6) and modern scholars are now returning to the idea that the gnostics *were*, in fact, rooted in Judaism.[2] It had been Reitzenstein's 'The Iranian Myth of the Redeemed Redeemer' which first started scholars hunting for the gnostic redeemer, the most fashionable and elusive snark of recent times and now recognized as 'the greatest hoax of the twentieth century'.[3] Scholars of gnosticism have, as one of their number has observed, now abandoned their epic journey to Persia![4] We are required to search the all too familiar texts of Judaism, too familiar because there is one particular way in which these texts are usually read and this may not have been that of all their first users. Others from the same family may not have been recognized for what they

167

really were. *The gnostic redeemer had originally been Yahweh*, but the wounds of history had caused the original system to disintegrate and the one figure had been divided into the evil creator archon and the descending redeemer. The evil archon seems to have taken over the roles of the more ancient Asael, the leader of the fallen angels, and one wonders what *his* significance might originally have been. He was the only supernatural being apart from Yahweh to whom an offering was made, viz. the scapegoat at Yom Kippur.⁵ Or had he been an aspect of Yahweh? If the Second Isaiah was assuming all divinities under the one Yahweh, what divinity necessitated his saying: 'I form light and create darkness, I make weal and create woe, I am Yahweh who do all these things' (Isa. 45.7)?

There had been a consistent tradition of dividing the roles of the second God. It was apparent in Philo's two powers of the Logos, the one of mercy and the other of justice. The Logos was neither the one nor the other, but above and between the two, invisibly enthroned above the cherubim on the right and on the left. In the gnostic texts these two powers became hostile to each other, one good and one evil, although there is a hint of the idea that the Logos was actually one who maintained the balance between these powers, just as in Philo (*On Planting* 10) or the Apocalypse of Abraham (Ap. Abr. 10.9–10, see chapter 7). The *Apocryphon of John* tells how the Great Archon seduced Eve who then gave birth to his two sons, Yave and Eloim. Yave was good and Eloim evil (Ap. John CG II.1.24). The *Tripartite Tractate* alludes to the same idea: 'If both of the orders, those of the right and those of the left, are brought together with one another *by the thought* which is set between them ...' (*Tripartite Tractate* CG.I.5.108), which was also part of the Valentinian system:

And they say she (Wisdom) first formed out of animal substance him who is Father and King of all things, both of these which are of the same nature with himself, that is, animal substances, which they also call right handed, and those which sprang from the passion, and from matter, which they call left handed. (*Against Heresies* I.5.1)

The ruler of the left was the Demiurge and of the right was the Father, even though both were apparently the same being. Theodotus taught the same:

And first of all things, Sophia put forth, as an image of the Father, the god through whom she made the heaven and the earth, that is the Heavenly and the Earthly, the Right and the Left. (*Excerpt* 47)

But the powers on the left, brought forth by her earlier than those on the right, were not formed by the advent of the light; those on the left were left to be formed by the Topos.' (*Excerpt* 34)

Those whom Epiphanius called Archontics taught that the Devil was the son of Sabaoth, the God of the Jews: '... and his father is not like him, nor again is he like the incomprehensible god whom they call the Father, but he belongs to the left hand power' (Epiphanius, *Panarion* 40.5), and thus we find again here the tradition implied in the Enochic texts, that Asael, the chief of the fallen angels, had not always been evil. The tradition, again attested only in the non-canonical texts, of the final battle between the Great Angel and the Evil Angel is reflected in the teaching of Basilides: 'he maintained that the God of the Jews was one of the angels; and on this account, because all the powers wished to annihilate his father, Christ came to destroy the God of the Jews' (*Against Heresies* I.24.2).

There were many gnostic systems; our purpose here is not to examine these in all their variety, but rather to sift through what seem to be the earliest expressions of these beliefs for evidence of motifs and patterns which could have come from the pre-exilic Hebrew religion. Such an exercise will, of necessity, be imprecise. The earliest gnostic teacher of whom we have any real evidence is Simon Magus, who was a contemporary of the apostles; the gnostic systems which existed at that time and later will have been as many centuries removed from their origins in the cult of the ancient temple as were the first expressions of Christianity, but the latter can be shown to have derived much of its form and content from memories of the pre-exilic cult. How these survived, and by what channels they were transmitted is not known, but the striking correspondences cannot be coincidence. Similarly, the first 'gnostic' teachings could have had ancient roots.

El Elyon, for example, appears in the gnostic texts as the unknown God, the high God of the First Father. This can be seen clearly in the *Letter of Eugnostos*, thought to be an early text and certainly one which has no Christian influences:

The one who is is ineffable ... For he is immortal. He is eternal, having no birth ... He is imperishably blessed. He is called the Father of the Universe. He was revealed in his likeness as Self Father [one of the names of the second deity], that is, Self Begetter, and Confronter, since he confronted the Unbegotten First Existing One. Indeed he is of equal age with the one who is before his countenance, but he is not equal to him in power. Afterward he revealed a multitude of confronting self begotten ones equal in age (and) power, being in glory, and without number. They are (called) 'the generation over whom there is no kingdom among the kingdoms that exist'. And the whole multitude there over which there is no kingdom is called 'the Sons of the Unbegotten Father' (*Letter of Eugnostos*, CG.III.3 71–5)

Without naming any heavenly power, this text describes the ancient Elyon and his sons, one of whom was pre-eminent. It continues with a description of the work of this pre-eminent being, which we shall consider later. Such a description of the far God and the nearer God is typical of the gnostic systems, even though there are variations in the names given to these deities. *Eugnostos* is especially valuable as an indication of the older strata since it has not yet adopted the hostility to the second God which came to characterize much of the later gnostic writing.

Menander, a disciple of Simon, taught that 'the first Power was unknown by all, but that he himself (i.e. Menander) was the one who was sent by the invisible as a saviour for the salvation of men' (*Against Heresies* I.23.5); Saturnilus, another follower of Simon, taught that there was 'one Father unknown to all who made angels, archangels, powers and authorities. The world and everything in it came into being from seven angels' (*Against Heresies* I.24.1) (note that there were seven creating angels). Cerinthus, according to Irenaeus, was a contemporary of the apostles, since John, seeing him in the bath house in Ephesus, refused to go in (*Against Heresies* III.3.4). He taught 'that the world was not made by the first God, but by a power which was widely separated and remote from that supreme power which is above all and did not know the God who is over all things' (*Against Heresies* I.26.1). Cerinthus taught that the second God was the creator, and that he did not know of the supreme God. Those whom Irenaeus called the Ophites said that Jesus came to proclaim the unknown Father (*Against Heresies* I.30.13). The Valentinians, according to Clement, expounded the prologue of the Fourth Gospel so as to teach that the Father was unknown, but desired to become known (*Excerpts* 6.1 and 7.1). *The Letter of Eugnostos* says 'The Lord of the universe is not rightly called Father but First Father' (*Letter of Eugnostos* CG.III.3.74), an important distinction since the second deity was also called 'Father' (*Against Heresies* I.17.1). Consistency such as this across so wide a spectrum in relatively early texts does suggest a common source: Elyon and his sons.

All the systems gave a prominent place to the second God, the one manifested in human form. Eugnostos described the second deity thus:

Before the universe the First was revealed. In the boundlessness he is a self-grown, self-constructed father who is full of shining, ineffable light. In the beginning he decided to have his form come to be as a great power. Immediately the beginning of that light was revealed as an immortal androgynous man. His male name is 'the [Begetting of the] Perfect One'. And his female name is 'All-wise Begettress Sophia'. It is also said that she resembles her brother and her consort ... Now from that man originated divinity and kingdom. Therefore he is called 'God of Gods', 'King of Kings'. (*Letter of Eugnostos* CG.III.3.76–7)

Note that the second deity has male and female aspects. Below this divinity were two further stages: the androgynous Image of the unbegotten First Father had an androgynous son, named Son of Man, and he in turn had a son named Saviour. All the lower deities had a consort named Sophia, often identified with Eve, and the second deity was also named Adam of the Light, thus linking this mythology to the Garden of Eden. Saviour and Sophia revealed six further androgynous heavenly beings who in their turn revealed in total three hundred and sixty powers. These various lesser powers, together with other even smaller ones, related to the passage of time; the second great deity was Time, and beneath him came the years, the months, the days, and so forth. This, again without any names, resembles the calendar system of 1 Enoch, where angels were in charge of the various portions of the year. It also affords a glimpse of how the various deities were believed to relate to each other; just as numerous days were a week, so numerous powers were a deity, the smaller being a separately comprehensible part of the greater. The angelic beings were the heavenly ones manifested in time and the material world, literally. The High God, whose title is usually translated 'The Ancient of Days', is rendered, in one modern translation, 'The Antecedent of Time'.[6] This expresses his role exactly. He was beyond all time and knowing. The imagery associated with these powers is drawn from the temple:

All the immortals ... have authority ... by the power of Immortal Man (another name for the second deity) and Sophia his consort ... The imperishables ... each provided for themselves great kingdoms in all the immortal heavens and their firmaments, thrones and temples corresponding to their greatness. Some indeed ... in dwelling places and in chariots, being in ineffable glory. And not being able to be sent into any nature, provided for themselves hosts of angels, myriads without number for retinue and glory, even ineffable virgin spirits of light. (*Letter of Eugnostos*, CG.III.3.80)

The Sophia of Jesus Christ, which is the Christianized version of this text, adds at this point that the Father of the Universe created *a curtain* between the immortals and those who came after them, an image drawn from the veil of the temple which separated heaven and earth. The first begetter was also named Yaldabaoth.

The Pleroma was the upper world, formerly represented by the holy of holies in the temple; the second deity was the one who came forth through the veil and was clothed in the material world which it represented. Thus the *Gospel of Truth* began by telling of the power of the Word that came forth from the Pleroma as the Saviour. Theodotus said (*Excerpt* 43) that the Saviour sent forth was 'the angel of Great Counsel' (the angel named in the LXX version of the messianic prophecy in Isa.9.6). He also said that the one who brought redemption was an angel of the pleroma who went forth beyond Horos (*Excerpt* 35). Horos here was the veil which separated the lower from the upper world. Redemption enabled the gnostic to pass through Horos and enter the Pleroma as his true angel self (*Excerpt* 22). Menander claimed to be this Saviour: 'he himself is the person who has been sent forth from the presence of the invisible beings as a saviour' (*Against Heresies* I.23.5). Several of the ancient roles of Yahweh can be seen in this figure.

The ancient Yahweh in the setting of his heavenly temple can also be detected in the *Untitled Apocalypse* in the Codex Brucianus,[7] which could be a second-century text. It distinguishes between the Primal Father and the second divinity who was called the Demiurge, Father, Logos and Man (chapter ix). The holy Pleroma is described as the heavenly city centred on the holy of holies (chapter xv). Each of its four gates has a Guardian who looks both inwards and outwards, and is also called the Servant. This fourfold Guardian is interesting since he seems to correspond to the Valentinians' Aeon of double nature named 'Christ and the Holy Spirit'. He stands at the boundary and is clearly derived from the four archangels who between them manifested aspects of the presence of Yahweh. Irenaeus also mentioned this fourfold aspect of the second divinity when he said that the cherubim had four appearances which figured the mode of operating of the Son of God (*Against Heresies* III.11.11). Later in the *Untitled Apocalypse* we read of the Only Begotten standing upon the altar (chapter xvii), which is reminiscent of the appearances of the Lord or the Angel of the

Lord in the temple standing on the bronze altar (e.g. Amos 1.1 'I saw the Lord standing upon the altar'). The Only Begotten is hidden within the Setheus, this text's name for the God who is King and Creator, who lives in the innermost part of the temple. The Only Begotten is surrounded by Powers which he wears like a crown and which transport him in a chariot (chapter xxiv). The Mother of the Universe gave her Firstborn a garment in which were all the elements and aspects of the creation and he then created the world before returning to the realm of the two Father Gods and the Mother. As with all the gnostic texts, the question we have to ask is: Why did they choose this particular set of images to describe their sundry bizarre systems if they had not derived ultimately from the ancient temple?

The *Pistis Sophia*,[8] a collection of texts some of which were probably written in the third century, has similar echoes. The texts describe a Highest Light World and below this the Middle Light World, then the Aeon World, the World of Mankind, and finally the Underworld. Among the many heavenly beings were Iao and Yew, both versions of the divine name, who inhabited the Middle Light World. A power of the Little Iao was was put into the body of John the Baptist (chapter 70). One named the Great Yew was the 'Great Guide of the Midst', the Middle Light World. One named simply Yew maintained the cosmic covenant: 'they were bound in all their bonds and in their places and in their seals, as Yew, the Overseer of the Light, had bound them at the beginning' (chapter 25). He was the Guardian or Overseer of the Light and came forth from the 'pure light of the first tree' (chapter 86), a reference to the presence of the Lord in the Tree of Life, the *Menorah*. There were two Books of Yew, given to Enoch in Eden. The Saviour, who is speaking at this point, says that *he* dictated them to Enoch from the Tree of Knowledge and the Tree of Life (chapter 99). Yew was an angel (chapter 50), but he was also described as the First Man (chapter 126). He had his own angels who acted as Guardians of the great dungeons (chapter 126). The angels of Yew brought souls to him for judgement: 'And when the ruler casteth out souls, straightway the angels of Yew, the First Man, who watch the dungeons of that region, hasten to snatch away those souls to lead them before Yew, the First Man, the Envoy of the First Commandment ... (and he) proveth them' (chapter 130). If the souls were worthy he then handed them over to the seven virgins of the light who eventually drew back the veil of the Treasury of the Light and allowed the souls to enter. The remotest ancestor of this piece must have been the Day

173

of Yahweh when Yahweh appeared in his temple as the Judge.

Saturnilus taught *explicitly* that the second God was the God of the Jews, one of the angels created by the unknown Father (*Against Heresies* I.24.2). Basilides taught that the angels of the last heaven, those who divided the earth between them, had as their chief the God of the Jews (*Against Heresies* I.24.3). The Ophites taught that the God of the Jews was this angel figure who was named *Yaldabaoth*. He had made a covenant with Abraham (*Against Heresies* I.30.10). Severus, an associate of Marcion, said that this Yaldabaoth was not only the son of the Good God, but was also the devil whose other name was Sabaoth (*Panarion* 45.1.4). The *Apocryphon of John* said he was an angel of three names: the other two were Saklas, the fool, and Samael, the blind one (Ap. John CG.II.1.11). He was the son of Sophia, and was the great archon who drew his power from his mother (Ap. John CG.II.1.10). Yaldabaoth ruled the seventh heaven, according to the Nicolaitans (*Panarion* 25.2.2), and was the firstborn of Barbelo, the female counterpart of the high God (*Panarion* 25.3.4). The *Hypostasis of the Archons* (HA) separated Yaldabaoth and Sabaoth, describing the latter as his son, but despite this variation, described the enthronement of Sabaoth in a familiar setting. He was enthroned on a huge chariot of cherubim, surrounded by ministering angels.

The name Yaldabaoth has exercised the ingenuity of scholars for a long time. Insofar as he was the God of Abraham, this archon must have been the equivalent of the Yahweh of the Old Testament. The earliest explanation of the name occurs in the *Untitled Work*, also known as *On the Origin of the World* (OOW): 'Then when Pistis Sophia saw him moving in the depth of the waters she said to him 'O youth pass over here' which is interpreted 'Yaldabaoth' (OOW CG.II.5.100). A sixteenth-century edition of the works of Irenaeus suggested that it should be read Jaldaboth, *born of the fathers*.[9] In the nineteenth century it became the fashion to derive the second part of the name from the word for chaos and 'son of Chaos' seemed set to survive the discovery of the Nag Hammadi texts. Scholem, however,[10] thought that the element *Yald* should be read as 'begetter' rather than 'born of' and the element *abaoth* as the common alternative form of Sabaoth. Yaldabaoth was thus the Father of Sabaoth. Black suggested that the name could have meant Son of Shame, in the manner of the older Hebrew writings which substituted *bošet* for abhorred names such as Baal (e.g. 2 Sam. 2.8). No conclusion has been reached or is possible but if we recall that we are actually looking for something which could have been one of the ancient titles of Yahweh it is perhaps worth considering the curious title given to him in 3 Enoch. Metatron, the exalted and transformed Enoch who has been installed as the greatest archangel, is given the name 'the little Yahweh' and also addressed as 'the youth', *na'ar*, exactly as in the Coptic text, albeit using another word for youth. Perhaps the explanation of the name given in the Coptic text should not be too lightly abandoned.

The second God was the creator, the archon who made the world (*Panarion* 26.1.9). This was a characteristic of western gnosticism.[11] Cerinthus had taught that the world was made not by the first God but by a power remote and separate from him (*Against Heresies* I.26.1). Irenaeus says that the Valentinians called him by many names. He was Metropator, one born only of his mother Achamoth (i.e. Wisdom); he was Apator, one who had no father; he was Demiurge, the Creator or Craftsman (cf. Prov. 8.30, where Wisdom is the Master Craftsman); and he was the Father. This latter was explained by saying that he was the Father of the animal substances, while as Demiurge he was craftsman of the material. He was king over them all. The whole creation was formed through the mother by the Demiurge, even though he was ignorant of his mother's role and thought himself to be independent and the sole creator (*Against Heresies* I.17.1). He created the seven heavens, above which he existed, an angel bearing the likeness of God (*Against Heresies* I.5.1–3). Clement gives a similar account of the Demiurge (*Excerpts* 47–8) but says also that the psychic Christ sits at the right hand of the Demiurge (*Excerpt* 62). All the prophets and the Law came from the Demiurge, according to Hippolytus, and the Demiurge was the power of the Most High which overshadowed Mary (Hippolytus, *Refutation* VI.35.1.3, although the text says that the Demiurge *was* the Most High). He was also the God of Abraham, Isaac and Jacob, the one who spoke to Moses at the burning bush (*Refutation*, VI.36.2). Again, there can be little doubt that this Archon was the Yahweh of the older cult.

The second God in his evil aspect sometimes had animal form as did all the archons. (This was a convention known also in the apocalypses, where the monstrous forms represented evil, animal forms the human, and human forms the divine). The *Hypostasis of the Archons* describes 'an arrogant beast resembling a lion. It was androgynous' (HA CG.II.4.94). It made seven offspring, also androgynous. The *Untitled Work* has a similar tradition; Pistis Sophia caused the existence of this great archon who was to rule over matter and its powers. It was lion-like, androgynous, and ignorant of the source of its power (OOW CG.II.5.100). A green jasper amulet has been found depicting this archon of many names; on the one side there is a lion-headed figure and the names Yaldabaoth and Aariel, and on the other the seven names Ia, Iao, Sabaoth, Adonai, Eloai, Oreos, Astapheos.[12] Equally significant for our purposes is the fact that the cherubim of Ezekiel's temple vision (probably a memory of the first temple where he had been a priest) were also of double aspect; they had the head of a man and the head of a lion (Ezek. 41.19).

The second God was also plural; as we have seen from *Eugnostos*, the deities were complex and contained many powers within themselves. Sometimes the second God was twofold, like the two chief powers of the Logos in Philo. Justin's *Baruch* (*Refutation* V.26ff.), for example, described three primal powers. The highest was 'The Good' (Elyon) who lived above everything in the kingdom of light, and then there were two others, Elohim and Eden, male and female, who produced a family of twenty-four angels. Sometimes the second God produced two sons, as in the *Apocryphon of John* where Eve bore two sons to the chief archon, Eloim and Yave, the one righteous and the other evil (Ap. John CG.II.1.24). Sometimes he was fourfold, as with the four light-givers of the Sethian systems, (to which we shall return later), and sometimes he was manifested in, or fathered, seven great powers of whom he was the chief. These were the six-plus-one of Philo's system, derived from the sevenfold *menorah*. These seven created the world. Closest to Philo's system must be the *Apocryphon of John* which describes the seven powers of Yaltabaoth over which he was lord: 'And he united the seven powers which were with him, *through his thought*. And when he spoke it happened. And he named each power ...' (CG II.1.12).

The *Megale Apophasis* is a work attributed to Simon, i.e. thought by Hippolytus to represent an early expression of gnostic thought. There is no proof of this, beyond the fact that Hippolytus himself believed it when he wrote in the early years of the third century, but whoever its author was, it gives a remarkable account of the creation which could have derived from the ancient temple symbolism. Beyond everything there was fire, but fire with two natures: one was unseen and one was manifest. There were *six powers* from this fire with whom there was *a seventh called the Logos* which 'stands, took his stand and will stand'. That Logos was the creative spirit of Gen. 1

which hovered over the waters: 'Now this seventh power is that which existed as a power within the infinite power and which came into being before all the ages ... the image of the infinite power ... an image of an incorruptible form which alone gives order to all things (*Refutation* VI.14.3–5). Yaldabaoth, according to Epiphanius's account of Ophite beliefs:

> begot seven sons who begot seven heavens. But Yaldabaoth closed off the area above him and hid it from view so that the seven sons he had emitted, who were lower down than he, would not know what was above him, but just him alone. And they say that he, Yaldabaoth, is the God of the Jews. But this is not so, heaven forbid!
>
> Then they say, since the heights had been closed off by Ialdabaoth's design, these seven sons he had begotten ... whether they were aeons, or gods or angels, they use various terms for them ... fashioned the man in the image of their father Yaldabaoth. (*Panarion* 37.3.6; 4.1)

Here we see the plural Elohim of Genesis 1 as the seven angels, Yahweh in his plurality, creating the man figure in his image. Like Philo, the Ophites regarded the different names and titles for the second God as indications of his different aspects or powers: 'He who was the first descendent of the mother is called Yaldabaoth; he, again, descended from him, is named Iao; he, from this one, is called Sabaoth; the fourth is named Adoneus; the fifth Eloeus; the sixth Oreus and the seventh and last of all Astanphaeus' (*Against Heresies* I. 30.5). All these names are recognizable: Iao is one of the variant forms of Yahweh; Adoneus is Adonai; Eloeus is God; Oreus is Light; and Astanphaeus is Crown (from the Hebrew *ha-tsaniph*, the royal/high-priestly turban). These seven are also give the more familiar names of the archangels and identified with the living creatures who surrounded the cherub throne. There is, as we have seen, a problem of numbers in the Hebrew texts; one tradition knew four archangels and four living creatures, another knew seven archangels. Here in the Ophite system there are also seven living creatures, the first four of which are familiar:

> ... the ineffable angel of the Demiurge ... is Michael the lion shaped ... the bull shaped one is Suriel ... the dragon shaped one is Raphael, the eagle shaped one is Gabriel ... the bear shaped one is Thauthaboth the sixth (Erathaoth) ... has the head of a dog ... one with the asses' shape is called Onoel or Thartharaoth ... (Origen, *Against Celsus* VI.30).

The living creatures of Ezekiel's vision had the face of a lion, an ox, a man and an eagle. John had seen the forms as separate beings, again

177

R Nov (stars)
— Water fire — Sun

as lion, ox, man and eagle; one called the *Lion* of Judah was worthy to open the sealed scroll (Rev. 5.5). The Barbelognostics had a different version of the seven archangels as the living creatures. When Sophia in her ignorance had borne the serpent-lion archon Yaldabaoth, he left his mother and went to a place of his own where he began the business of his own creation. He made many angels and powers among whom were those who ruled over the seven heavens:

> ... the first is Athoth, he has a sheep's face; the second is Eloaiou, he has a donkey's face; the third is Astaphaios, he has a [hyena's] face; the fourth is Iao, he has a [serpent's] face with seven heads; the fifth is Sabaoth, he has a dragon's face; the sixth is Adonin, he has a monkey's face; the seventh is Sabbede, he has a shining fire face. This is the sevenness of the week. But Yaltabaoth had a multitude of faces in addition to all of them, so that he could bring a face before all of them, according to his desire, being in the middle of the seraphs, he shared his fire with them; therefore he became lord over them ... (Ap. John CG.II.1.11)

The *Untitled Work* also describes these angel figures. There were seven androgynous beings each with two names, one masculine and one feminine: Yaldabaoth was also Pronoia Sambathas, Yao was Lordship, Sabaoth was divinity, Adonaios was kingship, Eloaios was envy, Oraios was riches, Astaphaios was Sophia:

> Now since the First Father Yaldabaoth had great authority, he created for each of his sons by means of the word, beautiful heavens as dwelling places and for each heaven great glories seven times more exquisite than any earthly glory thrones, and dwelling places and temples and chariots and spiritual virgins and their glories [looking] up to an invisible realm, each one having these within his heaven; [and also] armies of divine, lordly and angelic and archangelic powers, myriads without number, in order to serve. (OOW CG.II.5.102)

// to p. 17/

This heavenly world is just like that of the *Songs of the Sabbath Sacrifice. The Gospel of Truth* knew a similar system, but one which was significantly closer to the Old Testament tradition. There the second God was the first son of the High God, and the chief of his other sons. He was known as the Name: 'Since the Father is unengendered, he alone is the one who begot a Name for himself before he brought forth the aeons in order that the Name of the Father should be over their head as lord' (*Gospel of Truth*, CG.I.3.38). In some accounts, it was the seven angels who made the world. This was probably only another way of saying that the chief Archon made the world, since the angels seem to have functioned as did Philo's powers;

they were aspects of the greater power. Menander taught that the world was made by angels (*Against Heresies*, I.23.5), Saturnilus that 'the world and all things therein were made by a certain company of seven angels' (*Against Heresies* I.24.1). Carpocrates taught that the world was created by angels greatly inferior to the unbegotten Father (*Against Heresies* I.25.1).

The Creator Archon is invariably described as arrogant and ignorant. What is criticized throughout is this archon's claim to be *the only God*. Segal has suggested that the earliest evidence for this is the reports in Irenaeus and Hippolytus, who testified to 'transvaluing Judaism to create an evil demiurge in contrast to the saving grace of the gnostic redeemer'.[13] Bearing in mind what Philo had said about some people confusing the second God with God himself, it would seem that here again the tradition could be much older than the second century AD, and that the gnostics were in touch with something ancient. Philo does not say more than that the manifestation of God was foolishly taken for God himself, but it would be only a short step from this to saying that a second God who claimed to be the highest was arrogant. In the old mythology, it was exactly such a claim which had led to the proud angels being thrown from heaven, and this, surely, is a more likely source for the idea of the arrogant angel who was thrown down than any second-century transvaluing. What is most interesting is that the claims for which the arrogant archon was condemned were those very statements in the Second Isaiah which we have already seen were central to that prophet's declaration of monotheism:

I am the first and I am the last;
besides me there is no God. (Isa. 44.6)

and

I am Yahweh and there is no other,
besides me there is no God. (Isa. 45.5)

In other words, we can probably see underlying these later gnostic texts the reaction of the excluded devotees of the pre-exilic cult. Segal has suggested that since the gnostics focused on the first chapters of Genesis rather than on Deuteronomy or the Second Isaiah, they are more likely to have taken these texts from the rabbis' polemic than from the original works. This may be so, but it shows nevertheless that the gnostics were establishing their case within a Jewish context and arguing for a second God within that tradition:

Yaldabaoth ... is impious in his madness which is in him. For he said 'I am God and there is no other God beside me,' for he is ignorant of his strength and the place from which he had come.

And when he saw the creation which surrounds him and the multitude of the angels around him which had come forth from him, he said to them, 'I am a jealous God and there is no other God beside me.' But by announcing this he indicated to the angels who attended to him that there exists another God, for if there was no other one of whom would he be jealous? (*Ap. John* CG.II.1.11 and 13)

Their chief is blind; [because of his] Power and his ignorance [and his] arrogance he said with his [Power], 'It is I who am God; there is none [apart from me]. (HA CG.II.4.86)

When the androgynous lion-like archon was first formed, he became arrogant, saying, 'It is I who am God and there is none other apart from me' (HA CG.II.4.94). There are similar texts in OOW (CG.II. 5.103) and *The Second Apocalypse of James* (CG.V.4.56) The Second Treatise of the Great Seth is equally bitter: 'For the Archon is a laughing stock because he said, 'I am God and there is none greater than I. I alone am the Father and the Lord and there is no other beside me' (II Seth CG.VII.2.64). The *Trimorphic Protennoia* expresses the same theme differently: 'And the Powers all gathered and went up to the Archigenitor. [They said to] him, "Where is your boasting in which [you boast]? Did we not [hear you say], I am God [and I am] your Father and it is I who [begot] you and there is no other beside me?"' (*Trimorphic Protennoia* CG.XIII.1.43). The Great Archon created the chaotic material world. One wonders how old this idea might be since the Second Isaiah wrote:

> For thus says Yahweh
> who created the heavens
> (he is God!),
> who formed the earth and made it
> (he established it;
> he did not create it a chaos,
> he formed it to be inhabited!):
> I am Yahweh and there is no other.
> I did not speak in secret,
> in a land of darkness;
> I did not say to the offspring of Jacob,
> 'Seek me in chaos.' (Isa. 45.18–19)

Did these lines contradict an ancient belief about the role of Israel's God?

These bitter attacks upon the God of the Jews must have arisen as the result of a quarrel within the family. The arguments are based on the themes and even the words of the Old Testament, and yet they take issue with what we have come to read as its fundamental belief, monotheism. These must have been the sentiments of those who were Hebrews but not Jews.

There are also indications that the gnostic writers knew Jewish traditions which do not appear in our Old Testament. (The Old Testament as such would not have existed at the time when these gnostic texts were written, and so a distinction between knowledge of canonical and non-canonical is not appropriate.) Of particular interest are the Sethians, a group whose teachings were described by Irenaeus as 'a many headed beast generated from the school of Valentinus' (*Against Heresies* I.30.15). Modern scholars, on the other hand, are tending to see the Sethians as older than the Valentinians; in fact Sethianism 'has replaced "Ophitism" as a provisional generic term for some of the central and perhaps the earliest trends of gnostic mythology'.[14] Irenaeus says that Valentinus was himself an innovator 'who adapted the principles of the heresy called gnostic to the peculiar character of his own school' (*Against Heresies* I.11.1) and it is this earlier heresy which we may now be rediscovering from the 'Sethian' writings. If the Sethians *were* closer to the earliest Gnosis, their links with Jewish tradition become very significant indeed. Since we are only trying to establish the extent of traditions about the second God, it is not necessary to explore the teachings of the sect in detail but only to note those features which suggest that it had its roots in the temple traditions and remembered Yahweh as the second God.

First, the Sethians belonged to that group of gnostics whose system was based on three principles; Hippolytus described one group, the Peratae, thus: 'According to them the universe is Father, Son and matter; each one of these has innumerable powers within himself. Midway between matter and the Father there sits his Son, the Word, the serpent who is always moving towards the immovable Father and towards the movable matter.' The similarity to Philo's high priestly Logos figure is obvious, the one who moves between heaven and earth. Note too the serpent as the symbol of the second deity, another indication of the ambiguity of the Yahweh/Asael figure. The account continues:

And at one time he turns towards the Father and receives the powers in his own person and when he has received the powers he turns himself towards matter and the matter which is without quality or configuration is imprinted with the form from the Son which the Son printed off from the Father. (*Refutation* V.17.2–3)

This is the Son/Logos as the agent of the creation.

Another characteristic of the Sethian system was the four Light-Givers, four heavenly beings who were aspects of the second God, the Self-Begotten One. The texts which deal with these angels are not well preserved, but they seem to be the gnostic expression of the idea of the four archangels, the four living creatures who surrounded the cherub throne. These four, it will be recalled, were aspects of God rather than separate beings, just as the seven powers of Ialdabaoth were a part of him. Ezekiel had described them as part of the fire which *was* the presence of the Lord (Ezek. 1.5–14):

The Self Begotten God is the chief archon of his aeons and of messengers as his parts; for those who are four in him individually create the fifth aeon at one time. The fifth aeon exists in one. It is the four who [are] the fifth, part by part ... (*Zostrianos* CG.VIII.1.19)
As for the self begotten God, he stands within an aeon. There are within him four different self begotten aeons ... (*Zostrianos* CG.VIII.1.27)

Each of these aeons had a cluster of three names, a common feature for angels, but their main names were Harmozel, Oroiael, Davithe and Eleleth. The Melchizedek text describes Jesus Christ as the commander in chief of these four luminaries (Melch. CG.IX.1.6). Another text says he was also their source: 'Then the perfect Son revealed himself to his aeons who originated through him and he revealed them and glorified them and enthroned them ... (the four are then named) ... and these aeons received as well as gave glory' (TriPro CG.XIII.1.38, 39).

One of the four Light-Givers is described in detail. He rescues Norea, daughter of Eve, from the Rulers of Unrighteousness, the fallen angels who had attempted to rape her. He describes himself as Eleleth, the Great Angel who stands in the presence of the Holy Spirit; Norea is speechless:

Now as for that angel, I cannot speak of his power; his appearance is like fine gold and his raiment like snow. No truly my mouth cannot speak of his power and the appearance of his face ...
'It is I', he said, 'who am understanding. I am one of the four Light Givers, who stand in the presence of the Great Invisible Spirit. (HA CG.II.4.93)

This description of the Great Angel is familiar.

The Great Angel then reveals to Norea the secrets of the creation; they are also familiar. The setting for his account of the creation is the ancient temple, with the veil dividing the presence of God from the material world: 'A veil exists between the world above and the realms that are below; and Shadow came into being beneath that veil; and that Shadow became Matter; and that Shadow was projected apart' (HA CG.II.4.94). The arrogant lion archon was formed from the shadow and he, thinking that there was no other God, then proceeded to create a realm for himself. Yaldabaoth, the arrogant archon, has here become the fallen angel, for he was then bound and cast into the pit. His son Sabaoth recognized the power of Sophia and was reinstated as a ruler. He was placed in the seventh heaven, just below the veil: 'Now when these events had come to pass, he made himself a huge four-faced chariot of cherubim and infinitely many angels to act as ministers and also harps and lyres' (HA CG.II.4.95). The origin of the material is clear; what is not clear is how it came to be used in this way. This particular text has a curiously ambivalent attitude towards the archon Yaldabaoth; he himself is condemned but his son is reinstated and thus the text comes back to the traditional line with Sabaoth enthroned.

The origin of evil is described in terms of the myths of the fallen angels, and just as there are several versions of that myth in Jewish texts, so there are several versions of it in the gnostic writings. The Enochic version describes the rape of earthly women by the fallen angels; in HA CG.II.4.89 the powers planned to rape Eve, but in the end the demiurge and his powers tried to rape Norea her daughter. She was rescued by Eleleth the light-bringer. This doubtless corresponds to the sending of the four archangels to fight against the fallen ones (1 Enoch 9–10; Ap. Mos. 10.1–2). In the *Apocryphon of John* the chief archon and his powers seduce Sophia and produce all the evils of creation:

He made a plan with his authorities, which are his powers, and they committed together adultery with Sophia, and bitter Fate was begotten through them, which is the last of the terrible bonds ... For from that fate came forth every sin and injustice and blasphemy and the chain of forgetfulness and ignorance ... and thus the whole creation was made blind, in order that they may not know the God who is above them. (Ap. John CG.II.1.28)

This is then followed by an account of the events of Gen. 6 and 1 Enoch 6 showing that the one was the cosmic counterpart of the

183

other. The chief archon has the role of Asael, the leader of the fallen angels, just as he does elsewhere. In the Testament of Reuben there is a different version of the myth; there, the women 'allured the Watcher such that they changed their shape and became men for them' (Test. Reuben 5.6). This version appears in Epiphanius's account of the Nicolaitans; they described the mother of Yaldabaoth as one who seduced the archons (*Panarion* 25.2.4); the followers of Simon also said that the female power Barbelo had seduced the creator archons and had come to earth for that purpose (*Panarion* 21.2, 4). The result was violence on earth as the archons vied for her favours. The details of all these myths need not concern us; what is important is that none of this came simply from a gnostic exegesis of the early chapters of Genesis. These bizarre tales all stem from extra-biblical traditions, suggesting that the roots of gnosticism lie deep with those who kept the older mythology of the angels. The fall of Eve is not the result of disobedience, as in the biblical account, but as the result of being seduced by the evil archon, the serpent: 'And the chief archon seduced her and begot in her two sons ... Eloim and Yave. Eloim has a bear face and Yave has a cat face. The one is righteous the other is unrighteous .... And these he called with the names Cain and Abel in order to deceive' (Ap. John CG.II.1.24). Targum *Pseudo-Jonathan* also knew that Eve had conceived Cain from Samael, the angel of the Lord. The pure seed on earth were to be the descendents of Seth, the next son, and it is with this pure line that the Sethian gnostics identified themselves. This claim must have been known in New Testament times; Jesus alluded to this belief that the sons of Cain were demonic when he condemned the Jews: 'You are of your father the devil and your will is to do your father's desires. He was a murderer from the beginning and has nothing to do with the truth' (John 8.44). It was probably known a good deal earlier, since the sons of Seth, those who claimed to be the purer seed, were condemned in the oracles of Balaam. The Messiah would crush Moab and the sons of Seth (Num. 24.17), perhaps another indication that the Pentateuch was written in opposition to certain views.

The most striking evidence for gnostic roots in the ancient temple traditions is their detailed knowledge of the role of Sophia/Wisdom. Throughout the texts she appears either as the consort or the counterpart or the mother of the second deity, the great archon. She is clearly identical with the Wisdom figure of the biblical and non-canonical texts, and yet her role cannot be deduced entirely from them. The gnostic Sophia is all that remains of Israel's goddess. Christians knew that Christ was the power of God, i.e. the Angel, and also the Wisdom of God (1 Cor. 1.24); he was the incarnation of both aspects, but the female element had been purged from Israel's cult and from our reading of the Old Testament by the reformers of the seventh century BC. The most enigmatic of Enoch's histories of Israel says that wisdom was forsaken just before the destruction of the first temple by those who had become blinded (1 Enoch 93.8), and the refugees described by Jeremiah vowed that they would resume the worship of the queen of heaven since neglect of her had caused the disaster (Jer. 44.17–19). To say that Wisdom was 'personified' in later texts is to prejudge the issue, especially when there are inscriptions from the eighth century BC showing a consort for Yahweh.

Wisdom was one of the angels (1 Enoch 42.2), cf. 'Astaphaios's feminine name is Sophia. These are ... the powers of the seven heavens' (OOW CG.II.5.106); 'And the light Eleleth, which he set over the fourth aeon, has three aeons within it which are Perfection, Peace and Sophia' (Ap. John CG.II.1.8); Wisdom was the female counterpart of the great archon: 'His male name is the [Begetting of the] Perfect One. And his female name [is] All-wise Begettress Sophia. It is also said that she resembles her brother and her consort ...' (*Letter of Eugnostos*, CG.III.3.76); Wisdom was an emanation from God (Wisd. 7.25–6), cf. '... from the first angel who stands by the side of the Only Begotten, the Holy Spirit has been sent forth whom they term Sophia' (*Against Heresies* I.29.4).

As the Holy Spirit, Wisdom was the agent of creation (Prov. 3.19; 8.27–30; Wisd. 7.7, 22, 23) and the tradition in the Targums interpreted Gen 1.1 as 'By Wisdom God created ...', cf. 'Sophia Zoe sent her breath into Adam who was without a soul ...' (OOW CG.II.5.102), 'Sophia who is called Pistis, wanted to create something, alone without her consort ...' (HA CG.II.4.94). She was the 'master workman' (Prov. 8.30), cf.

For (the Demiurge) was foolish and without understanding, and believed that he himself was creating the world, unaware that Sophia ... was accomplishing everything for the creation of the world without his knowledge ... (*Refutation* VI.34.7)

The heaven has been consolidated along with the earth by means of the Sophia of Yaldabaoth. (OOW CG.II.5.103)

She was the consort: 'and his (the second deity's) consort was the great Sophia' (*Sophia of Jesus Christ* CG.III.4.101). She shared the divine throne, living in the clouds (Wisd. 9.4; Sir. 24.4; 1 Enoch 84.3): 'But he (Sabaoth, ruling in the seventh heaven on his chariot throne) sits on a throne concealed by a great light cloud. And there was none with him in the cloud except Pistis Sophia' (OOW CG.II.5.106). She descended into the world in order to give knowledge and revelation and then reascended (Wisd. 9.11; 1 Enoch 42.2), cf.

They [Adam and Eve] discovered foods under the guidance of Sophia (*Against Heresies* I.30.9)
Sophia herself also uttered many things through (the prophets) concerning the First Man, the imperishable Aeon ... (*Against Heresies* I.30.11)
... the power ... fell downward from the place occupied by its progenitors ... and they call it Sinistra, Prunicus and Sophia as well as masculo-feminine. This being in its simplicity, descended into the waters while they were yet in a state of immobility and imported motion to them also ... (*Against Heresies* I.30.3)

She was the guide and guardian of Israel's history, forming Adam and protecting the patriarchs (Wisd. 10.1–21), cf. 'So Sophia first brought forth a spiritual seed in Adam' (*Excerpt* 53); 'But in this also Sophia opposed (Yaldabaoth) and those who were with Noah in the ark were saved' (*Against Heresies* I.30.10). She was identified with Life (Prov. 8.35), cf. '... our sister Sophia ... was called life which is the mother of all living' (Ap. John CG.II.1.23) and thus also with Eve, (who is Zoe in the LXX): 'Sophia Zoe who is beside Sabaoth' (OOW CG.II.5.113). She was a tree in Paradise (1 Enoch 32.3–6; Prov. 3.18); cf. Sophia, pursued by the evil archons, 'laughed at them for their witlessness and their blindness and in their clutches she became a tree' (HA CG.II.4.89); 'But what they call the tree of the knowledge of good and evil, which is the Epinoia of light ...' (Ap. John CG.II.1.22). There were hints in the Old Testament, as we have seen, that Wisdom was the mother of the manifested one, and this too appeared in some gnostic texts where Yaldabaoth was the son of Sophia.

The myth of Eden had originally described the holy mountain and the judgement of the proud heavenly beings, but the historicization of Israel's religion, along with its new emphasis on personal responsibility for sin and the centrality of the Mosaic law, led to this myth being incorporated into the *history* of Israel. It described the disobedience of human beings, rather than the cosmic disaster of disobedience in heaven. The gnostic texts suggest that there had been some within Israel who applied the ancient myth of the judgement on the arrogant heavenly beings to the angel of Israel; the claims to rule alone were on a par with those of the star angel of Babylon who had been thrown down and of the angel king of Tyre. If the angel of Israel had had a double aspect, then Wisdom too would have fallen from heaven. Several of the motifs from this older myth come through into the gnostic texts. Hippolytus's description of the teachings of Valentinus shows that Sophia tried to create on her own, like the Unbegotten Father; in other words, to be like God:

[When Sophia] perceived that all the other aeons, being begotten, were procreating in pairs, but that the Father alone was procreating without a partner, she wished to emulate the Father and to produce offspring of herself alone, without a partner, *in order that she might achieve a work which would not be in any way inferior to that of the Father*. She did not know that he, being uncreated ... is capable of procreating alone but that Sophia, being begotten and born after many others, cannot have the power of the unbegotten one. (*Refutation* VI.30.6)
Sophia who is called Pistis wanted to create something alone, without her consort ... (HA CG.II.4.94)

The result was an unformed chaos.

She had wanted to comprehend the Father and this passion was her undoing: 'This passion, they say, consisted in a desire to search into the nature of the Father, for she wished, according to them, to comprehend his greatness. When she could not attain her end, insomuch as she aimed at an impossibility' (*Against Heresies* I.2.2). The disasters of a misformed creation were the result. This must have been the female version of the arrogant archon myth; here it was Sophia who wanted to create on her own and wanted to be like God. This was echoed in the Genesis account where it was Eve who was tempted by the serpent to be like God, knowing good and evil. The result was a world of pain, thorns and thistles. Wisdom which came to earth without the blessing of the Most High corrupted the creation, according to 1 Enoch, although this version of the myth already knew wisdom as a body of teaching rather than as a heavenly being. It was probably related to the tradition that Sophia was the mother of the rebel archons. The separation of Yahweh and his female consort by the seventh-century reformers of Israel's cult was probably recorded in the tradition that the archon became arrogant and claimed to be the only God when he lost sight of the power of his mother and did not realize that she existed. He claimed the powers of creation for himself alone:

historic mythogem

187

Water of Life

Now when Pistis Sophia desired [to cause] the one who had no spirit to receive the pattern of a likeness and rule over the matter ... a ruler appeared out of the waters, lion-like in appearance, androgynous ... but not knowing whence he came into being ... When the ruler saw his greatness ... then he thought that he alone existed ... (OOW CG.II.4.100)

Sophia was reinstated in the gnostic mythology; she was helped back to the upper world, grieving at the dire state of her offspring: 'When these were generated, the mother Sophia deeply grieved, fled away, departed into the upper regions and became the last of the Ogdoad ... On her thus departing, he [the arrogant archon] imagined he was the only being in existence' (*Against Heresies* I.29.4). This is exactly the tradition of 1 Enoch 42, where Wisdom returns in despair to the heavens and takes her place among the angels. Enoch had also prophesied that there would be an evil generation of sinners who would find no place for Wisdom (1 Enoch 94.50), but that Wisdom would be given back to the elect at the end of time when they awoke from their sleep (1 Enoch 91.10). Here, surely, is a root of the gnostic myth: the gift of Wisdom and resurrection are closely linked. The possession of knowledge was the key to eternal life.

Hebrew

The gnostic texts, for all their opacity at certain points, show that their system originated in the temple cult. There had been several influences on it over the centuries in which it developed and the texts cited in this chapter will have been influenced by the culture of hellenized Egypt. Fragments of many philosophies can be seen; we even recognize some of the ancient gods of Egypt. But underlying all (and this is the important point, *underlying all*) is the world of the ancient temple. Aspects of that cult which we no longer fully understand, e.g. the conflicting traditions about the archangels (four or seven), are both represented in the gnostic systems. Aspects which we can only deduce by measuring gaps and watching shadows (e.g. the female aspect of the second God) are represented in complex but consistent form in the gnostic texts. Perhaps gnosticism is what happened to the religion of those who fled to Egypt after the fall of Jerusalem? They would have known only the pre-exilic cult of the temple and taken this, or rather, its mythology, into their new way of life. Philo, the leading Jewish thinker of his community, certainly suggests that it was a development of the old angel cult that he was adapting for his Greek readers. The gnostic texts, perhaps, are that same Judaism adapted with other considerations in mind.

Both Philo and the Gnostics testify to the belief in the second God, the creator, the Logos, the Man. The Gnostics show that both far God and near God were known as Father (which will doubtless have led to confusion in exactly the same way as modern scholars' failure to distinguish between the sons of Elyon and the sons of Yahweh has obscured some vital points). The crucial information which the gnostic texts afford is that they identify the second God with the God of the Jews in a way that Philo does not; sometimes he is named with a version of the divine name and *sometimes he is identified with Jesus.*

Notes to chapter nine

1 G.A.G. Stroumsa, *Another Seed: Studies in Gnostic Mythology*, London 1984, p.19.

2 B.A. Pearson, 'Jewish Elements in Gnosticism and the Development of Gnostic Self-Definition', in E.P. Sanders, ed., *Jewish and Christian Self Definition I: The Shaping of Christianity in the Second and Third Centuries*, London 1980, p.151 and notes.

3 G. Quispel, 'Judaism, Judaic Christianity and Gnosis', in A.H.B. Logan and A.J.M. Wedderburn, eds, *The New Testament and Gnosis. Essays in Honour of G.McL. Wilson*, Edinburgh 1983, p.59.

4 Stroumsa, op.cit., p.9.

5 See above chapter 3, p.45.

6 In the translation of E. Isaac, in *The Old Testament Pseudepigrapha*, vol.1, ed. J.H. Charlesworth, New York and London 1983.

7 C.A. Baynes, *A Coptic Gnostic Treatise from the Codex Brucianus*, Cambridge 1933.

8 Tr. G.R.S. Mead, London 1921.

9 M. Black, 'An Aramaic Etymology for Jaldabaoth?' in Logan, op.cit., n.3.

10 G.G. Scholem, *Jewish Gnosticism, Merkabah Mysticism and Talmudic Tradition*, New York 1960, p.143.

11 W. Foerster, *Gnosis*, vol.I, Oxford 1972, p.11.

12 See C. Bonner, *Studies in Magical Amulets, chiefly Graeco Egyptian*, Michigan 1950, pp.135–8.

13 A.F. Segal, *Two Powers in Heaven*, Leiden 1978, p.256.

14 Stroumsa, op.cit., p.5.

Chapter ten The Evidence of the First Christians

Several writers of the first three Christian centuries show by their descriptions of the First and Second persons of the Trinity whence they derived these beliefs. El Elyon had become for them God the Father and Yahweh, the Holy One of Israel, the Son, had been identified with Jesus. In order to demonstrate this I shall look at four aspects: (i) evidence for the survival of belief in Elyon and his sons; (ii) the interpretation of the Old Testament which recognized in the appearances of Yahweh or the angel of Yahweh a manifestation of the pre-incarnate Christ; (iii) the widespread belief that Jesus had been a high angelic figure and survivals in Christian texts of angel symbolism from the temple cult; and (iv) the use of the term *the Name*.

The clearest texts developing the ideas of Deut. 32.8 are found in the pseudo-Clementine writings where Simon Magus debates with Simon Peter the nature of the faith, and it is significant that the interpretation of the sons of God text is crucial to both their understandings of the role of Christ. The point of difference between them is the old one: is Yahweh identical with the High God or is he not? Simon Magus kept to the view that Yahweh was one of the sons of God, their chief, but distinct from God Most High. Peter's position is not so clear; he asserts that the God of the Jews is called the God of gods, implying that there is none higher, but later adds that *the God of gods is Christ.* In other words, although the two differ as to the exact status of the God of the Jews in the heavenly hierarchy, both agree that the God of the Jews is Christ. In the *Recognitions* Simon Magus argues on the basis of the Jewish Scriptures that there are many called gods:

There are also many other testimonies which might be adduced from the law, not only obscure but plain, by which it is taught that there are many gods. One of these was chosen by lot, that he might be the God of the Jews. But it is not of him that I speak, but of the God who is also his God, whom even the Jews themselves did not know. For he is not their God, but the God of those who know him. (*Recognitions* II.39)

Peter implies that the God of the Jews is the God of gods, the only God, creator of heaven and earth, and goes on to explain that the name God has several meanings. Here his point resembles that of Philo who emphasized the difference between the supreme God, described as THE God and the angelic intermediaries who were called simply God (see chapter 7, n.7):

For every nation has an angel to whom God has committed the government of that nation; and when one of these appears, although he be thought and called God by those over whom he presides, yet being asked he does not give such testimony to himself. For the Most High God, who alone holds the power of all things, has divided the nations of the earth into seventy two parts and over these he hath appointed angels as princes. But to the one among the archangels who is greatest, was committed the government of those who, before all others, received the worship and knowledge of the Most High. (*Recognitions* II.42)

Thus, says Peter, the princes of the various nations, by which he means the angelic princes such as appear in Daniel, are called gods and Christ is the God of these princes.

Simon Magus takes up the same point in the *Homilies* and shows that the God of gods, although the ruler of the other gods, is, nevertheless, not Elyon but the chief of his sons, the one known as Yahweh. Starting from Matt. 11.27, 'no one knows the Son except the Father, and no one knows the Father except the Son and any one to whom the Son chooses to reveal him', he says:

He would not have made this statement had he not proclaimed a Father who was still unrevealed, whom the law speaks of as *the Highest* ... who also limiting the nations to seventy languages according to the number of the sons of Israel who entered Egypt, and according to the boundaries of these nations, gave to his own Son, who is called Lord, and who brought into order the heaven and the earth, the Hebrews as his portion, and defined him to be God of gods ...

Accordingly at this moment you yourself, in assigning the special attributes of the unrevealed Most High to the Son, do not know that he is the Son, being the Father of Jesus, who with you is called the Christ. (Hom. XVIII.4)

This resembles the gnostic practice known elsewhere of naming both the first and second Gods as Father, the Son being the Father of the one in whom he made himself known, and likewise the first God being the Father of the Son in whom he made himself known. Origen in the middle of the third century had testified to a confusion between God Most High and the Son on the part of some people:

... there may be some individuals among the multitudes of believers who are not in entire agreement with us, and who incautiously assert that the Saviour is the Most High God; however, we do not hold with them, but rather believe him when he says, 'The Father who sent me is greater than I.' (*Against Celsus* VIII.14)

Even pagans, he said, had recognized the distinction:

But even in regard to those who, either from deficiency of knowledge or want of inclination or from not having Jesus to lead them to a rational view of religion, have not gone into these deep questions, the Most High God and in His only-begotten S (*Against Celsus* VII.49)

Eusebius, writing about AD 320, shows in that the distinction between the two deities his time and that the second God was identi quoted Deut. 32.8 he says of it:

In these words surely he [Moses] names first Supreme God of the Universe, and then, as Lord, His Word, Whom we call Lord in the second degree after the God of the universe ...
... to One beyond comparison with (the angels), the Head and King of the Universe, I mean to Christ Himself, as being the Only Begotten Son, was handed over that part of humanity denominated Jacob and Israel ... (*Proof of the Gospel* IV.9)

Yahweh the God of Israel was the Son, the Christ. The Word of God, he says, called people to worship the Father, 'Who is Most High, far above all things that are seen, beyond the heaven and the whole begotten essence, calling them quietly and gently, and delivering them to the worship of God Most High alone, the Unbegotten and the Creator of the Universe' (*Proof of the Gospel*, IV.9). *In the older disputes about the nature of Yahweh, whether he was identical with the High God or one of his sons, can be found the seeds of later trinitarian controversies.* There was no doubt that Jesus was identified with the God of the Jews. The problem was: Who was this God of the Jews and what was his place in the hierarchy?

The evidence that the first Christians identified Jesus with the God of the Jews is overwhelming; it was their customary way of reading the Old Testament. The appearances of Yahweh or the angel of Yahweh were read as manifestations of the pre-existent Christ. The Son of God was their name for Yahweh. This can be seen clearly in the writings of Paul who applied several 'Lord' texts to Jesus (see chapter 11). Now Paul, though completely at home in the Greek world, claimed to have been the strictest of Jews, educated in Jerusalem and zealous for the traditions of his people. How was it that he, of all people, could distinguish between God and Lord as he did in 1 Cor., if this was not already a part of first century Jewish belief? He emphasized that this distinction was fundamental to his belief: 'there is one God, the Father ... and one Lord, Jesus Christ' (1 Cor. 8.6). This is, to say the least, a remarkable contradiction of Deut. 6.4, *if he understood that verse in the way that we do, as a statement of monotheism.* If, on the other hand, it was a statement of the unity of Yahweh as the one inclusive summing up of all the heavenly powers, the *'elohim*, then it would have been compatible with belief in God Most High also.

The first writer of the sub-apostolic period whose works survive in any quantity is Justin. His *Dialogue with Trypho* is a set piece dispute with a Jew, written about the middle of the second century. Justin was himself a native of Palestine, having been born at Flavia Neapolis (the biblical Shechem). He became a Christian in adulthood in Ephesus and also lived in Rome. Thus he was well acquainted with Christian belief in the period immediately following the death of the first disciples, and his witness to the Church's use of the Old Testament is very important. For him, the appearance of Yahweh or the angel of Yahweh were *appearances of the pre-existent Christ and proof that there was a second God mentioned in the Scriptures.*

His first example is the appearance of the three men to Abraham at Mamre (Gen. 18):

Moses therefore, that blessed and faithful servant of God, declares, that he who was seen by Abraham at the oak of Mamre was God, accompanied by two angels who were sent, for the condemnation of Sodom, by Another, namely by Him Who always remains above the heavens Who has never been seen by any man and Who of Himself holds converse with none, whom we term the Creator of all things and the Father ... (*Trypho* 56)

Trypho, naturally, is not happy with this assertion, and so Justin continues to demonstrate from the Scriptures: 'That there both is, and that we read of, another God and Lord under the Creator of all things who is also termed an angel in that he bears messages to men, whatever the Creator, above Whom there is no other god, wills to be borne to them.' There are further instances in the Scriptures of the appearance of this second being called God. When Jacob wrestled with the angel (Gen. 32) he encountered God and named the place of his struggle Peniel, 'the Face of God'. The One whom he had seen at Bethel when he fled from Esau's anger was also the Lord, the Angel: '... when Jacob fled from his brother Esau, the same Angel and God

193

and Lord, appeared to him, Who also appeared to Abraham in the form of a man and afterwards wrestled with Jacob in the same form' (*Trypho* 58). This same Angel as 'God, Lord and *Man*' (*Trypho* 59: note *the Man*) appeared to Moses at the burning bush and was addressed by God at the creation when he said 'Let Us make man in our image' (*Trypho* 62). He was the warrior who met Joshua (Josh. 5.13–15), and was also the angel who went before Israel bearing the name of the Lord (Exod. 23.21). Justin believed that this angel was present in the person of Joshua himself, since he emphasised that the one who in fact led Israel into the promised land was named Jesus (the Greek form of Joshua).

Further, the Angel was the subject of the enthronement psalms. Passages such as:

> Yahweh reigns; let the peoples tremble.
> He sits above the cherubim, let the earth quake. (Ps. 99.1–2)

or

> Give the King thy justice, O God,
> and thy righteousness to the royal son. (Ps. 72.1)

referred to this Angel (*Trypho* 64). The disputed passage in Isa. 42.8, 'my Glory I give to no other', was not, said Justin, to be taken out of context. The passage as a whole showed that the glory was to be given to the servant of Yahweh, *and to no other*. In other words, one of the strongest of Trypho's arguments was shown to add weight to Justin's position provided that the text was read in its natural setting.

Justin returns to his arguments at the end of the *Dialogue with Trypho*. He feels that he has demonstrated that the Old Testament bears ample witness to the existence of the Angel God who acts as emissary for the unknown Father: 'If you had known ... who he is that is called at one time the Angel of Great Counsel, and a Man by Ezekiel, and like the Son of Man by Daniel and a little Child by Isaiah ... you would not have blasphemed Him who has already come' (*Trypho* 126). (Note the recognition that Angel of Great Counsel, Man and Son of Man are synonymous.) Justin then reiterates all the anthropomorphic passages of the Old Testament which the Magharians had also attributed to the presence of the Angel; how, he said, could the ineffable Father have come down to close Noah into the Ark (Gen. 7.16)? 'You should not suppose that the Unbegotten God Himself descended or went up from any place; for the Ineffable Father and

Lord of all things neither comes to any place, nor walks nor sleeps nor rises up ...' (*Trypho* 127). The Angel had been present on Sinai, had filled the tabernacle and the temple with his glory, had spoken from the burning bush and brought judgement upon Sodom:

... then neither Abraham nor Isaac nor Jacob nor any other man ever saw the Father and Ineffable Lord of all things whatever and of Christ Himself; but (they saw) Him who according to his will, is both God his Son and his angel from ministering to his will. (*Trypho* 127)

The next generation of writers continued to interpret the Scriptures in this way. Irenaeus of Lyons used the same arguments for the pre-existent Christ in his *Proof of the Apostolic Preaching*, but the memory of the distinction between God Most High and the Son had begun to blur. It was the Word who said to Moses at the burning bush 'I am He Who is', a clear indication that the God named with the sacred name was thought to be the Second, not the First person (*Proof* 2), and yet Irenaeus could also say that the God of Abraham, Isaac and Jacob was the Father, God Most High (*Proof* 8). It was the Son who had been the agent of the creation (*Proof* 43), and the Son who had appeared to Abraham at Mamre:

So Abraham was a prophet, and saw what was to come to pass in the future, the Son of God in human form, that he was to speak with men and eat food with them and then bring down judgement from the Father, having received from Him Who is Lord over all, power to punish the men of Sodom (*Proof* 44)

Similarly, it was the Son who appeared to Jacob at Bethel:

And all visions of this kind signify the Son of God in his speaking with men and his being with them. For it is not the Father of all, who is not seen by the world, the Creator of all, who said: *Heaven is my throne and the earth is my footstool; what manner of house will you build for me, or what is the place of my rest?* and *who holds the land in his fist and the heavens in his span* ... it is not He who would stand circumscribed in space and speak with Abraham, but the Word of God who is always with mankind ... (*Proof* 45)

It was the Word who spoke to Moses and led Israel out of Egypt.

Irenaeus was a self-proclaimed guardian of orthodoxy; he wrote against heretics and he ended his *Proof* with a solemn warning against the ways of those who were wandering away from the truth. *The truth, for him, must have been this way of reading the Old Testament.*

Approximately contemporary with Irenaeus, but on the other side of the Mediterranean world, was Clement of Alexandria, expounding his Old Testament in the same way, even though it was for a very different purpose. His treatise *The Instructor* owes a great deal to Philo. Like his predecessor in Alexandria, Clement transformed the ancient Angel of the Old Testament and presented him as the guide for all reasonable people. Philo's Logos became Clement's Instructor but with the added detail that this Instructor was known to have been Jesus: 'But our Instructor is the Holy God Jesus, the Word who is the guide of all humanity' (*The Instructor* I.7). This guide had already been manifested in the Old Testament: he had led his people out of Egypt, he had appeared to Abraham and guided him; he had protected Jacob; he had given the law of Moses; he had sent his angel to lead them into the promised land; and he would also be their judge: 'For the same who is Instructor is also Judge, and judges those who disobey him' (*The Instructor* I.7). Clement knew that his Instructor was the second God, the Son; '... our Instructor is like His Father God, whose Son he is, sinless, blameless and with a soul devoid of passion; God in the form of man, stainless, the minister of his Father's will, the Word who is God' (*The Instructor* I.2). Clement, like Philo nearly two centuries before him, took the ancient belief in the second God and adapted it for his own purposes, What is important to notice is that this belief in the second God, by this time clearly identified with Jesus for the purposes of Christian apologetic, was in no way an invention of the Christian community. The identification of the manifested God of the Old Testament with the Word, the second God, was the basis on which Clement could argue, and was not, as in Justin's case, a position he had to demonstrate.

Hippolytus, another contemporary who lived in Rome, wrote a commentary on Daniel. Expounding Dan. 10, he said that the man clothed in linen who revealed the future to Daniel was in fact Yahweh:

And the Father in truth heard me, and sent His own Word, to show what should happen by Him. And that took place by the great river. For it was meet that the Son should be manifested there, where also He was to remove sins. *And I lifted up mine eyes* he says, *and behold a man clothed in linen.* In the first vision he says, *Behold the Angel Gabriel was sent.* Here, however, it is not so; but he sees the Lord, not yet indeed as perfect man, but with the appearance and form of man ...

Commenting on the vision of Dan. 7, he explained that the Ancient of Days was 'the Lord and God and Ruler of all, and even of Christ himself' and that the son of man figure was the Son of God, the Lord of the angels.

Novatian, the first theologian of the Roman church, wrote an treatise on the Trinity in the middle of the third century and he read the Old Testament in the same way. In several texts he found reference to the second God. Thus of Hos. 1.7 'I will deliver them by Yahweh their God', he said that the speaker was God the Father, promising to send help by means of the Lord (*On the Trinity* XII). This second God, he said, was Christ, the agent of the creation, the one who appeared in all the theophanies. It was the second God who came down to Babel and appeared to Abraham, spoke to Hagar, destroyed Sodom and wrestled with Jacob:

We are led to understand that it was not the Father, Who never has been seen, that was here seen, but the Son, Who repeatedly descended to this earth and so was seen. For he is the image of the invisible God, being so in order that weak and frail human nature might in time become accustomed to see, in Him, Who is the Image of God, that is, in the Son of God, God the Father. (*On the Trinity* XVIII)

Novatian was careful to note that the second God had often been called an angel:

He who calls to Hagar out of heaven was God. And yet he is called 'Angel' ... The only intelligible explanation is that He is both angel and God. Such a description cannot be appropriate and suitable to the Father, who is God only; but it can be appropriately applied to Christ, Who has been declared to be not God only, but also angel. It is obvious, therefore, that it was not the Father Who spoke to Hagar in the present passage, but Christ; since he is not only God but One to Whom the title of angel is appropriate, by virtue of His being made 'the angel of great counsel' ... (*On the Trinity* XVIII)

The Angel of Great Counsel was one of the many ways in which the Christians referred to the second God. Theophilus of Antioch, at the end of the second century, explained to Autolycus that the theophanies in the Old Testament were not of the Father of All, but of his Logos who inspired Moses and all the prophets. For him, it was the Logos who was the Son of God (*To Autolycus* II.10.22).

Most remarkable of all is Eusebius, who shows how this reading of the Old Testament survived into the fourth century. In the *Preparation* and throughout the *Proof* he both assumes and argues systematically for the belief that the God of the Jews was the second God who appeared in human form and was finally manifested in Jesus. Commentaries on his work label his more explicit statements as Arian,[1] but they are in fact consistent with, and developed from, the ancient and unbroken tradition of reading the Old Testament in this way. The second God was the Great Angel, King, High Priest and Anointed One. Much of his language is close to that of Philo, but, since Philo did not originate the idea of the second God this similarity is not significant. In the *Preparation* he wrote of the Second Cause: 'the Hebrew oracles teach [him] to be the Word of God and God of God, even as we Christians also have ourselves been taught to speak of the Deity' (*Preparation* XI.14) and of the Beginning: 'the Image of God and Power of God and Wisdom of God and Word of God, nay further "the great captain of the host of the Lord" and "Angel of great Counsel"' (*Preparation* VII.15). Moses, he said, spoke of two Lords (two named Kyrios, both Yahweh in the Hebrew) in the account of the destruction of Sodom. David spoke of two Lords in Ps. 110.1, 'the Lord said to my Lord ...' (two named Kyrios in the Greek which he used, but only the first is Yahweh in the Hebrew). This second Lord, he said, was the agent of the creation known either as the Word, Ps. 33.6, or as Wisdom, Prov. 3.19. Eusebius also knew that this second God was the one whom Philo had called the Logos (*Preparation* XI.14).

In his *Proof* he began by stating his case:

Remember how Moses calls the Being, Who appeared to the patriarchs and often delivered to them the oracles written down in Scripture, sometimes God and Lord and sometimes the Angel of the Lord. He clearly implies that this was not the Omnipotent God but a secondary Being, rightly called the God and Lord of holy men, but the Angel of the Most High his Father. (*Proof* I.5)

The Lord was the visible second God:

And if it is not possible for the Most High God, the invisible the Uncreated, and the Omnipotent to be said to be seen in mortal form, the being who was seen must have been the Word of God, Whom we call Lord as we do the Father. (*Proof* I.5)

Eusebius knew, then, the tradition apparent in several texts, that both Father and Son could be called Lord, just as the gnostics knew that both could be called Father. He distinguishes throughout between God Most High and another Lord, and shows in his treatment of Ps. 91 that God Most High was the Father addressed by Jesus (*Proof* IX.7). The psalmist had addressed the second God, later manifested as Jesus, when he spoke of the Lord who had made his refuge with God Most High. Eusebius here has read the Hebrew more accurately than modern translators since the text of Ps. 91.9 does actually say:

You, O Yahweh, are my refuge,
You have made Elyon your dwelling place.

which clearly distinguishes Elyon from Yahweh, God Most High from the Lord. As has happened so often, translators have altered the text in order to give what they think it should have said.

The second figure was the anointed one, the heavenly reality with an earthly counterpart who was both King and High Priest. Moses had seen the true High Priest in his vision of the tabernacle on Sinai, and the instruction to reproduce everything in accordance with what he had seen (Exod. 25.40) included installing a high priest:

And Moses himself, having first been thought worthy to view the divine realities in secret and the mysteries concerning the first and only Anointed High Priest of God, which were celebrated before him in His theophanies, is ordered to establish figures and symbols on earth of what he had seen in his mind in visions ... (*Proof* IV.15)

When the psalms spoke of the Anointed One they referred not to the king but to the second God anointed by his father Elyon:

Wherefore in the Psalms this oracle says thus to this same Being anointed of the Father
Thy throne O God, is for ever and ever ...
Wherefore God, thy God, hath anointed thee ... (Ps. 45.6–7).

Eusebius discusses the finer nuances of the Greek and Hebrew of this verse and concludes:

So the whole verse runs: 'Thou hast, O God, loved justice and hated impiety: therefore in return, O God, the highest and greater God, Who is also thy God ...'
... so that the Anointer, being the supreme God, is far above the Anointed, he being God in a different sense. And this would be clear to anyone who knew Hebrew.
Therefore in these words you have it clearly stated that God was anointed and became the Christ ...
And this is He who was the beloved of the Father and his Offspring and the eternal Priest and the being called the Sharer of the Father's throne. (*Proof* IV.15)

In earlier times the heavenly anointed One had been known to the prophets: 'Therefore the prophetic word ... referring to the Highest Power of God, the King of Kings and Lord of Lords, calls him the Christ and the Anointed' (*Proof* IV.15). He had been manifested particularly in the high priests: '... among the Hebrews they were called Christs who long ago symbolically presented a copy of the first (Christ)' (*Proof* IV.10). This is exactly what Philo describes, when he says the Logos was the high priest, the second God present with his people, passing through the veil of the temple to pass into heaven. The ancient Christs had also been anointed with the Holy Spirit. David, said Eusebius, had spoken of this anointed high priest when he wrote Ps. 110.1, 'The Lord says to my Lord': 'David ... knows an eternal priest of God and calls him his own Lord and confesses that he shares the throne of God Most High' (*Proof* IV.15). The second God had been named throughout the Old Testament, 'already hymned as God and Lord in the sacred oracles' (*Proof* IV.10). Eusebius knew and used all the examples which earlier writers had employed; there was Another present at the Creation, there were two Lords in the story of Sodom, the angel who met Jacob was the Lord and the angel who led Moses was the Lord.

When Origen had spoken of the Son as High Priest he too had been careful to name the one worshipped as God Most High: 'To the Son we present [our petitions] and beseech him, as the propitiation for our sins, and our High Priest, to offer our desires, and sacrifices, and prayers, *to the Most High*' (*Against Celsus* VIII.13; cf. VIII.26).

Eusebius also dealt with the problem of the vision of God (*Proof* V.18). If the Gospel could say 'No man has seen God at any time' (John 1.18), was the Gospel incorrect? No, because the appearance in the Old Testament had been not of God, meaning God Most High, but of the Lord:

But if they be understood, like our former quotations, of the Word of God, Who was seen by the fathers 'In many ways and in sundry manners', no contradiction is involved. The God of Israel here seen is shown to be the same Being who wrestled with Jacob ... I have shown in the proper place that this was no other than the Word of God. (*Proof* V.18)
The Almighty God Himself, Who is One, was not seen in his own person ... so that the Father was seen by the fathers through the Son according to his saying in the Gospels 'He that hath seen me hath seen the Father'. (*Proof* V.13)

The third task is to show how the first Christians identified Jesus with the Great Angel not only in their reading of the Old Testament but also in their new writings. It is not necessary to demonstrate that the first Christians thought of Jesus as an angel; many have done this already, notably M. Werner,[2] who regarded angel terminology, especially as used by Origen, as evidence of authentic early Christology. Although criticized at several points by later scholars,[3] the possibility remains that angel terminology derives from the most ancient descriptions of Yahweh as the Angel who was both God and Son of God. What I propose is to show how Jesus was identified with this particular Angel, and how these early Christian texts have preserved the ancient cultic patterns and traditions associated with this Angel.

The prologue to Revelation is the earliest detailed recognition of Jesus as the Great Angel. Both the description and the setting are unmistakable. The Angel was a human figure with flaming eyes and feet like burnished bronze, appearing in the temple. He was in the midst of the seven lampstands, meaning, surely, not that he stood among seven separate lamps but that he was the central stem of the sevenfold lamp, as Philo's Logos had been. He introduced himself as Yahweh: 'I am the first and the last and the living one' (Rev. 1.17), with which we should compare:

> Thus says Yahweh the King of Israel,
> and his Redeemer the Lord of Hosts:
> I am the first and I am the last;
> besides me there is no god. (Isa. 44.6)

The monotheism of the last line is the Second Isaiah's own and this verse was, as we have seen, crucial to the two powers arguments of the early Christian centuries. But the other titles were traditional; Yahweh the King of Israel, Redeemer, Lord of Hosts, First and Last: 'I am He, I am the First and the Last. My hand laid the foundation of the earth and my right hand spread out the heavens' (Isa. 48.12–13).

The Angel of John's vision was the one whom Isaiah had called Yahweh, the Redeemer of Israel. Job had trusted in a similar being. In a passage which is now suspiciously obscured, Job expressed confidence in a living Redeemer, and apparently in the vision of God and in the sword of the Lord's judgement. The line in question could be read 'I know my Redeemer is the Living One and the Last One shall rise up' (Job 19.25–9). The Angel of John's vision was Jesus, for he had died and was alive again (Rev. 2.8), although in all other respects he was the ancient Yahweh. He could permit people to eat from the tree of life (2.7), he had the sharp sword of judgement (2.12), he was the Son of God (2.18), he had the seven spirits of God (3.1), and he was the scribe of the Book of Life (3.5; cf. 21.27, the Lamb's book of life), he sat on a throne and had a Father also enthroned. Most opaque in the

English is the title rendered '*Amen*, the faithful and true witness, the beginning of God's creation' (3.14). The Semitic original behind this vision would probably have had here not Amen but *Amon*, the heavenly master workman. In Prov. 8.30 the *Amon* is Wisdom who assisted at the creation and later appeared in the gnostic texts as the Demiurge, the agent of the creation. The faithful and true witness was yet another title for Yahweh (Jer. 42.5), perhaps also concealed by the English translations of Ps. 89.37 and Job 16.19. In the former the Hebrew has 'a faithful witness in the clouds' guaranteeing the royal line of David, and in the latter Job cries out to his 'witness in heaven' to plead with God for justice. The 'witness' of the Old Testament appeared later in the Testaments of the Twelve Patriarchs as the mediating Angel. The *Beginning* of the creation was, as we have seen, one of the titles of Philo's Logos and also the way in which the first verse of Genesis was interpreted in some Targums. *In the beginning* was read as 'By means of the Beginning (or the Firstborn) ... God created ...'

Like Yahweh, the figure in John's vision both was and had an angel; he says that Jesus sent his angel to bring the revelation (1.1, 22.16), just as Yahweh had sent his angels as messengers (but compare the Ethiopic of the *Epistle of the Apostles* 14 where Jesus declares that he was his own messenger when he came to Mary at the Annunciation).

In the central section of Revelation there are several other titles which confirm that the Jesus-Angel was Yahweh. The lamb had seven horns and seven eyes (5.6); in Zechariah's vision the seven eyes were the seven spirits, the seven eyes of Yahweh. The lamb, then, symbolized the same as the lamp, the presence of Yahweh with his people (cf. Rev. 21.23: 'for the glory of God is its light and *its lamp is the lamb*'). The lamb, too, may have lost some of its older associations in the course of being transferred from a Semitic original into Greek. Lamb (Heb. *tale'* Aram. *talya'*) can also mean a youth, which was, as we have seen, the inexplicable title given to the human figure in 3 Enoch, when he was taken up to heaven, transformed into the Great Angel, made the agent of the judgement and given the name 'the Lesser Yahweh'. 3 Enoch used a different word for youth, but the word play in John's vision on lamb/youth and the sacrificial imagery carried by the former could explain this. John's vision also testified to the double naming which we have seen already in the tradition of the 'two Yahwehs' (see chapter 5); in 14.1, the lamb and his Father have the same name and this name is the mark on the forehead of those who have been saved. According to Ezek. 9.4 this mark was a *tau*, which, in the Samaritan and old Hebrew scripts, was a diagonal cross, X, the sign of Yahweh. The One who Is and Was was also the Holy One and the judge (16.5). The Lamb was explicitly identified as Lord of Lords and King of Kings (17.14). The Faithful and True rode out from heaven as the warrior judge (19.11–16), i.e. he was the Yahweh of Deut. 32.43. He was crowned and named with the secret Name, the sword issued from his mouth, and he was called the Word. He trod the winepress of wrath, another of Yahweh's roles in Isa. 63.3–6. The Lamb was also married to the heavenly city (21.9–10), just as Isaiah had seen Jerusalem wed to the Lord:

> For your Maker is your husband,
> Yahweh of Hosts is his name.
> and the Holy One of Israel is your Redeemer. (Isa. 54.5)

The bejewelled city who had been the bride of Yahweh (Isa. 54.11–12) became the heavenly city of Rev. 21. *There can be no doubt that for John the heavenly Christ was the ancient Yahweh.*

Revelation had a temple setting for the son of man/lamb/angel figure; the great judgement was a heavenly liturgy spilling over onto the earth. Vestiges of the temple setting passed into many early Christian writings, but their variety is such that they cannot have been transmitted because of John's vision. Many of the older patterns discernible in these writings were not present in Revelation, showing that they were drawing on a broader and older tradition which had from the beginning set Jesus in the heavenly temple. First, there are traditions derived from the sevenfold lamp which in its entirety represented plural manifestation of Yahweh. Philo knew that the Logos was particularly associated with the central stem of the lamp. Hermas similarly saw a glorious Man flanked by six others. He was told: 'The glorious man is the Son of God and the six are glorious angels supporting him on the right hand and on the left' (Hermas Sim. ix.12.8). Similarly the pseudo-Cyprianic text *The Threefold Fruit of the Christian Life* described the seven angels created from fire, one of whom was the Son of God seen by Isaiah in his vision: 'When the Lord created the angels from the fire he decided to make one of them his son, he whom Isaiah called the Lord of Hosts' (*Fruit* 216–19). There has also been found an engraved amethyst bearing the names of the seven archangels: Raphael, Renel, Uriel, Ichtys, Michael, Gabriel and Azael. Ichtys was the common acronym for Jesus Christ Son of God Saviour, and thus we have again the Great Angel as the central one of seven.[5] The sevenfold tradition appeared in a slightly different form in the tradition of the seven spirits which rested upon the Messiah: 'The golden lamp conveys another enigma as a symbol of Christ ... and they say the seven eyes of the Lord are the seven spirits resting on the rod that springs from the root of Jesse' (Clement, *Stromata* V.6). Irenaeus knew something similar: 'The spirit of God in his indwelling is manifold and is said by the prophet Isaiah to rest in seven forms on the Son of God, that is, on the Word in his incarnation ... And Moses revealed the pattern of this in the seven branched candlestick' (*Proof* 9). The original conception was probably that all seven were aspects of Yahweh (cf. Yahweh our Elohim is one) because, as we shall see later, Yahweh could be described as Michael or as Gabriel.

Yahweh was also the angel among the four living creatures of the divine throne. The earliest description of the four creatures around the throne is in Ezek. 1.1–4, where it is clear that the four, who each had four faces, are a part of the fire which *is* the glory of Yahweh. This tradition of the four appeared in several forms. By the time of John's vision the four had only one face each (Rev. 4.7), but they were obviously the creatures of Ezekiel's throne. The four were known to the gnostics: Apelles who had been a disciple of Marcion said that there were four gods called angels, to whom Christ was added as the fifth (*Refutation* X.20); the Sethians spoke of the four Light-Givers who were aspects of the second God, the Self-Begotten One. The unity of the four, however, is seen most clearly in an otherwise obscure passage in Irenaeus, dismissed by commentators as one which cannot be taken too seriously![6] Irenaeus argues thus for there being only four Gospels. The Word, he said,

... gave us the gospel *under four forms but bound together by one Spirit.* As also David says, when entreating His presence, Thou that sittest upon the cherubim, shine forth. *For the cherubim too were four faced and their faces were the images of the dispensation of the Son of God.* (*Against Heresies* III.2.2)

Irenaeus must have known that the four living creatures were manifestations of the One.

The tradition of the two powers represented by the two cherubim of the throne also survived, but the variety of forms in which it survived suggests that the Christian tradition drew on one older than that in Philo, i.e. was not derived from him. The earliest example is in the Ascension of Isaiah, which depicts the Lord and the Angel of the Holy Spirit on either side of the Lord. Here there is the tradition of the double naming, with both the central figure and his attendant named as the Lord, but also there are two angelic figures on either side of the throne: 'And I saw how my LORD and the angel of the Holy Spirit both together praised the LORD' (Asc. Isa. 9.40).[7] The second Lord having lived his life on earth, he went back to heaven and there took his place at the right hand of the great Glory; the angel of the Holy Spirit sat on the left (Asc. Isa. 11.32–3). In 2 Enoch, however, it is Gabriel who sits on the left of the throne (2 Enoch 24.1), showing how the archangels were passing into the Christian Trinity. Jewish tradition remembered that there was something special about Gabriel and Michael; *Genesis Rabbah* 78.1 knew that, unlike the other angels who were being demoted to insignificant spirits renewed each morning, Michael and Gabriel did not change. There was also an ancient version of the trinity which comprised Christ, Michael and Gabriel: 'In Syria there was a solemn formula XMΓ (Christos, Michael, Gabriel) which can be recognised in epitaphs, on seal stones, amulets as well as on amphorae and such like dating in part back to the fourth century.'[8]

Origen knew a very similar tradition and, interestingly, said that it came from a *Jewish source*:

My Hebrew master used to say that the two six-winged seraphim in Isaiah ... were the only-begotten Son of God and the Holy Spirit. And we ourselves think that the expression in the song of Habakkuk* 'in the midst of the two living creatures shalt thou be known' is spoken of Christ and the Holy Spirit. (*On First Principles* I.3)

In his commentary on Romans 3.8 Origen discussed the cherubim over the mercy seat and said that they symbolized the Word and the Spirit *in* the soul of Christ. This is very close to Philo's two powers, not separate beings but aspects of the One who spoke to Moses from between the cherubim. Such an association of the two powers with the Word and the Spirit is very significant since it could be evidence of a tradition even older than that found in Philo, where the two powers are both 'masculine'. Here in Origen we see the Word as the masculine power and the Spirit as the feminine, the ancient Wisdom. The

(* Hab. 3.2 in the Greek version differs from the Hebrew and reads 'In the midst of the two living creatures you will be known'.)

twofold second God is presupposed by the creation story of Gen. 1.27 where the Lord created *male and female in his image.* Christ was, said Paul, both the power of God and the Wisdom of God (1 Cor. 1.24), the complete manifestation of both aspects of Yahweh. The twofold nature of the second God as Word and Wisdom was known to Origen and inspired his explanation of the cherubim as Word and Spirit who were both found in Christ. This teaching, that the cherubim were aspects (*epinoiai*) of the Son was later condemned as heresy.[9] The Elchasaites, an ancient Jewish Christian sect also remembered as heretics, kept the memory of this twofold angel; they told of a book revealed by an angel of enormous stature: 'And there was with him also a female ... the male is the Son of God and the female the Holy Spirit' (*Refutation* IX.13). Theophilus of Antioch knew the twofold angel; he was careful to state that Logos and Sophia/Wisdom were the same (*To Autolycus* II.10.22)

There were variant traditions, too, about the baptism of Jesus when he had been declared to be the beloved son. We assume that the voice from heaven was the voice of God, but the Gospels do not actually say whose voice it was. *The Gospel of the Hebrews*, as recorded in Jerome on Isa. 11, shows that it was the *Spirit* who spoke to Jesus and called him her son: 'the whole fount of the Holy Spirit descended and rested upon him and said unto him: My Son ... my Mother the Holy Spirit.' Further, Origen's *Commentary on John* II.12 reveals that this *Gospel of the Hebrews* recorded that Jesus spoke thus: 'even now did my mother the Holy Spirit take me by one of my hairs and carried me away.'

The memory of the four archangels as aspects of the One survives in the texts which identify Jesus either with Gabriel or with Michael. In the *Epistle of the Apostles* it was the Lord himself who appeared to Mary as Gabriel; he had descended through the heavens and left Michael, Gabriel, Uriel and Raphael to perform his priestly functions in heaven during his absence. This implies that Gabriel, too, was a plurality. The same identification with Gabriel occurs in the Sibylline oracles: 'In the last times [the Word] came upon earth ... First of all he showed himself as Gabriel in pure and mighty form; then, as an archangel he spoke these words to the young maiden: receive God in your spotless womb, O Virgin' (VIII.456–61). In *The Shepherd of Hermas*, however, Christ the glorious angel is Michael but also the Holy Spirit: 'the great and glorious angel is Michael' (Hermas Sim. viii.3.3); cf. 'the glorious man is the Son of God' (Hermas Sim.

ix.12.8), and 'the Holy Spirit ... that Spirit is the Son of God' (Hermas Sim. ix.1.1). Commentators despair of constructing a neat christology for this text, but if the Son of God was the *four* angels, this fluidity is no problem. In John's Revelation both Michael (Rev. 12.7) and the Word (Rev. 11.16) lead the heavenly host in the great battle.

For the first Christians Jesus was the Angel of Great Counsel (LXX Isa. 9.6). Novatian, as we have seen, explained carefully that the Angel of Great Counsel was more than just an angel: 'The name God has never been granted to angels ... He is entitled 'The Angel of Great Counsel' (*On the Trinity* XVIII). The gnostic Theodotus, according to Clement in his *Excerpts from Theodotus*, had identified the Angel of Great Counsel as the Jesus of Col. 1.16 and Phil. 2.10:

... he is sent forth as the angel of the counsel and becomes the head of the whole after the Father. 'For all things were created by him, things visible and invisible, thrones, dominions, kingdoms, divinities, services'. 'So God also exalted him and gave him a name which is above every name ...' (*Excerpt* 43)

Origen explained that Jesus was 'not simply an angel but the Angel of Great Counsel' (*Against Celsus* V.53, cf. VIII.27). Eusebius knew that this was not a Christian innovation; the anointed heavenly figure was the Angel of great Counsel: 'And when, as the Captain of the Angels he leads them he is called: The Angel of Great Counsel, and as Leader of the Armies of heaven: Captain of the Host of the Lord' (*Proof* IV.10). The Hebrews, he said, also believed that this angel was the Messiah (*Preparation* VII.14–15), but the difference between the Jews and the Christians was that the Jews did not believe he had already appeared. This implies that the belief in two deities in the Old Testament was not unique to Christians; the point of dispute was whether or not Jesus *was* the second God. Elsewhere Christ was the 'first among the archangels', and 'being himself God, the Commander in Chief and Shepherd of all that is in heaven', all rational creatures gave him homage (Methodius, *Symposium* iii.4, 6). Melito named him as the captain of the angelic army (*New Fragments* 15). Justin listed the titles as 'the Glory of the Lord, at another time a Son, at another Wisdom, at another an Angel, at another God, and at another Lord and Word. He once calls himself *Captain of the Host* when he appeared to Joshua the son of Nun in the form of man' (*Trypho* 61).

The most telling of all the Christian descriptions of Jesus is that of Origen in his homily on Luke, because it shows how faithfully the early Church had adhered to temple traditions. He describes Jesus as standing in the river of fire beside the flaming sword. Now the biblical description of the gate of Eden says only that it was guarded by cherubim and a flaming sword, but the Palestinian Targums remembered where this story originated. Both *Neofiti* and the *Fragment* Targums recall the temple setting and render Gen. 3.24, 'And he cast out Adam and made the Glory of his Shekinah to dwell at the front of the east of the Garden, above the two cherubim.' Origen knew, then, that Jesus was the one who guarded the gate of Eden, above the cherubim. He was the Glory of the Shekinah. This understanding must date back to the time when the Church had still been within Judaism, perhaps to the first or second generation.

Finally, we see that the first Christians used 'the Name' in a highly significant way. One strand of the Old Testament tradition shows that *the Name* had been used as a substitute for the presence of the Lord in the temple, but those who did not accept this new convention of the Deuteronomists kept to more ancient ways. For them the Name was simply one of the many ways of describing Yahweh. Thus in Philo, as we have seen, the Name was one of the titles of the Logos. Early Christian writings kept to the non-Deuteronomic ways and are evidence that not only was the Name used as a designation of Jesus but also that the cultic patterns associated with the Name in the Old Testament were retained in a new Christian context. Yahweh was the Name, the chief of the sons of El Elyon. Jesus was the Name, the chief of the archangels and the Son of God. If the distinction between the ancient El Elyon and his sons is kept in mind, and also Justin's statement that 'To the Father of all ... there is no name given ...' (*Apology*, II.6), we see in these early Name texts, too, a clear expression of the belief that Jesus had been the manifestation of Yahweh. Further, his followers, in that they *were* the body of Christ, continued to be that manifestation (cf. 'he gave them power to become children of God' John 1.12). It is a mistake to read these texts with the conclusions of later Christian teachers in mind; left to speak for themselves they say something very interesting.

As early as the Fourth Gospel we find 'Father glorify thy Name' (12.28) and 'Glorify the Son' (17.1). John knew that the Name was the Son; he said that Jesus had 'manifested the Name in the world' (17.6), almost as though the Name had been something separate which Jesus took upon himself. This is exactly how other early writers described the process; the Name was 'put on'. The most frequent imagery was that of robing or of being marked on the forehead. Clement of Alexandria had known the significance of the high priestly vestments. His *Excerpts from Theodotus* record that the golden plate was removed and left on the altar of incense in front of the veil before the high priest entered the holy of holies. Possession of this engraved tablet, the Name, gave the high priest the right to enter the holy of holies and in the material world he was the one who was *wrapped around* with the Name (*Excerpt* 27). That obscurest of passages in Zechariah describes the vesting of the high priest (Zech. 3). Joshua stands in front of the Lord and the heavenly attendants vest him (3.1–5); he is given the right of access to the heavenly place (3.7); before him is set a stone with seven eyes engraved by the Lord (3.9, a literal rendering of the Hebrew text). Immediately associated with this stone is the promise that Yahweh will remove the guilt of the land. Now removing guilt was the purpose of the Day of Atonement rituals when the high priest entered the holy of holies. This cryptic text must refer to the heavenly vesting of the high priest with the seven eyes, i.e. the seven spirits or powers of Yahweh, as a result of which *Yahweh* could remove the guilt of the land. I suspect that this is the earliest reference to the significance of the vesting.

The description in the Testaments of the Twelve Patriarchs of Levi being vested by the seven archangels (Test. Levi 8) has elements which are also those of an early Christian baptism, viz. anointing, washing, feeding with bread and wine, clothing with a white robe. There are two possible explanations for this: either certain details were a Christian addition to an earlier text, in which case it is interesting that they should have associated baptism with the vesting of the priest; or the text has not been augmented and the ancient vesting ritual was that on which a baptism was modelled. Whatever the explanation, the fact of the similarity remains. Thus it was that the sacred Name worn on the forehead of the high priests came to be marked on the forehead of the Christian at baptism. He was robed with Christ. Paul said that at baptism the believer 'put on Christ' (Gal. 3.27, cf. 'Put on the Lord Jesus Christ,' Rom. 13.14).

The *Odes of Solomon*, which, even if they were not baptismal hymns, are full of baptism imagery, show time and again how common this way of describing Christian initiation was:

The Lord is on my head like a crown (Odes 1.1)
Because thy seal is known ...

> the elect archangels are clothed with it. (Odes 4.7, 8)
> In form he was considered like me, that I might put him on. (Odes 7.4)
> And the Lord renewed me with his garment ... (Odes 11.11)
> I put on immortality through his Name. (Odes 15.8)
> I am a priest of the Lord ...
> But put on the grace of the Lord generously
> and come into His Paradise ... (Odes 20.7)
> ... the sign on them is the Lord
> and the sign is the way for those who cross in the Name of the Lord.
> Therefore put on the Name of the Most High and know him
> And you shall cross without danger. (Odes 39.7–8)

The Name of the Most High is the Lord; it does not mean that this is the way that the Most High is addressed, but rather that the Lord was the Son/Name of the Most High. Further, the Lord could be worn as a sign, just as the high priests wore the golden plate. Narsai, who lived in Edessa in the fifth century, described anointing as the time when the priest 'signs the flock with the sign of the Lord and seals upon it his hidden name (in outward form)'.[10] This was the secret Name worn by the Word when he rode out from heaven in Revelation (Rev. 19.12). Although riding as a warrior, he wore many diadems and his secret name was 'inscribed', we assume on the diadem.

As early as *Hermas* we see that bearing the Name was a way of describing Christianity, 'those who bear the Name of the Son of God' (Hermas Sim ix.14.5), but there was a distinction between being sealed with the Name and being robed with the power (the heavenly spirits in this text are described as maidens):

A man cannot be found in the kingdom of God, except they (the holy spirits) clothe him with their clothing. For if you receive the name alone but do not receive the clothing from them, you will benefit nothing for these maidens are the powers of the Son of God. If you wear the Name but do not bear his power you are bearing his name in vain.
'What', said I, 'is their raiment, Sir?'
'Their names themselves', said he, 'are their raiment. Whoever bears the Name of the Son of God must also bear their names; for even the Son himself bears the names of these maidens.' (Hermas Sim. ix.13.2–3)

The original dwelling place of the Name was remembered too; the *Didache* records as a part of the eucharistic prayer: 'Thanks be to Thee, Holy Father, for thy sacred Name which Thou hast caused *to tabernacle* in our hearts' (*Didache* 10). The Name was the invisible second God who could become visible. Thus Clement of Alexandria recorded in his *Excerpts from Theodotus*: 'The visible part of Jesus is

Wisdom and the Church ... but the invisible part is the Name which is the Only Begotten Son' (*Excerpt* 26). This is not far removed from the *Gospel of Truth*, where the Name of the Father is the Son. The Name was also the dove which descended at Jesus's baptism (*Excerpt* 22). That Son, Name and Spirit could be thus interchanged shows the fluidity of the early years when so many of the older designations for the second God were still being used. Thus in the *Acts of Thomas* the apostle summons the *Name* at the baptismal anointing:

Come thou holy Name of the Christ that is above every name
Come thou power of the Most High. (*Acts of Thomas*, 27)

Note that the Name functions where we should expect the Spirit and it is a power of El Elyon. There is another baptism recorded later:

Glory be to thee hidden one that art communicated at baptism
Glory to thee the unseen power that is in baptism.
Glory to thee renewal whereby are renewed they that are baptised ...
Glory to thee Name of Christ,
Glory to thee power established in Christ. (*Acts of Thomas*, 132)

The renewer would have been an exact recollection of the original meaning of the name Yahweh, 'the One who causes to be'.

Sometimes the Name was no more than a synonym for Jesus. Ignatius wrote that he was a prisoner for the Name (Eph. 1, 3); Hermas was told of those who had suffered for the Name (*Hermas Vision* iii.1.9); he used the Son of God and the Name of the Son of God as equivalents, both designating the power which upheld the creation (Hermas Sim. ix.14.5). Clement of Rome exhorted: 'Let us show ourselves obedient to his all-holy and glorious Name, so that we may escape the doom that was pronounced of old by Wisdom upon the ungodly' (1 Clem. 58). Just as the elect of Ezekiel's time were signed with the sign of Yahweh, the X, so too the Christians were signed on the forehead with the same sign. It is interesting, as Daniélou observed, that neither the name Jesus, nor any of its abbreviations such as IHS, was used for the baptismal signing. Christians chose to use the sign of Yahweh, the sign of the Name, touching 'the very oldest stratum of the rite of signatio in Jewish Christian circles, where the Jewish X comes to represent Christ as God'.[11]

We can trace this signing even further. The rabbis remembered that the anointed high priests, those who had been consecrated before the sacred oil had been hidden in the time of Josiah's reform (see chapter 2), had been anointed with the sign of a diagonal cross. The Talmud describes this as 'in the shape of a Greek *chi*' (b. *Horayoth* 12a) but there can be no doubt that they too were anointed with the sign of Yahweh, whose name they wore on their crown and whose manifestation they became.

Notes to chapter ten

1 W.G. Ferrar, *The Proof of the Gospel*, London 1920, on *Proof* III, pp.15 and 16.

2 M. Werner, *The Formation of Christian Dogma*, ET London 1957.

3 For discussion see J.W. Trigg, 'The Angel of Great Counsel: Christ and the Angelic Hierarchy in Origen's Theology' in JTS 42.1 1991, pp.36-7.

4 Published in translation by R. Reitzenstein, in ZNW 15 (1914).

5 J. Daniélou, *A History of Early Christian Doctrine before the Council of Nicaea, I: The Theology of Jewish Christianity* (1958) ET London 1964, p.122.

6 J. Stevenson, *A New Eusebius*, London 1963, p.122.

7 M.A. Knibb's translation in *The Old Testament Pseudepigrapha* vol. 1, ed. J.H. Charlesworth, New York and London 1983. In the note to Asc. Isa. 1.7 he says that he has rendered by LORD the Ethiopic word which commonly translates the Hebrew Yahweh, to distinguish it from other divine titles.

8 Werner, op.cit., p.136.

9 P. Nautin, *Origène: sa vie et son oeuvre*, Paris 1977, p.132. He believes he has identified Pamphilus' *Apologia* in Photius' *Bibliotheca*.

10 Quoted, with other examples, in J.E. Fossum, *The Name of God and the Angel of the Lord*, Tübingen 1985, p.101.

11 Daniélou, op.cit., p.154-5.

Chapter eleven The Evidence of the New Testament

The New Testament has been left until last so that evidence from all the other chapters can be used to provide as broad a context as possible within which to set several vital questions. What did the first Christians mean when they said that Jesus was Lord, Son of God? How was it possible for a Jewish community to worship Jesus? And, before either of these is answered, by what date were Christians claiming that Jesus was Lord and Son of God and offering him devotion? If it can be shown that the claims and the worship were not known to the first Palestinian community, then, and only then, is it legitimate to look for an explanation in a pagan Greek context. If the titles and the worship were part of the earliest Palestinian tradition, then their original significance cannot be sought in anything other than a Jewish setting.

The hymn in Phil. 2.5–11 is an early composition; when Paul wrote to Philippi and quoted it, it is unlikely that the teaching in the letter differed from that given on his first visit. In other words, the confession 'Jesus Christ is Lord' must have been current in the Christianity which Paul brought with him, at the very least from Antioch. Thus a first-generation community believed that Jesus had been exalted, given the divine Name and then proclaimed Lord. The pattern is unmistakable: it is that of the exaltation and transformation of the Davidic king, part, perhaps, of the royal theme common to all the Gospels, that Jesus had been the King of the Jews. The same pattern occurs in Rom. 1.3, which all scholars agree contains an early confession. Jesus had descended from David according to the flesh but had been designated Son of God by the resurrection, his exaltation. Behind the confession lies the Davidic covenant, 'I will be his father and he shall be my son' (2 Sam. 7.14), and 'You are my Son; today I have begotten you' (Ps. 2.7). Luke 1.32–3, Acts 13.33–7 and Heb. 1.5 all set the divine sonship in this royal context, suggesting that Jesus was believed to be whatever the kings had been or had foreshadowed. Both Phil. 2 and Rom. 1 express the same belief but not in the same words; in the former Jesus was given the Name and recognized as

213

Lord, in the latter he was designated Son of God. 'Lord' and 'Son of God' must, then, have been synonymous in the early Christian community, as indeed they were in the case of Yahweh the Son of God Most High. The congruence of both these early confessions with the royal theology of Israel makes it unlikely that they originated outside a Palestinian community.

This is confirmed by Paul; although both titles were used to describe the exalted Jesus, Paul used 'Lord' far more frequently than he used 'Son'.[1] Had Son of God been a title adopted from the pagan world, one might have expected that the apostle to the Gentiles would have used it more frequently in his letters. In fact, as Hengel observed, '"Son of God" appears most frequently in the letters where the controversy with the *Jewish* tradition is at its height, in Romans and Galatians.'[2] It has even been suggested that since Paul used 'Son of God' mainly in stereotyped formulas drawn from tradition, the real significance of the term may have been *lost* on a Gentile congregation and therefore it was not used, just as 'Son of Man' was not used. Paul had received a tradition that the pre-existent Son had been sent into the world that he might be the firstborn of many sons of God (Rom. 8.3, 29, 32; Gal. 4.4–7), a Son who, in the near future, would return from heaven to save the faithful from 'the wrath to come' (1 Thess. 1.10). Hengel summarized the situation thus:

Paul's conception of the Son of God, which was certainly not his own creation but goes back to earlier community tradition before Paul's letters, thus proves to be quite unique. Jesus, the recently crucified Jew, whose physical brother James ... Paul himself had personally known well (Gal. 1.19; 2.9; cf. 1 Cor. 9.5) is not only the Messiah whom God has raised from the dead, but much more. He is identical with a divine being before all time, mediator between God and his creatures.[3]

A divine being? If the context of this first proclamation was a Palestinian Jewish community, what divine being could have been proclaimed Lord and Son of God? Further, the title 'Son of God' in the tradition which Paul received was set within the apocalyptic tradition; the Son sent forth *when the time was fulfilled* (Gal. 4.4) *to deliver from the wrath to come* (1 Thess. 1.10) cannot reasonably be placed in any other context. Since the apocalyptic tradition had developed from the older royal theology, the glimpses which Paul gives of the tradition he received are mutually consistent, and strengthen the case for that tradition having come from the Palestinian Christians.

214

The divine being, the firstborn of the sons of God, the Son who had come forth and delivered his people had been Yahweh the Son of God Most High emerging from his holy place for the sake of his people. The people of Israel had long hoped for his appearance and had summoned their Lord to come and help them:

> Arise, O Yahweh! Deliver me, O my God! (Ps. 3.7; cf. 7.6)
> Arise, O Yahweh! Let not man prevail;
> let the nations be judged before thee. (Ps. 9.19; cf. 10.12)
> Our God comes, he does not keep silence (Ps. 50.3)
> ... Yahweh ... comes to judge the earth. (Ps. 96.13; 98.9)
>   when wilt thou come to me? (Ps. 101.2)
> Behold your God will come ... and save you. (Isa. 35.4; cf. 59.20)
>   that thou wouldst rend the heavens and come down. (Isa. 64.1; cf. Ps. 144.5)
> For behold Yahweh will come in fire ... (Isa. 66.5)

In Christian worship there was a very similar 'Come Lord Jesus' (Rev. 22.20); since the Aramaic original of this prayer has survived, *Maranatha*, 'Come Lord' (1 Cor. 16.22; *Didache*, 10.6), both the form and the language of the prayer suggest that the Palestinian community worshipped Jesus as Yahweh. Scholars have found this worship of Jesus hard to explain and have even been driven to suggest that the veneration of Jesus was an unfortunate development, introduced by the Hellenistic communities who needed to have a cult deity as good as that of their neighbours.[4] This hypothesis is not necessary.

There is other evidence of worship; there are doxologies ascribed to Christ: '... our Lord and Saviour Jesus Christ. To him be the glory both now and to the day of eternity' (2 Pet. 3.18); 'To him who loves us and has freed us from our sins by his blood ... to him be glory and dominion for ever and ever' (Rev. 1.5–6). It is possible that Rom. 9.5 also referred to Christ as 'the God who is over all, blessed for ever', but the lack of punctuation makes the reading ambiguous.[5] Other ambiguous examples are Heb. 13.20–1, where the glory seems to be ascribed to Christ, and 2 Tim. 4.18, where the glory is ascribed to the Lord of the heavenly kingdom, presumably meaning to Christ even though there is nothing in the context to put this beyond doubt. The fact that there are two clear examples (2 Pet. 3.18 and Rev. 1.5–6), however shows that doxologies ascribed to Christ did exist. There are also early benedictions: 'May our God and Father himself and our Lord Jesus direct our way to you and may the Lord make you increase and abound in love' (1 Thess. 3.11–12; also 2 Thess. 3.5 and 3.16).

215

Prayers were offered to the Lord: the disciples worshipped Jesus after the ascension (Luke 24.52);[6] they prayed to him for guidance when choosing a replacement for Judas (Acts 1.24); the dying Stephen prayed, presumably to the heavenly judge, since he said 'Lord do not hold this sin against them' (Acts 7.60); and Paul prayed to him three times about the 'thorn in the flesh' which was troubling him (2 Cor. 12.8). Christians were exhorted to 'reverence Christ as Lord' (1 Pet. 3.15) and even the heavenly host was exhorted to worship the Son (Heb. 1.6, a quotation from the LXX of Deut. 32.43 which had originally referred to Yahweh). Jesus also interceded for his followers (Heb. 7.25; 1 John 2.1), at the right hand of God (Rom. 8.34), just as the unnamed angel had done in the Testament of the Twelve Patriarchs (Test. Levi 5.6; Test. Dan. 6.1). Hymns were sung to Christ; there are several in John's vision (Rev. 4.8, 11; 5.9–10; 15.3–4)[7] and Pliny wrote of Christians singing hymns to Christ as God (*Letters* X.96). Hymns were also sung about Christ; John 1.1–18; Phil. 2.5–11; Col. 1.15–20 are widely thought to be fragments of such early hymns as are Eph. 2.14–16 and 1 Tim. 3.16.

Not only was Jesus Son of God, he was also God. In the Fourth Gospel 'the Word was with God and the Word *was God*' (John 1.1). Several early versions have 'the only begotten *God* who is in the bosom of the Father' instead of 'the only begotten Son' (John 1.18).[8] Thomas recognized Jesus as 'My Lord and my God' (John 20.28). Rom 9.5, as we have seen, may refer to Christ as God, and Heb. 1.8 quotes of Jesus the LXX of Ps. 45.6, which can be read: 'Your throne, O God, is for ever and ever.' Eusebius was later to use this psalm to demonstrate that there were two Gods in the Old Testament and he was adamant that any other reading showed a defective knowledge of Hebrew! Titus 2.13 can be read: '... the appearing of the glory of our great God and Saviour Jesus Christ,' and 2 Pet. 1.1 can be read: 'the righteousness of our God and Saviour Jesus Christ'. Other possible references are 2 Thess. 1.12; Col. 2.2; Jas. 1.1.[9] Ignatius in AD 106 wrote of 'Jesus Christ our God' (Eph. 18, cf. Eph. 1) and applied to him Ps. 33.9, which had originally described Yahweh: 'One such Teacher there is; He who *spoke the word and it was done*' (Eph. 15). Those who had no faith, the Docetists, were said to have denied 'the sufferings of God' (Trall. 10).

Jesus had also been recognized as the Saviour and his work described as redemption but his ability to be both Saviour and Redeemer, the effectiveness of whatever he did, must have depended initially on who he was believed to be. Traditional treatments of christology deal with the person and then with the work of Christ, since the latter obviously depends on the former. Retrojected into the earliest Palestinian community, this implies that it was a conviction who Jesus was which made it possible to proclaim what he had done as Saviour and Redeemer. This may be stating the obvious, but the obvious must not be overlooked. *In the Old Testament the Saviour had been Yahweh.* The saving actions of Yahweh are its theme. The psalmist's most frequent prayer had been 'Save me, Yahweh', his most frequent assertion of faith that Yahweh had saved him. A major theme of the prophets had been that Yahweh was Israel's Saviour; in Isaiah the Saviour was Yahweh the King (e.g. Isa. 33.22; 43.12) present in his angel (Isa. 63.9). The Saviour was Yahweh's title (e.g. Isa. 43.3, 11; 49.26; 60.16; 63.8).

Jesus was recognized as that Saviour. The name itself meant Saviour, and was associated in Matthew with the prophecy of the presence of God with his people (Matt. 1.21–3). The Christ was expected to save (Luke 2.11; 23.29; John 4.42).[10] Speeches attributed to Peter (Acts 5.31) and Paul (Acts 13.23) say that Jesus was the Saviour. Paul hints at the process by which 'saving' was achieved; the Saviour, the Lord Jesus Christ, was awaited from heaven to transform the believer's body into a body of glory like his own (Phil. 3.20–1). This is the same process as that described by the Jewish mystics who believed that they had been transformed by the sight of the presence of Yahweh, the presence which the prophets had described as a human form, the likeness of the glory of Yahweh (Ezek. 1.28, cf. John 1.14).

Later writings indicate that Saviour became one of the accepted designations of Jesus (2 Tim. 1.10), a Saviour who *appeared* just as Yahweh had appeared. 1 John 4.14 is clear that it was the Father who sent the Son as Saviour, but other passages show that the Saviour-Son was also known as God (e.g. Titus 1.3). This may be evidence of early confusion in the texts, or it may be further proof that it was the Lord, the Son of Elyon who had come as Saviour to his people. The two expressions 'Our *God* and Saviour Jesus Christ' and 'Our *Lord* and Saviour Jesus Christ' were interchangeable (e.g. 2 Pet. 1.1; cf. 2 Pet. 1.11).

Jesus, like Yahweh, was also the Redeemer. Again, the fact that redemption is such a major theme in the Old Testament should not lead to its being overlooked in the quest for establishing who Jesus was believed to be. Yahweh was the Redeemer (Ps. 19.14). Another unnamed Redeemer, who is clearly *not the supreme deity* since he is to plead the cause of the afflicted, presumably in some heavenly judgement, is mentioned in Job 19.25 and Prov. 23.11. The title is most frequent in Isaiah; Israel's Holy One and Redeemer is Yahweh (Isa. 41.14; 43.14; 44.6, 24; 47.4; 48.17, etc.) coming with judgement (Isa. 63.4), just as did Yahweh, the Warrior-Priest of Deut. 32.43. Zechariah sang of the Lord redeeming his people (Luke 1.68). The disciples had hoped that Jesus was the promised Redeemer (Luke 24.21); if this is an accurate reflection of the situation immediately after the crucifixion, then the problem lay not in who Jesus was, but in the manner in which his work was effected.

It is possible that there was no consistency in early Christian thought, and that nothing theological happened to the new faith until it encountered paganism. It is more likely, however, that all the apparent contradictions and fragments which we find in the New Testament are so perceived only because their original significance has been lost. As Deissmann observed, 'The origin of the cult of Christ is the secret of the earliest Palestinian community'.[11] Such evidence as there is demands a divine figure who could have been called both Son of God and God, Son of Man and Messiah, Saviour and Redeemer, and who could be worshipped. His followers chose apocalyptic/royal theology to express their beliefs about him and summarized their new faith in the words 'Jesus is Lord' (Rom. 10.9; 1 Cor. 12.3) or 'Jesus Christ is Lord' (Phil. 2.11). Their earliest creed, then, was the affirmation of *who Jesus was* and to treat 'Lord' as a description of his function rather than as a statement of his identity is the root of much confusion.

Given that there is evidence for a second God in pre-Christian texts and in both Jewish and Christian writings of the early Christian era, the 'secret of the earliest Palestinian community' must be this identification of Jesus as *Kyrios*, the Lord. Investigations of this problem, if they are not purely theological, usually centre on linguistic evidence rather than on literary and theological context, and in particular they concentrate on the study of Greek translations of the Old Testament. The Septuagint most commonly translates Yahweh by *kyrios*, Lord, or *ho kyrios*, the Lord. The LXX's usage is not entirely consistent, however. Yahweh Elohim in Gen. 2–3, for example, became *kyrios ho theos*, whereas Yahweh in Gen. 4.1 became *ho theos*, in Gen. 4.3 *ho kyrios*, and in Gen. 4.6 simply *kyrios*. In Lev. 23.1–2

Yahweh became *kyrios* but in Lev. 23.3–6 *ho kyrios*. In Isa. 1.2 Yahweh is *kyrios*, in Isa. 1.4 *ho kyrios*, but in Isa. 2.2 *ho theos*. Nevertheless, *the title most commonly used for Yahweh in the Old Testament became that of Jesus in the New*. This created enormous problems for later orthodoxy once it had lost sight of the older distinction between Yahweh and Elyon. When it was believed that Yahweh was the Father and yet Jesus was not the Father, various expedients had to be devised to explain how 'the Lord' could possibly have been used of Jesus. When we set all the linguistic evidence in the context of the widely held belief in the second God such ingenuity is redundant. The New Testament identified Jesus with Yahweh, the second God, but not with Elyon, the Father.

The most extreme conclusion drawn from linguistic evidence suggested that, since many copies of the Greek Old Testament did not use the title *the Lord* but retained the Hebrew letters of the divine name, the practice of using *the Lord* in the Old Testament texts was a Christian innovation.[12] Quotations from the Old Testament preserved in the New had originally retained the older practice of using the Hebrew letters, but, in the course of time, when Christianity became separated from its Jewish roots, the divine name of the Old Testament quotations came to be written in Greek as *kyrios*, the Lord, the form of address already used for Jesus: 'This removal of the tetragram, in our view, created a confusion in the minds of early Gentile Christians about the relationship between the Lord God and the Lord Christ which is reflected in the MS tradition of the NT itself.'[13] Thus the basis of much Christian theology, it was implied, was a confusion, a mistake. Such a theory illustrates well the dangers of over-specialization since even the most cursory perusal of contextual evidence would have shown that this was an untenable thesis.

At the other end of the spectrum is the article by J. Fitzmyer which has become a classic, 'The Semitic Background of the New Testament Kurios Title'. The evidence for Jesus being addressed with the divine name is carefully presented, but the conclusion of the article shows how such studies can founder at the last fence because of the failure to recognize the fact that Judaism at that time was not monotheistic. He wrote that if 'Jesus is Lord' was part of the earliest Jewish Christian proclamation in Palestine,

... then it at least implies that the early Christians regarded Jesus as sharing in some sense in the transcendence of Yahweh, that he was somehow on a par with him. This, however, is meant in an egalitarian sense, not in an identifying sense, since Jesus is never hailed as Abba.[14]

Quite so; but 'Abba' was Father and Jesus was 'Marana', Our Lord.

The problem centres on the use of *kyrios* in the Septuagint. Most of the surviving texts, however, are Christian, which raises the possibility that they have been reworked. Surviving Jewish texts of the Greek Bible have the divine name in Hebrew, in much the same way as some of the Qumran scrolls write the divine name in the old Hebrew script. Outside the Septuagint, *kyrios* was in fact an unusual designation for God. Unfortunately, as can be seen from a comparison of the pre-Christian and post-Christian *Hebrew* text of Deut. 32.8, it was not only the Christian scribes who reworked sacred texts on sensitive issues. It could be argued that it is suspicious that *kyrios* does *not* appear in Jewish manuscripts if *kyrios* was a name for the Lord adopted by Christians rather than invented by them. If the *Christians* were responsible for writing *kyrios* into the Old Testament, this only confirms in the text what they had been doing in their interpretations from the beginning, namely identifying Jesus with the God manifested in the Old Testament.

Thus one question is replaced by another: What made Christians choose *kyrios* as a translation for the divine name if nobody else was using it at the time? There *are* in fact a few instances of *kyrios* in Jewish texts. In the Letter of Aristeas, for example, the author alludes to Deut. 7.18–19 which in the Hebrew has the tetragrammaton, but in the allusion has *kyrios*. In the fragments of Aquila's translation found in the Cairo Geniza there is one example of *kyrios*, in 2 Kings 23.24, even though he usually retained the Hebrew letters. Most interesting for our purposes is the fact that Luke 10.27 quotes Deut. 6.5, 'you shall love the Lord your God', and renders the divine name of the Hebrew original by *kyrios*. Luke and his community must have had an Old Testament which used *kyrios* for the divine name.

Nor is it only what they wrote that matters; if those who knew Hebrew did not pronounce the sacred name but replaced it with *Hashem*, the Name, or *Adonai*, the Lord, what did a Greek-speaking Jew actually pronounce when he saw the Hebrew letters of the sacred name? Did he use the Greek equivalent of *Adonai*? If he did, he will have said *kyrios* even when the text in front of him had the Hebrew letters. The Hebrew of Ps. 151, found at Qumran, writes *Adon* as a synonym for Yahweh, proof that these synonyms were written into the text as well as substituted when it was being read.

Then there is the question of the Aramaic-speaking Jews of Palestine, and what equivalents they had for the divine name. There is some evidence that they used *mr'*, the Lord, which appears in the New Testament invocation *Marana tha*, 'Our Lord Come!' In the *Genesis Apocryphon* there are two instances of *mr'* (1QApGen 20.12–13; 15) and in the Aramaic fragment of 1 Enoch 10.9 it seems that *mr'* stood where the Greek version has the abbreviated form of *kyrios*. This is paralleled by two New Testament texts; in 1 Cor. 16.22 there is preserved the transliterated Aramaic *Marana tha*, and in Rev. 22.20 what is clearly the equivalent in Greek, *Come, Kyrios Jesus*. It would be hard to make a good case that Yahweh was not represented by both the Aramaic *mr'* and the Greek *kyrios* before the advent of Christianity and thus to suggest that the first Christians had not intended to identify Jesus with Yahweh.

This identification happened in the very earliest period; it was, in fact, what the Christians were proclaiming when they said that Jesus was Lord. Jesus was Yahweh, the second God, but, since there were various traditions as to how Yahweh manifested himself, so there were several versions of how it was that Jesus came to be that second God. There were manifestation traditions and there were exaltation traditions, although those who were at home in this world would doubtless have known how the two were aspects of one belief. The former recorded the manifestation of Yahweh in angels, the latter implied that divine status was conferred on certain human beings, e.g. Moses, when they were exalted into the presence of God. The royal/high priestly traditions, such as we can still glean from the Old Testament, seem to have been a combination of the two: the Lord was present, manifested in his son, although the sonship was achieved not at birth but at the moment of installation or recognition. The king was raised up (Ps. 89.19), perhaps a mystical experience, and then set on the holy hill (Ps. 2.6) as the son. The combined traditions appear in the pre-Pauline hymn about Jesus quoted in Phil. 2.6–11, which describes both the existence of the second God before his coming into human form and then his exaltation to receive the great name which the whole creation honours. The hymn alludes to Isa. 45.23: 'To me every knee shall bow, every tongue shall swear', originally uttered of Yahweh but by the Christians here of Jesus. It complicates matters to read these texts in the light of what came to be Christian orthodoxy; the first Christians recognized that Jesus *was* Yahweh, not that he was in some way equivalent but not identical. Later complications arose when the distinction between God Most High and the Lord had been lost and it was assumed, along with one strand of Judaism, that God Most High and the Lord were identical. This is not to suggest that the very first disciples called by Galilee immediately recognized Jesus in this way; the Gospel traditions themselves make clear that right to the very end the disciples had failed to recognize Jesus (Luke 24.25–7). Such recognition as we have in the accounts of the ministry must have come from a later stage of realization, when the stories were recalled and retold with the wisdom of hindsight.

It is perhaps best to read the New Testament in the light of Philo's usage; he knew that *kyrios* and *theos* were the main aspects of the chief of the angels, the Word. *Kyrios* was the Word as ruler and *theos* was the Word as creator. *Kyrios* dominates in the New Testament since so much is expressed in terms of the royal traditions; there is no need to search through the contemporary cults of divine kingship and suggest that the title *kyrios* is evidence of the hellenization or paganization of early Christianity. The same is true of *theos*; it is used wherever it is appropriate and need not be a sign of the *later* deification of Jesus, where *later* implies 'in a Greek or pagan context'. The prologue to the Fourth Gospel deals with the mystery of the creation and therefore calls the Word *theos*, God. Philo's distinction between God (the second God) and *the* God (God Most High) is there too: the Word was with *the* God, and was God. Thomas exclaimed 'My Lord and My God', not because he thought that there was a difference between the two but because, as Philo said (*Questions on Genesis* IV.87), he was uttering a double invocation to the powers, the creative and the kingly.

Paul, who had been most zealous for the traditions of his people, was able to quote Old Testament Yahweh texts to describe Jesus: 'Everyone who calls upon the name of the Lord' (Rom. 10.13) was originally said of Yahweh (Joel 2.32). 'Blessed is the man against whom the Lord will not reckon his sin' (Rom. 4.8) was originally said of Yahweh (Ps. 32.2). 'When he ascended on high he led a host of captives' (Eph. 4.8) was originally a description of Yahweh's appearing in his holy place and then 'returning to heaven' (Ps. 68.18), and the allusion in Phil. 2.10, as we have seen, was also originally to Yahweh. Equally unambiguous are the other titles and roles of Jesus in the epistles traditionally ascribed to Paul: he is the power and the wisdom of God (1 Cor. 1.24); he sits at the right hand (Eph. 1.21); he has a 'Day' (1 Cor. 1.8; 5.5; Phil. 1.6); he is the image of the invisible God, the firstborn of all creation, he holds all things together and is the mystery now manifest (Col. 1.15–20); he is to be revealed from heaven with mighty angels to bring judgement (2 Thess. 1.7); he would kill the Lawless One with the breath of his mouth (2 Thess. 2.8; originally said of the Messiah, Isa. 11.4, but then of the Man from the sea, the son of Elyon, 2 Esd. 13.10 and 32); he is the one mediator between God and men (1 Tim. 2.5); he is the bridegroom of the Church (Eph. 5.21–33; cf. John 3.29 and 2 Cor. 11.2), just as Yahweh had been the 'husband' of his people (Isa. 54.5; Hos. 2.20). All these were the roles and titles of the second God. He even equates Jesus with an angel of God (Gal. 4.14: 'You received me as an angel of God, as Christ Jesus'). We should also consider the account of his conversion. According to all three versions in Acts (8.5; 22.8; 26.15) Paul says to the great light: 'Who are you, Lord?' and the Lord replies: 'I am Jesus'. Now it may be that Paul is not using 'Lord' in any technical sense here, but it would be interesting to know what word Paul used before it was put into Greek. Was he asking the Lord who he was? And his version of the *Shema'* was equally puzzling: how could he say that he believed in One God, the Father, *and* One Lord, Jesus Christ if *the Lord* was the name by which he knew the Father?[15]

Paul also knew that Christ had been present in the events of the Old Testament.[16] The clearest example of this is 1 Cor. 10.1–11, where he describes the desert wanderings of Israel and says that the rock was Christ. In the Song of Moses *the Rock* is one of the names of Yahweh (Deut. 32.4, 31). Similarly Moses had seen the glory of Yahweh and had himself been transformed by it such that he had to wear a veil; Christians had also seen the glory of the Lord which was transforming them into his likeness (2 Cor. 3.12–18). And then it was the Lord to whom Isaiah spoke: 'Yahweh, who has believed what he has heard from us?' (Isa. 53.1) and Yahweh who said: 'I have been found by those who did not seek me' (Isa. 65.1). Paul uses these and many other quotations in Rom. 10 to show how it was that Israel's rejection of Yahweh in former times had been repeated in their rejection of Jesus.

The Epistle to the Hebrews gives another vivid picture of Jesus as the second God, and, although dwelling mainly on his role as the high priest, it reveals most of his other aspects too. He was the agent of the creation (1.2; 1.10), the Son (1.2; 1.5) and the royal figure (1.5 quotes two royal texts, Ps. 2.7 and 2 Sam. 7.14). He was enthroned on high (1.3) and was greater than the angels. The writer demonstrates this in two ways: first, he receives the homage of the angels, and second, he

223

commands the angels as his servants (1.6–7). The first text quoted is the Greek of Deut. 32.43, which, in its original context, described Yahweh the warrior priest coming to his people. The second is Ps. 104.4, which described the power of Yahweh the creator, riding on the chariot throne attended by the heavenly hosts. For the writer of this epistle these texts described Jesus, and no amount of ingenuity can avoid the conclusion that for him, Jesus was Yahweh.

It is the role of the high priest which is most fully explored in Hebrews, and since the writer is clearly relating the work of Jesus to an existing pattern of belief, we must assume that this was what was believed of the high priests. Like Philo's Logos, the true high priest had to take material form: 'Therefore he had to be made like his brethren in every respect, so that he might become a merciful and faithful high priest in the service of God, to make expiation for the sins of the people' (Heb. 2.17). It was the temple veil which *was* his flesh (10.20). The true high priest passed through the heavens and was the Son of God (4.14). Jesus had become that high priest, in the manner of Melchizedek (6.20), and would continue as high priest for ever (7.24). He was a priest in the heavenly sanctuary (8.1), the mediator of the new covenant. It had been promised that the Lord would establish a new covenant (8.8–12) and this he had done with his own blood.

The true high priest was also the heavenly judge, as can be seen from the Qumran *Melchizedek* text, in which history culminates on the great Day of Atonement at the end of the tenth jubilee. Melchizedek is the God who takes his place in the heavenly council to preside at the great judgement. He is the God of whom Isaiah said to Zion: 'Your God reigns' (Isa. 52.7). But he was also Melchizedek the high priest. Melchizedek must have been one of the titles or manifestations of the second God. The heavenly priest/judge in Hebrews is the Lord, and those who spurn the Son of God and the blood of his covenant incur his wrath. The texts used to describe this judgement are, again, texts which in their original setting described the judgement of Yahweh (10.29–30; cf. Deut. 32.35–6). It would seem, although the text is not clear, that the description of the heavenly city in 12.22–4 also describes Jesus as the judge, God of all and mediator of the new covenant.

Finally, there are passages in Hebrews where Christ is regarded as present in the Old Testament. Moses, we are told, 'considered abuse suffered for the Christ greater wealth than the treasures of Egypt' (11.26). The Israelites were punished when they refused 'him who warned them on earth'; how much greater would be the punishment when the warning came from heaven (12.25). There has been much debate about this mysterious passage, but the simplest reading seems to be that it is a contrast between the two warnings, one on earth and one from heaven. The first warning was on Sinai, when the Law was given; the second was predicted by Haggai: 'For thus saith Yahweh of Hosts: Once again in a little while I will shake the heavens and the earth' (Hag. 2.6). In each case the speaker was Yahweh, yet the setting in Hebrews implies that this was Christ.

The Gospels also depicted Jesus as the second God. Gabriel announced that Jesus would be the Son of God Most High, to be given the Davidic throne by Yahweh, exactly the old pattern of the human king being installed as divine (Luke 1.32). John the Baptist warned of imminent judgement as the prophets before him had warned of the Day of Yahweh. 'Prepare', he said, 'the way of Yahweh' (Matt. 3.3; Luke 3.4). Then he sent to Jesus to ask if he was the indeed the one who was to come (Luke 7.18–23). Jesus implied that he was. The demoniac recognized Jesus as the Son of God Most High (Mark 5.7), come before 'the time' (Matt. 8.29). The crowd who saw the widow's son raised to life said, 'God has visited his people' (Luke 7.16). A comparison of Matt. 23.34 and Luke 11.49 shows that Jesus spoke as Wisdom.

Clearest of all are the Son of Man sayings. Even if 'Son of Man' is not a title but simply an idiomatic way of saying 'a man', when the Gospel passages are read in the light of the anthropomorphic tradition suppressed by the Deuteronomists, a great deal is explained. Son of Man meant the manifested second God, the Man, as well as being simply a way of referring to oneself. Doubtless the Son of Man traditions grew and became more refined as the Christian community developed, but the nuances of this process need not concern us. What is important is that the development was in a particular way, not limited simply to an expansion of the vision of Dan. 7, but all within what was known to be the roles and functions of the second God. In Dan. 7 he had risen on the clouds of heaven and had received the kingdom from the Ancient of Days, a tradition reminiscent of El and Ba'al. In 2 Esd. 13 he had risen from the sea, destroyed the wicked with his fiery breath, and been named as the hidden son of God Most High. Several Gospel passages are based on these:

225

I – warrior *avoids "I AM"*

i   The Son of Man comes on the clouds: e.g. Matt. 24.30; 26.64; Mark 13.26; 14.62.

ii   The Son of Man is enthroned: e.g. Matt. 19.28; 25.31.

iii The Son of Man is the heavenly judge: Matt. 25.32.

Other texts have a more tenuous link, but their additional material is significant.

iv   The Son of Man comes with his holy angels: e.g. Matt. 16.27; 25.31; Mark 8.38; Luke 9.26.

v   He sends the angels out as the agents of judgement: e.g. Matt. 13.41; 24.31; Mark 13.27.

In parallel sayings, the Kingdom of God (Mark 9.1) is the Kingdom of the Son of Man (Matt. 16.28). The Son of Man has a day like the Day of Yahweh. The time of the Day of the Son of Man is not known but it will come like a thief in the night (Matt. 24.43; Luke 12.39). Exactly the same is said of the Day of the Lord (1 Thess. 5.2) and of the time of the coming of Jesus (Rev. 3.3; 16.14–15). It would be hard to argue that the Day of the Lord, the Day of the Son of Man and the coming of Jesus were not identical, especially as the Day of the Son of Man is described in language drawn from the Old Testament descriptions of the Day of Yahweh. Whoever wrote Matt. 24, Mark 13 and Luke 17.22–7 must have had a reason for taking the imagery from Isa. 13.10, Ezek. 32.7, Joel 2.10–11 and Zeph. 1.14–16. The obvious reason is that he was describing the same event. *bar enash*

Further, the coming of the Son of Man with his angels resembles closely the coming of Yahweh for the judgement as described in Deut. 33.2, Zech. 14.5, and Hab. 3. It occurs also in 1 Enoch 1.9 where the Great Holy One, i.e. the Great Angel, comes forth for the judgement. Jude 14 testifies to Enoch's judgement scene having been an important part of early Christian teaching. Matthew records Jesus's own version of the judgement theme in Matt. 25.31–46. The language is very revealing, as are the presuppositions that scholars bring to it. The Son of Man comes with his angels and takes his place on the throne as judge. He is the King acting for another whom he names as his Father (Matt. 25.34). There is no need to suggest that the ancient role of Yahweh the King has been altered and given to the Son of Man, thus causing complications and making it necessary for Matthew to alter the story so as to make a place for 'the Father':

firey

In verse 34 the Son of Man is referred to as 'the king'. This may be a trace of an earlier state of the parable, in which the reference was to God himself. If so, the address to those on the right hand as 'blessed of my Father' must be regarded as a Matthaean adjustment.[17]

None of this is necessary if we recognize that Yahweh *was* the Son of Elyon, the Man. The Son of Man as vicegerent is exactly like the role of Philo's Logos and this is corroborated in Mark 2.10 and parallels where the Son of Man has authority to forgive sins on earth and in John 5.27 where the Father has given authority to the Son of Man to act as judge. Mark hints at this identification of Yahweh and the Son of Man in Mark 2.28; the Son of Man is Lord *even* of the Sabbath.

There are yet more points of contact with the second God; the Son of Man was to be the heavenly advocate of the faithful (Matt. 10.32–3; Luke 12.8–9); and his life was to be a 'ransom' (Matt 20.28; Mark 10.45). This latter has caused acute problems; it is hard to establish exactly what *lutron* meant. In the LXX it was used to translate *kopher* (e.g. Exod. 21.30; 30.12), a noun formed from the root *kpr* meaning 'expiate' or 'atone for'. Now making expiation (this verb) was one of Yahweh's roles when he came as the heavenly Warrior-Priest (Deut. 32.43), an association confirmed by the sequence of ideas in 1 Tim. 2.5–6; Jesus is described as the one mediator who gave himself as a 'ransom'.[18] The high priest's question at the trial does not necessarily reflect the later Christian conflation of titles. 'Are you the Christ the Son of God?' and 'Are you the Christ the Son of the Blessed?' and Jesus's reply, 'You will see the Son of Man ...' fit perfectly the picture of the second God who was the Son of God Most High, manifested as the Man in the person of the anointed king and high priest.

The Fourth Gospel does not use the same Son of Man sayings as the synoptics, but the Son of Man is recognizably the same figure, suggesting that there was a great deal more to this Son of Man tradition than a simple growth on the vision of Dan. 7. John's Son of Man comes from heaven (John 3.13) and will return there (John 6.62). He is the vicegerent (John 5.25–7) and the angels of God will descend on him as they did on Yahweh when he appeared to Jacob at Bethel (Gen. 28.12–13; see below). The total picture of Jesus in this Gospel is consistent with his being presented as the second God. He was the Word who became flesh and tabernacled on earth such that people could see the Glory. Thus his body was the Temple (2.21) and he was the visible God, the revealer of the Father. Throughout there is the theme of manifested glory: the miracles manifest the glory (2.11;

[handwritten margin notes: "End by Fire", "Me as Future 'New cosmic Beginning by rain", "Me"]

11.4, 40), as does the Son of Man (13.31), who shared the Father's glory before the creation (17.5). As in Philo, the Glory was the power manifested in the creation. Jesus healed the blind man so that the works of God could be seen (9.3). The second God had come from heaven (3.13; 6.38; 8.23) where he had been in the Father's bosom (1.18). He alone had seen the Father (6.46); the Jews had never heard his voice nor seen his form (5.37; cf. 1.18). The one manifested in their Scriptures had been the second God: 'They bear witness to me' (5.39); 'If you believed Moses you would believe me, for he wrote of me' (5.46). He it was whom Abraham had known (8.56–8), perhaps when he saw Yahweh at Mamre (Gen. 18), and he whom Isaiah had seen enthroned in the temple (12.41). As in Isaiah's prophecies (Isa. 1.4), so in the Gospel, he was known as the Holy One (6.69). He could speak of heavenly things (3.12–13). He was the image of the Father (14.9). He was the Man, the human form of the Glory descended to earth (3.13) on whom the angels of God would descend (1.51), possibly a reference to Jacob's dream at Bethel when he saw the angels on the ladder above Yahweh who was standing beside him (Gen. 28.13 can be read: 'The Lord stood beside him'). As in Ezekiel's vision (Ezek. 8.2; 9.3, 5–6), so too in the Gospel it was the Man, the Glory, who was to be the judge (5.26–7). He would be exalted (8.28) as the ancient kings had been exalted (Ps. 89.19) and then his real identity would be known. 'You will know that I am he' (8.28) is the great claim of Yahweh in the Second Isaiah: 'I, Yahweh, the first, and with the last; I am he' (Isa. 41.4); 'I, I am he who blots out your transgressions' (Isa. 43.25).

[handwritten margin note: "Me"]

There are also the I AM sayings, and the otherwise inexplicable incident at the arrest: 'When he said to them, "I am he", they drew back and fell to the ground' (18.6). The Son of Man was also the Name: 'The hour has come for the Son of Man to be glorified' (12.23); cf. 'Father glorify thy Name' (12.28). He was the light of the world (8.12; 9.5) and the vine with its branches (15.1–6), both images drawn from the *menorah* which represented the presence of the Lord. The plural presence of the ancient Yahweh had become the plural presence of Yahweh living in his followers. Like Yahweh, Jesus was the Shepherd of his people (10.11; cf. Isa. 40.11; Ezek. 34) and he was the high priest, interceding for them (ch. 17).

There is further indirect evidence that the Palestinian community did not draw its Son of Man theology simply from Dan. 7, but from a more broadly based expectation of a second divine figure. In the

[handwritten note at bottom: "me – Warrior: raincloud throne – New Beginning"]

Similitudes of Enoch there is a Messianic title 'The Righteous One' (1 Enoch 38.2; 53.6) given to the heavenly figure who is named elsewhere in same text as Son of Man and Chosen One. Without any explanation, this title is used of Jesus in the speeches attributed to Christian teachers in Jerusalem: 'The Holy and Righteous One ... the Author of Life' (Acts 3.14); '... the prophets announced ... the coming of the Righteous One' (Acts 7.52); '... the God of our fathers appointed you ... to see the Righteous One (Acts 22.14). It was also used in 1 Pet. 3.18, 'Christ died ... the Righteous One for the unrighteous' and in 1 John 2.1, 'We have an advocate with the Father, Jesus Christ the Righteous One.' Such usage suggests that this was an established messianic title,[19] and a variant reading in 1QIs[a] confirms that there were some who regarded the Judgement, Righteousness and Salvation mentioned in Isa. 51.4–5 as designations of the Messiah. This raises further possibilities: at two places in Jeremiah there is the name 'Yahweh is our Righteousness', given at Jer. 23.6 to the Messiah and at Jer. 33.16 to Jerusalem. Was Yahweh the original Righteousness, the Righteous One? Two cryptic verses at the beginning of Isaiah mention a personified Righteousness, thought by some to indicate the memory of an older Canaanite deity named Zedek (i.e. Righteousness), but showing clearly that Jerusalem was the place where Righteousness had his abode: 'Righteousness lodged in her' (Isa. 1.21); '... you shall be called the city of Righteousness' (Isa. 1.26). The high priest of the city was named Melchizedek, 'My king is Righteousness' (Gen. 14.18; Ps. 110.4). In isolation this would be insufficient evidence to establish anything, but taken in the context of the considerable body of evidence which suggests that Jesus was Yahweh, it is at least consistent.

Further evidence of this identification is found in the allusions and symbolism of Revelation (see chapter 10). It was also the Spirit of Christ which inspired the prophets to predict the sufferings of Christ (1 Pet. 1.11); the Old Testament had said that *the Spirit of Yahweh* inspired them. Jude, like Paul in 2 Cor., implies that Christ was present at the Exodus. The text is not entirely clear, but the Lord Jesus Christ of v.4 seems to be the one who saved the people from the land of Egypt, v.5. Most ancient texts have *the Lord saved a people from the land of Egypt* but two important ones, the fourth-century Vaticanus and the fifth-century Alexandrinus, have *Jesus saved a people from the land of Egypt.* Since we know that this is how the Old Testament was understood by the first Christians, it comes as no surprise to find Jesus actually in the text.

What would the titles Son of God, Lord and Messiah have meant to a first-century Galilean? Whatever they meant must have been clear, straightforward and obvious. When we look at the origins of Christian belief about Jesus, we are not contemplating the learned conclusions of professional scholars who had access to all contemporary learning and infinite time to speculate on theological matters. The Christianity to which Paul was converted was the faith of those whom the authorities had declared ignorant of the Law (John 7.47) and yet it was claimed to be the fulfilment of existing expectations, those of the Old Testament. How diverse and inchoate were those expectations? The implication of much that is written about the origin of Christology is that the Christians were the first to gather together a rag bag of expectations and forge from them, within a very short period, a powerful theological position with which they were prepared to confront the Jewish establishment and change the whole world. They had been forced in the process, and at great speed, to create for themselves a whole new mythology in order to explain their chosen designation for Jesus as Son of God, and they had had to alter the meaning of many other key words such as Messiah which they adopted from their native Judaism. Richard Longenecker expressed the problem well: 'But we are faced with a much more difficult problem in expliciting how these strands and motifs became fused into a Christology more or less structured. Here there are no explicit pointers as to the process'.[20] Quite so. But there are no pointers in the apostolic period because the process of fusion was much older than the origin of Christianity. This whole collection of titles and expectations existed already, part of the religion of those strata in Palestine from which Jesus's first followers came.

The earliest statement of their faith was 'Jesus is Lord', and 'Lord' must have meant in this context what it already meant to these people. If it meant 'Jesus is the manifestation of Yahweh', then all the beginnings of Christology can be explained. The quotations from the Old Testament will not have been applied to Jesus with a whole series of mental caveats and theological scruples; the texts about Yahweh were about Jesus. Justin, an early Christian interpreter of the Old Testament whose home was in Palestine, will have been repeating what the Palestinian Christians were saying about Christ in the Old Testament. Philo can be seen as relevant to our understanding of the Judaism of Christian origins, and not as the exponent of a remote and degenerate form of Judaism. The ferocity of the rabbinic debates

230

about the second power in heaven can be understood; the finest minds in Judaism are not likely to have been engaged against something which was cobbled together from pagan mystery cults and woolly misunderstandings of the Old Testament. The threat they addressed was a threat from within. The worship of Jesus and his designation as God is no longer a problem if the Christians were proclaiming him to be a manifestation of Yahweh. Much of the imagery and theology assumed by New Testament writers is explained: the plurality of the ancient Yahweh accounts for the plurality of the body of Christ; the high priestly theme of Hebrews is drawn from the centre of the older tradition; Revelation is no longer an embarrassing difficulty, which cannot be positioned in the scheme of things, but it is the Christians' vision of the Day of the Lord. The roots of Christianity can be seen to go deep into the religion of Israel, and will not be properly recovered and understood simply by reading the authorized version of what that religion was.

To suggest that Jesus was seen as Yahweh raises many questions about our understanding of Christian origins. If those questions cannot be faced, then the alternative is to assert that all this evidence is no more than coincidence.

... it is a good thing that the true historical Jesus should overthrow the modern Jesus, should rise up against the modern spirit and send upon earth not peace but a sword. He was not a teacher, not a casuist; He was an imperious ruler. It was because He was so in His inmost being that He could think of Himself as the Son of Man. That was only the temporally conditioned expression of the fact that He was an authoritative ruler. The names in which men expressed their recognition of Him as such, Messiah, Son of Man, Son of God, have become for us historical parables. We can find no designation which expresses what He is for us.[21]

Albert Schweitzer

Notes to chapter eleven

1 Lord occurs 184 times, Son of God 15 times.

2 M. Hengel, *The Son of God*, London 1976, p.7.

3 Ibid., p.15.

4 W. Bousset, *Kyrios Christos*, ET Nashville 1970, p.151.

231

5   W. Sanday, and A.C. Headlam, *The Epistle to the Romans*, ICC
    Edinburgh 5th edn 1902, pp.233–4.

6   This is the reading of several early manuscripts: Sinaiticus,
    Vaticanus, Freerianus (fourth century) and Alexandrinus (fifth
    century).

7   See chapter 10 where it is shown that Jesus is presented as the
    Lord.

8   The reading is found in p.66, early third century, the original text
    of Sinaiticus, fourth century, Vaticanus, fourth century, and parts
    of Irenaeus and Origen.

9   L.W. Hurtado, *One God, One Lord*, London 1988, pp.101–4.

10 R.N. Longenecker, *The Christology of Early Jewish Christianity*,
    London 1970, p.143, shows that 'Saviour' whilst also used in
    Hellenistic cults, was not used in this way in the New Testament
    but was a part of the Jewish heritage.

11 Hengel, op.cit., p.59, attributes this line to A. Deissmann, but
    without any further reference.

12 G. Howard, 'The Tetragram and the New Testament', JBL 96
    (1977), pp.63–83.

13 Ibid., p.63.

14 J.A. Fitzmyer, 'The Semitic Background of the New Testament
    Kurios-title', in *A Wandering Aramean: Collected Aramaic Essays*,
    SBL Monograph 25, Missoula 1979, p.130.

15 *Didache* 16 uses Zech. 15.5, the coming of Yahweh with his holy
    ones, to describe the second coming of Jesus.

16 Most of my examples on this theme are taken from A.T. Hanson,
    Jesus Christ in the Old Testament, London 1965, and A.W.
    Wainwright, *The Trinity in the New Testament*, London 1962.

17 B. Lindars, *Jesus Son of Man*, London 1983, p.126.

18 A different word is used, *antilutron*, but the meaning is the same.

19 Longenecker, op.cit., p.46.

20 Ibid., p.152.

21 A. Schweitzer, *The Quest of the Historical Jesus*, tr. W.
    Montgomery, London 1948, p.401, the final page.

Bibliography Primary Sources

Compendia of texts are: *The Apocrypha and Pseudepigrapha of the Old Testament,* ed. R.H. Charles, vol 2 *Pseudepigrapha* (Oxford 1913), *The Old Testament Pseudepigrapha,* ed. J.H. Charlesworth, vols 1 and 2 (New York and London 1983), *The Dead Sea Scrolls in English* by G. Vermes (3rd edn London 1987), *Discoveries in the Judaean Desert* by M. Baillet, J. Milik and others (Oxford 1955–68), *The Nag Hammadi Library,* ed. J.M. Robinson (Leiden 1977), *The Ante-Nicene Christian Library* ed. A. Roberts and J. Donaldson (Edinburgh 1868–72; Grand Rapids 1950–52) and *The Apocryphal New Testament,* tr. M.R. James (Oxford 1924, 1980).

The Acts of Thomas in James.

Al-Qirqisani's Account of the Jewish Sects containing translations of his *Book of Lights and Watchtowers* in A. Nemoy. HUCA 7 (1930).

The Angelic Liturgy at Qumran. J. Strugnell. SVT VII (1960).

The Apocalypse of Abraham in Charlesworth.

The Apocryphon of James (CG I.2) Williams and Mueller in Robinson.

The Apocryphon of John (CG II.1) Wisse in Robinson.

The Ascension of Isaiah in Charlesworth.

Assumption of Moses in Charles and Charlesworth.

Babylonian Talmud. tr. I. Epstein. Soncino, London from 1936.

The Babylonian Targum: Onkelos in J.W. Etheridge *The Targums to the Pentateuch.* London 1862; New York 1968.

1 Enoch in Charles and Charlesworth.

A Coptic Gnostic Treatise from the Codex Brucianus. C.A. Baynes. Cambridge 1933.

Clement of Alexandria: Excerpts from Theodotus. R.P. Casey. Studies and Documents 1. London 1934.
    The Instructor ANCL vol IV.
    The Miscellanies ANCL vol XII.

Clement of Rome: First Epistle ANCL vol I.

Pseudo-Clementine Homilies ANCL vol XVII.
    Recognitions ANCL vol III.

Corpus de tablettes en Cuneiformes alphabetiques decouvertes a Ras Shamra-Ugarit de 1929 à 1939. A. Herdner, Paris 1963.

The Damascus Rule (CD) in Vermes.

2 Enoch in Charles and Charlesworth.

3 Enoch in Charlesworth and in *3 Enoch or the Hebrew Book of Enoch*. H. Odeberg. Cambridge 1928.

Epiphanius of Salamis. Panarion. tr. F. Williams. Leiden 1987.

Letter of Eugnostos (CG III.3) Parrott in Robinson.

Eusebius: The Proof of the Gospel. W.G. Ferrar. London 1920.
   The Preparation of the Gospel. E.H. Gifford. Oxford 1903.

Ezekiel the Dramatist in Eusebius, ed. E.H. Gifford. Oxford 1903.

Genesis Rabbah. ed. H. Freedman and M. Simon. Soncino London 1939.

The Gospel of the Ebionites in James.

The Gospel of Philip (CG II.3) Isenberg in Robinson.

The Gospel of Truth (CG I.3) MacRae in Robinson.

Hippolytus: On Daniel. M. Lefevre. Sources Chretiennes, Paris 1947.
   Refutation. F. Legge. London 1927.

Hypostasis of the Archons (CG II.4) Bullard and Layton in Robinson.

Irenaeus: Against Heresies ANCL vols V and IX.
   The Proof of the Gospel. J. Armitage Robinson. London 1920.

Isaiah Targum. J.F. Stenning. Oxford 1949.

Job Targum (11Qtg Job) in J.A. Fitzmyer and D.J. Harrington.
   A Manual of Palestinian Aramaic Texts. Rome 1978.

Jubilees in Charles and Charlesworth.

Justin Martyr: Dialogue with Trypho ANCL vol II.

Magical Texts in *Amulets and Magic Bowls*. J. Naveh and S. Shaked. Jerusalem and Leiden 1985, and in K. Preisendanz *Papyri Graecae Magicae*. Berlin 1928. tr. as *The Greek Magical Papyri in Translation*. H-D Betz ed., Chicago 1986.

The Manual of Discipline (1QS) in Vermes.

The Mekhilta of R Ishmael. J.Z. Lauterbach. Philadelphia 1933.

The Memar Marqah. J. MacDonald. 2 vols BZAW 84 Berlin 1963.

The Mishnah. H. Danby. Oxford (1933) 1989.

Novatian: On the Trinity. H. Moore. London 1919.

The Odes and Psalms of Solomon. J. Rendel Harris. Cambridge 1909.

Origen: On John. tr. C. Blanc. Sources Chretiennes, Paris 1966.
   On First Principles. tr. G.W. Butterworth. New York 1966.
   Against Celsus. tr. H. Chadwick. Cambridge 1953.

On the Origin of the World (CG II.5) Bethge and Wintermute in Robinson.

Philo, Works. tr. R. Marcus and others. 9 vols. Loeb Classics London 1961–5.

The Pistis Sophia. G.R.S. Mead. London 1921.

The Second Treatise of the Great Seth (CG VII.2) Gibbons, Bullard and Wisse in Robinson.

The Shepherd of Hermas ANCL vol I.

Songs of the Sabbath Sacrifice in Vermes and in C. Newsom. HSS 27 Cambridge, Mass. 1985.

The Sophia of Jesus Christ (CG III.4) Parrott in Robinson.

The Palestinian Targums: Neofiti in A. Diez Macho. Madrid 1970–8.
    Pseudo-Jonathan in *The Targums to the Pentateuch*. J.W. Etheridge. London
    1862; New York 1986.

Testaments of the Twelve Patriarchs in Charles and Charlesworth.

Theophilus of Antioch: Ad Autolycum. tr. R.M. Grant. Oxford 1970.

The Trimorphic Protennoia (CG XIII.1) Turner in Robinson.

The Tripartite Tractate (CG I.5) Attridge, Pagels and Mueller in Robinson.

The War Scroll (1QM, 4QM) Y. Yadin. London 1962, also in Vermes.

Zostrianos (CG VIII.1) Sieber in Robinson.

Secondary Literature

Ahlstrom, G.W., *Aspects of Syncretism in Israelite Religion*. Horae Soderblomianae V Lund 1963.

Albright, W.F., 'Astarte Plaques and Figurines from Tell Beit Mirsim', in *Melanges syriens offerts a M Rene Dussaud*. Paris 1939.

Alexander, P.S., 'The Targumim and early Exegesis of the Sons of God in Gen 6', JJS 23 (1972).

——, 'The Historical Setting of the Hebrew Book of Enoch', JJS 28 (1977).

——, 'Rabbinic Judaism and the New Testament', ZNW 74 (1983).

Barr, J., 'Theophany and Anthropomorphism in the Old Testament', SVT vii Leiden 1960.

Barrett, C.K., *The Gospel According to John*. London 1978.

Bernard, J.H. *The Odes of Solomon*. Cambridge 1912.

Black, M., 'The Christological Use of OT in NT', NTS 18 (1971).

——, 'An Aramaic Etymology for Ialdabaoth?', in Logan, *Essays*.

Blumenthal, D.R., *Understanding Jewish Mysticism*. New York 1978.

Bonner, C., *Studies in Magical Amulets, chiefly Graeco Egyptian*. Michigan 1950.

Borgen, P., 'God's Agent in the Fourth Gospel' in Neusner, *Religions*.

Bousset, W., *Kurios Christos*. ET Nashville 1970.

Box, G.H., 'The Idea of Intermediation in Jewish Theology', JQR xxiii (1932).

Brownlee, W.H., 'The Ineffable Name of God', BASOR 226 (1977).

Bultmann, R., *The Gospel of John*. Oxford 1971.

Chernus, I., 'Visions of God in Merkabah Mysticism', JSS 13 (1983).

Chilton, B.D., *The Glory of Israel. The Theology and Provenience of the Isaiah Targum*. Sheffield 1982.

Clifford, R.J., 'Prov 9: a suggested Ugaritic Parallel', VT xxv (1975).

Cross, F.M., *Canaanite Myth and Hebrew Epic*. Cambridge Mass. and London 1973.

Cross, F.M., and others, ed. *Magnalia Dei. The Mighty Acts of God. Essays in Memory of G.E. Wright*. New York 1976.

Dahl, N.A., and Segal, A.F., 'Philo and the Rabbis on the Names of God', JJS ix (1978).

Danielou, J., *A History of early Christian Doctrine before the Council of Nicaea I. The Theology of Jewish Christianity*. ET London 1964.

Day, J., 'Asherah in the Hebrew Bible and North West Semitic Literature', JBL 1986.

De Jonge, M., and Van der Woude, A.S., '11Q Melchizedek and the New Testament', NTS xii (1965-6).

De Lacey, D.R., 'Jesus as Mediator', JSNT 29 (1987).

Dever, W.G., 'Asherah, Consort of Yahweh', BASOR 255 (1984).

Dix, G.H., 'The Influence of Babylonian Ideas on Jewish Messianism', JTS 26 (1925).

——, 'The Seven Archangels and the Seven Spirits', JTS 28 (1927).

Dunn, J.D.G., *Christology in the Making*. London 1980.

Eaton, J., *Liturgical Drama in Deutero-Isaiah*. London 1979.

Edersheim, A., *The Life and Times of Jesus the Messiah*. London 1890.

Eissfeldt, O., 'El and Yahweh', JSS 1 (1956).

Eliade, M., *Myths, Dreams and Mysteries*. London 1960.

Emerton, J.A., 'The Origin of the Son of Man Imagery', JTS New Series ix (1958).

——, 'New Light on Israelite Religion', ZAW 94 (1982).

Etheridge, J.W., *Targums to the Pentateuch*. London 1862.

Fallon, F.T., *The Enthronement of Sabaoth. Jewish Elements in Gnostic Creation Myths*. Leiden 1978.

Finnegan, R., *Oral Literature in Africa*. Oxford 1970.

solar — twofaced throne

Fitzmyer, J.A., 'The Contribution of Qumran Aramaic to the Study of the New Testament' and 'The Semitic Background of the New Testament Kurios title' both in *A Wandering Aramaean: Collected Aramaic Essays*. SBL Monograph 25, Missoula 1979.

Foerster, W., *Gnosis*. 2 vols Oxford 1972.

Fossum, J., *The Name of God and the Angel of the Lord*. Tübingen 1985.

——, 'Colossians 1.15–18a in the Light of Jewish Mysticism and Gnosticism', NTS 35 (1989).

Freedman, D.N., 'The Name of the God of Moses', JBL 79 (1960).

Frohlich, I., 'Les Enseignements des Veilleurs dans la Tradition de Qumran', RQ 13. 49–52 (1988).

Ginzberg, L., *Legends of the Jews*. 7 vols Philadelphia 1909–38.

Goldin, J., 'Not by means of an Angel and not by means of a Messenger', in Neusner, *Religions*.

Goodenough, E.R., *By Light, Light. The Mystic Gospel of Hellenistic Judaism*. New Haven 1935.

Grant, R.M., 'Theophilus of Antioch to Autolycus', HTR 40 (1947).

Grunwald, I., *Apocalyptic and Merkabah Mysticism*. Leiden 1980.

Habel, N.C., '"Yahweh, Maker of Heaven and Earth"; a Study in Tradition Criticism', JBL 91 (1972).

Hadley, J.M., 'Yahweh's Asherah in the Light of Recent Discovery', unpublished thesis in the Cambridge University Library.

Hanson, A.T., *Jesus Christ in the Old Testament*. London 1965.

Hanson, R.P.C., 'The Transformation of Images in the Trinitarian Theology of the Fourth Century', in *Studies in Christian Antiquity*. Edinburgh 1985.

Hayman, P., 'Monotheism: A Misused Word in Jewish Studies' JJS 42 (1991).

Hayward, C.T.R., 'The Memra of Yahweh and the Development of its Use in Targum Neofiti I', JJS xxv (1974).

——, 'The Holy Name of the God of Moses and the Prologue of St John's Gospel', NTS 25 (1978).

Hengel, M., *The Son of God*. London 1974.

Hooker, M.D., 'The Johannine Prologue and the Messianic Secret', NTS 21 (1974).

Horbury, W., 'The Messianic Associations of "The Son of Man"', JTS New Series 36 (1985).

Horton, F.L., *The Melchizedek Tradition*. Cambridge 1976.

Howard, G., 'The Tetragram and the New Testament', JBL 96 (1977).

Hurtado, L.W., *One God, One Lord*. London 1988.

Kenyon, K., *Digging up Jerusalem*. London 1974.

Kohler, K., *Jewish Theology Historically and Systematically Considered*. New York 1918.

Lindars, B., *Jesus Son of Man*. London 1983.

Liver, J., 'The Doctrine of the Two Messiahs', HTR 52 (1959).

Logan, A.H.B., and Wedderburn, A.J.M., ed. *The New Testament and Gnosis, Essays in Honour of G McLaren Wilson*. Edinburgh, 1983.

Longenecker, R.N., *The Christology of Early Jewish Christianity*. London 1970.

MacRae, G.W., 'Some Elements of Jewish Apocalyptic and Mystical Tradition and their Relationship to the Gnostic Literature', unpublished thesis in the Cambridge University Library 1966.

——, 'The Jewish Roots of the Gnostic Sophia Myth', NT xii (1970).

Maier, W.A., *Aserah. Extra Biblical Evidence*. HSM 37 Atalanta 1986.

Marmorstein, A., *The Old Rabbinic Doctrine of God*. 2 vols London 1920 reprinted New York 1968.

——, 'Philo and the Names of God', JQR 22 (1931).

McCarter, P.K., 'Aspects of the Religion of the Israelite Religion; Essays in Honour of F.M. Cross. Ed. P.D. Miller and others Philadelphia 1987.

McKane, W., *Proverbs*. London 1970.

Meeks, W.A., 'Moses as God and King' in Neusner, *Religions*.

——, *Jews and Christians in Antioch in the first four Centuries*. SBL Seminar Papers, Missoula 1976.

Mettinger, T.N.D., *The Dethronement of Sabaoth*. Lund 1982.

Miller, P.D., 'El the Creator of earth', BASOR 239 (1980).

Moore, G.F., 'Intermediaries in Jewish Theology', HTR xv (1922).

——, *Judaism in the First centuries of the Christian Era; the Age of the Tannaim*. 3 vols Cambridge Mass. 1927–30.

Murray, R., *Symbols of Church and Kingdom*. Cambridge 1975.

——, *The Cosmic Covenant*. London 1992.

Nautin, P., *Origène: sa vie et son oeuvre*. Paris 1977.

Neusner, J., ed., *Religions in Antiquity; Essays in memory of E.R. Goodenough*. Leiden 1970.

——, *The Incarnation of God. The Character of Divinity in Formative Judaism*. Philadelphia 1988.

Newsom, C., *Songs of the Sabbath Sacrifice*. HSS 27, Cambridge Mass 1985.

Nickelsburg, G.W.E., *Resurrection, Immortality and Eternal Life in Intertestamental Judaism*. Cambridge Mass 1972.

Oden, R.A., 'The Persistence of Canaanite Religion', BA 39 (1976).

Olyan, S.M., 'Some Observations concerning the Queen of Heaven', U-F 19 (1987).

——, *Asherah and the Cult of Yahweh in Israel* SBL Monograph 34, Atlanta 1988.

Otto, E., 'El und Yhwh in Jerusalem. Historische und theologische Aspekte einer Religionsintegration', VT xxx (1980).

Pagels, E., *The Gnostic Paul*. Philadephia 1975.

Patai, R., *The Hebrew Goddess*. New York 1947.

Pearson, B.A., 'Jewish Elements in Gnosticism and the Development of Gnostic Self-Definition', in Sanders, *Definition*.

Petuchowski, J.J., 'The Controversial Figure of Melchizedek', HUCA xxviii (1957).

Porten, B., *Archives from Elephantine*. Berkeley 1968.

Quispel, G., 'Judaism Judaic Christianity and Gnosis' in Logan, *Essays*.

Reventlow, H. Graf 'A Syncretistic Enthronement Hymn in Isa. 9.1–6' U-F 3(1971).

Rowland, C.C., *The Open Heaven*. London 1982.

Sanday, W., and Headlam, A.C., *The Epistle to the Romans*. ICC 5th edn Edinburgh 1902.

Sanders, E.P., ed., *Jewish and Christian Self-Definition I: the Shaping of Christianity in the Second and Third Centuries*. London 1980.

Sawyer, J.F.A., 'The Daughter of Zion and the Servant of the Lord in Isaiah. A Comparison', JSOT 44(1989).

Schmid, H.H., 'In Search of New Approaches in Pentateuchal Research', JSOT 3 (1977).

Schmitt, J.J., 'The Motherhood of God and Zion as Mother', RB 92 (1985).

Schnackenburg, R., *The Gospel of John*. London 1968.

Scholem, G.G., *Jewish Gnosticism, Merkabah Mysticism and Talmudic Tradition*. New York 1960.

——, *Major Trends in Jewish Mysticism*. 3rd edn New York 1961.

——, *On the Kabbalah and its Symbolism*. tr. R. Mannheim. London 1965.

——, *Origins of the Kabbalah*. ET Princeton 1987.

Schweitzer, A., *The Quest of the Historical Jesus*. tr. W. Montgomery. London 1948.

Segal, A.F., *Two Powers in Heaven*. Leiden 1978.

Skehan, P.S., 'A Fragment of the "Song of Moses" (Deut 32) from Qumran', BASOR 136 (1954).

Smith, J.Z., 'The Prayer of Joseph', in Neusner, *Religions*.

Strack, H.L., and Billerbeck, P., *Kommentar zum neuen Testament aus Talmud und Midrasch*. Munich 1924.

The Great Angel

Stroumsa, G.G., 'Form(s) of God: Some Notes on Metatron and Christ', HTR 76 (1983).

——, Another Seed: Studies in Gnostic Mythology. London 1984.

Stone, M.E., 'Lists of Revealed Things in Apocalyptic Literature', in Cross, Magnalia Dei.

Sumney, J.L., 'The Letter of Eugnostos and the Origins of Gnosticism', NT xxxi (1989).

Suter, D.W., 'Fallen Angel, Fallen Priest. The Problem of Family Purity in 1 Enoch 6–16', HUCA 50 (1979).

Thunberg, L., 'Early Christian Interpretation of the Three Angels in Gen 18', SP vii.i (1966).

Trigg, J.W., 'The Angel of Great Counsel: Christ and the Angelic Hierarchy in Origen's Theology', JTS 42 (1991).

Urbach, E.E., The Sages: their Concepts and Beliefs. Jerusalem 1979.

van der Horst, P.W., 'Moses' Throne Vision in Ezekiel the Dramatist', JJS 34 (1983).

van Seters, J., Abraham in History and Tradition. New Haven 1975. 'The Religion of the Patriarchs in Genesis', Biblica 61 (1980).

——, 'Confessional Reformulation in the Exilic period', Biblica In Search of History: Historiography in the Ancient World and the Origins of Biblical History. New Haven and London 1983.

Vawter, B., 'Prov 8.22: Wisdom and Creation', JBL 99 (1980).

von Rad, G., Studies in Deuteronomy ET D. Stalker SBT 9 London 1961.

Wainwright, A.W., The Trinity in the New Testament. London 1962.

Walton, F.R., 'The Messenger of God in Hecataeus of Abdera', HTR 48 (1955).

Weinfeld, M., 'The Worship of Moloch and the Queen of Heaven and its Background', U-F. 4 (1972).

Werner, M., The Formation of Christian Dogma. ET London 1957.

Westcott, B.F., An Introduction to the Study of the Gospels. 4th edn London 1872.

——, The Gospel According to St John. London 1908.

Whybray, R.N., Wisdom in Proverbs. London 1965.

——, The Making of the Pentateuch. JSOT Supplements Series 53, Sheffield 1987.

Wolfson, H.A., Philo: Foundations of Religious Philosophy in Judaism, Christianity and Islam. 2 vols Cambridge Mass. 1948.

——, 'The Pre-Existent Angel of the Magharians and Al-Nahawandi', JQR 51 (1960–61).

Wright, G.E., Biblical Archaeology. London 1957.

York, A.D., 'The Dating of Targumic Literature', JSJ v.i (1974).

Index of Names and Subjects

Index of Primary Sources

HEBREW

Genesis
1.2 62
1.27 206
2.10–14 65
3.5 58, 164
3.14–19 163
3.22 164
3.24 128
6.2–4 4, 5
7.16 194
12.7 32, 136
14.9 18, 54
14.18 229
14.19 88
14.22 88
16 34
16.9 121
17.1 136
18 34, 193, 228
18.1 33, 136
19.1 34
22.10 85
24.7 31
26.23 32
28.12–13 227
31.13 119
32 193
35.1 32, 136
48.3 136
48.15–16 33, 35

Exodus
3.2–3.7 34
3.15 16, 17
4.22 4, 9
4.24 86
6.2–3 16–17
12.12 32, 115
12.29 115
13.21 86
14.19 32, 86
15.11 30
15.26 36

16.10 136
20.2 154
21.30 227
23.20, 23 31, 98, 120, 122
23.21 31, 79, 194
24.9–11 119–21
24.17 136
25.22 15, 129
25.40 199
28 123
28.37 78
30.12 227
32.32–3 31, 91
32.34 31
33.2 31
33.23 127
39 122
39.28 78

Leviticus
9.4, 6, 23 136
9.6 134
16.22 45

Numbers
6.25 36
9.15–16 136
11.12 49
11.26–9 64
12.8 100
14.10, 14 136
16.19, 42 136
20.16 31
22.31 121
24.2 64
24.3–9, 15–24 100
24.17 184

Deuteronomy
4.6 13, 51, 61, 165–6
4.12 30, 100, 165–6
4.19–20 13, 165
4.39 128
6.4 50, 165, 193
6.5 5, 220

6.6–9 61
7.5 55
7.9 18
7.18–19 220
11.18–21 61
12.3 55
14.1–3 4, 9
16.21 55
19.12 13
28.36 15
30.12–14 67
32.8–9 4, 5, 6, 8, 21, 54, 64, 130, 190, 192, 220
32.11, 18 49
32.35–6 32, 225
32.43 43, 45–6, 64, 75, 203, 218, 227
33 30
33.2–5 29, 38, 226

Joshua
5.13–15 35, 194
22.22 18

Judges
2.2 32
5.23 33
6 34
6.34 98
13 34, 135
13.6 136

1 Samuel
3.21 136
10.10 64

2 Samuel
2.8 174
7.5, 13 102
7.14 4, 213, 223
14 9
14.20 63, 164
15.7 50
22.11 136
23.1–2 8, 101
24 31

GREEK OLD TESTAMENT

DEAD SEA SCROLLS

SAMARITAN TEXTS

OTHER ANCIENT TEXTS